Popular Religion in America

PRENTICE-HALL STUDIES IN RELIGION SERIES

PETER W. WILLIAMS
Miami University
Oxford, Ohio

Popular Religion in America

Symbolic Change and the Modernization Process in Historical Perspective

PRENTICE-HALL, INC., *Englewood Cliffs, New Jersey 07632*

Library of Congress Cataloging in Publication Data

WILLIAMS, PETER W
Popular religion in America.

(Prentice-Hall studies in religion series)
Includes bibliographical references and index.
1. United States—Religion. I. Title.
BL2530.U6W54 200'.973 79-22986
ISBN 0-13-686113-X

Printed in the United States of America

10 9 8 7 6 5 4 3 2 1

Editorial/production supervision: Robert Hunter
Manufacturing buyer: John Hall

PRENTICE-HALL INTERNATIONAL, INC., *London*
PRENTICE-HALL OF AUSTRALIA PTY. LIMITED, *Sydney*
PRENTICE-HALL OF CANADA, LTD., *Toronto*
PRENTICE-HALL OF INDIA PRIVATE LIMITED, *New Delhi*
PRENTICE-HALL OF JAPAN, INC., *Tokyo*
PRENTICE-HALL OF SOUTHEAST ASIA PTE. LTD., *Singapore*
WHITEHALL BOOKS LIMITED, *Wellington, New Zealand*

Contents

Series Foreword

The volumes in this series are intended to contribute to the development of the study of religion. It seems to us that it is especially important that appropriately conceived and well-written materials be available for use in undergraduate and graduate instruction. Moreover, it is our hope that this series will not only be useful as teaching instruments within the formal curriculum, but also play an important role in shaping the study of religion.

Individual volumes fall into one of three subsections in the series. One set of studies, small in number, will be concerned with theories of religion or methodological approaches to the study of religion. Our attempt will be to offer books where none are available or where the existing materials are inadequate. A second group of books, also small, will deal with general aspects of religion in various traditions. Mysticism, symbol and myth, religious ethics, and other comparable topics deserve theoretical and systematic treatment not available at present. The third section of the series consists of particular studies of various religious traditions, periods, or movements. The editors will try to identify areas of study to which sufficient attention has not been given, as well as classical subjects which deserve or even require fresh approaches at the present time.

We hope that each of the volumes in the series will be sufficiently lucid to be readily used by undergraduates, while sufficiently rigorous to contribute to the work of specialists as well. Scholarly apparatus and bibliographies will be included as appropriate to provide directions for further study. Throughout the project the editors will seek out studies which manifest unquestioned quality in scholarship and writing.

John P. Reeder, Jr.
Brown University

John F. Wilson
Princeton University

Preface

This book might best be described as a tentative synthesis. It is synthetic in that it attempts to arrange a considerable body of materials in a perspective that is both novel and useful. Many synoptic treatments of religion in America have been attempted over the past century, with each adding a new perspective to materials which in some measure are already familiar to students in the field.[1] Each has necessarily depended upon the monographic literature contributed by historians, sociologists, and other laborers in highly particular vineyards, and each has been more or less valuable insofar as it has—or has not—succeeded in arranging those particular materials in such a fashion that they form a coherent whole, a unity within a broad interpretive framework which transcends the specific vantage points of individual studies.

More particularly, this book is intended to stand in dialectical counterpoint with a far more ambitious work of synthesis, Sydney E. Ahlstrom's *A Religious History of the American People.*[2] My graduate study was carried out under Ahlstrom's direction, and the impact of his work on my own thought—as well as that of the profession as a whole—has been profound. During the past several years, however, I have found myself working less in the field of religious history as such, and have become increasingly interested in the possibilities of interpreting the religious and symbolic life of an historically self-conscious people—that is, Americans—from the perspectives offered by the socially oriented behavioral sciences. This resultant effort is an attempt to utilize these perspectives to filter Ahlstrom's data through a rather different sort of prism, in the hope that the light cast thereby will provide an illumination of another, complementary sort.

Because I deal in very brief span with a wide range of materials, the reader will perhaps feel the need for further immersion in historical (and, from time to time, ethnological) accounts of the phenomena I am trying to analyze. In order to aid this process, I have provided what I hope to be ample suggestions for further reading in the notes, which are designed to constitute a sort of running bibliographical essay and commentary on the monographic and interpretive sources on which I am drawing. More particularly, I have given references to corresponding sections in Ahlstrom's *Religious History* both to provide supplementary readings and to illustrate where possible the divergences in interpretation which arise from an historical standpoint in contrast with one that depends extensively on insights from the behavioral sciences.

Because this study is synthetic, it is almost necessarily tentative as well. Students of religion have only very recently begun to apply categories derived from anthropology to contemporary societies, and the methodological problems are abundant. I hope to demonstrate herein that, all the problems notwithstanding, the approach is potentially fruitful and rewarding. This is, in any case, a beginning, and is designed to serve a heuristic function rather than to be an attempt at making any definitive statements. Also, the work is tentative because of my necessary dependence upon previous scholarship. Where historians have attempted to address questions relating to the social composition of religious movements, I feel fairly confident in utilizing an interpretive method that seeks to correlate symbolic expression with social experience and structure. Where little is known about such matters, however, I fear that I have at many points risked describing what ought to have been the case rather than that which actually was. My only defense is that such speculations may serve to stimulate interest in more detailed researches in order to demonstrate whether theory does in fact have predictive value.

In a work of this sort which draws on the writings and thoughts of literally hundreds of others—past and present, living and dead, friends, acquaintances, colleagues, and strangers—I can only begin to acknowledge the aid and comfort provided by those most immediately and directly connected with this enterprise. The footnotes must stand as a testimonial to the indirect (and often unwitting) aid of the more extended community of scholars. First, I must thank the one person without whom quite literally this work would not have been possible. John F. Wilson first suggested this project to me at the annual meeting of the American Academy of Religion in St. Louis in 1976, and provided encouragement and counsel at every stage of its execution. My debt to him simply cannot be expressed in words. Next, I must thank the teachers who trained me in the historian's craft—Sydney E. Ahlstrom, whose influence should be visible at many points along the way; Jeremy duQ. Adams; Daniel Walker Howe; and Thomas N. Pappas. Third, my acquaintance with the behavioral sciences which I have attempted to apply herein to historical data is the result in large measure of my interaction with a number of colleagues over the past decade—Wayne Elzey and Alan Miller of Miami; Paul Antze, with whom my association goes back two-and-a-half decades; and my associates in the American Academy of Religion Consultation on American Popular and Devotional Religions, especially Carlyle Haaland, Catherine Albanese, Charles Lippy, and Sandra Sizer. Charles Wallace, Jr., merits mention not only for continued support, but for introducing me to the delights of Gospel hymnody during our mutual days at Yale Divinity School. Wayne Elzey, Harold Forshey, Dennis McGucken, Bradford Simcock, Kathleen Spencer, and Baird Tipson deserve special thanks for reading and commenting on large chunks of manuscript at various stages in its composition. Roy Bowen Ward and C. K. "Bud" Williamson deserve thanks for helping to create an academic climate in which a work of this sort might thrive. Kathi Fields and Lucille Hautau, secretaries extraordinary, contributed to the preparation of a long series of manuscript materials above and beyond the call of duty. The Miami Faculty Research Committee generously funded the final preparation of the manuscript. Curt and Barb Ellison, Harold and Carol Forshey, John and Francie Irvine, and Ruth Ann Schneider provided support and comfort at various periods of trial. Finally, I would like to acknowledge the company of Mistress Margaret Brent, who lay on the floor of my office chewing an endless series of tennis balls while I worked on what follows. Her distinctively canine outlook on my enterprise helped me to keep it in perspective.

PETER W. WILLIAMS
Miami University

NOTE ON NOTES

Where possible, I have attempted to give the date of first publication of a work when the edition I cite is a reissue. I have also indicated which books are, or at least have at one time been, available in paperbound editions by an asterisk (*) following the complete citation.

NOTES

1. Such works include ROBERT BAIRD, *Religion in America* (New York: Harper Torchbooks, 1856/1970);* LEONARD WOOLSEY BACON, *A History of American Christianity* (New York: Scribner's, 1970); WILLIAM WARREN SWEET, *Religion in the Development of American Culture* (New York: Scribner's, 1952); CLIFTON

E. Olmstead, *History of Religion in the United States* (Englewood Cliffs, N.J.: Prentice-Hall, 1960);* Sidney E. Mead, *The Lively Experiment* (New York: Harper & Row, 1963); Winthrop S. Hudson, *Religion in America* (New York: 1965/73);* Edwin Scott Gaustad, *A Religious History of America* (New York: Harper & Row, 1966); William A. Clebsch, *From Sacred to Profane America* (New York: Harper & Row, 1968); and Martin E. Marty, *Righteous Empire* (New York: Dial, 1970).*

2. New Haven, Conn.: Yale University Press, 1972.*

INTRODUCTION

Popular Religion and Its Study

RELIGION IN AMERICA: FORMAL AND INFORMAL

Religion is all around us here in America. For all the talk about our having become a secularized society, we have only to drive around our towns and highways, open a newspaper, or turn on the radio to realize that G. K. Chesterton may not have been far off in describing us as "the nation with the soul of a church." European observers have continued to be surprised not by our secularity, but rather by the enthusiasm with which we take our religion. A "born-again" prime minister would be unthinkable in England or France; in America, such a president arouses only mild suprise even among the skeptical. Whatever the rise and fall of fortunes of specific denominations, it is certainly premature to conclude with some now nearly forgotten theologians of the 1960s, that religion (if not God) is in fact dead.

The religion that surrounds us so pervasively is not just that which is found in the churches and denominations. Revivalists have been pitching their tents and tabernacles now for generations, and Billy Graham still conducts his massive crusades. Preachers from Bishop Sheen through Oral Roberts and Robert Schuller have been taking advantage of the huge audiences which television commands, and the powerful signal of radio station WWVA in Wheeling brings nonstop "old-time religion" to millions of potential listeners. Catholic priests, Baptist evangelists, and positive thinkers vie with Jack Anderson and Ann Landers as newspaper columnists and givers of advice. Shopping centers and supermarkets dispense mass-circulation paperbacks by faith healers, evangelical antifeminists, transcendental meditators, and astrologers on how to bring one's life into harmony with any number of versions of the Ultimate. Billboards tell us that "God Makes House Calls," and bumper stickers let the world know that the driver has been joyfully reborn.

Almost from their collective beginnings, Americans have been reluctant to accept the established religions of the Old World without question or dissent. Even in colonial days, such refuges as Pennsylvania and Rhode Island made possible the expression of the religious beliefs of those who did not accept the official teachings of the established churches. While the latter certainly maintained themselves and generally thrived, those who thought themselves the bearers of new insights and revelations found themselves increasingly free to spread their teachings without regard to tradition or institutions after the Bill of Rights prevented any group from exercising a monopoly on belief and practice. The demands of the frontier, where men and women were free to pick and choose among any number of competing options, forced those who wanted to spread their faith to adapt themselves to circumstances unparalleled in Europe since the Middle Ages. With the development of mass media, beginning with the printed word, whole new means—which could scarcely be confined to the control of the established denominations—of spreading the Word became available.

"American religion" can thus be seen as an interplay—a dialectic—between two different forces. On the one hand, most Americans belong to one of the three major religious communities—Protestant, Catholic, Jewish—and, if Protestant, to a particular denomination. On the other, many of these believers supplement their participation in formal worship by attending revivals, practicing various forms of devotion, reading books, watching television, or partaking in any number of forms of religious activity which are not directly provided by the formally organized religious bodies to which they belong. Others abandon these traditional groups entirely, and follow new leaders or join loosely organized movements which may not even be explicitly religious, but which look very much like religion when examined closely. All of these phenomena, which exist apart from the organized structures of the churches and the teachings of their seminaries, seem to form a class of related belief and behavior which we may loosely call "popular religion."

"EXTRA-ECCLESIASTICAL" RELIGION

These examples of "popular religion"—revivals, newspaper columns, radio programs—are all present in the common culture in which most Americans participate, and are familiar enough by heresay if not by direct experience. They are probably all good examples of what the term "popular religion" means for most of us, even though we may never have thought very carefully about the term. They may be popular in two principal senses. On the one hand, they have "mass appeal," they "sell." On the other hand, they are "of the people": they are examples not of the kind of religion that is taught by theologians in seminaries, but rather of that which appeals to a wide variety of people of no special theological sophistication outside the context of formal "Sunday-morning" worship in the churches.

These familiar examples of popular religion are the proverbial tip of the iceberg in terms of the broader religious experience of the peoples who have made up the American nation. The story of formal, organized religion has been told and retold by generations of historians, and has over the years come to include progressively more and more groups until the complexity of our religious institutions has been adequately recognized. Historians of religion no longer write from narrow denominational or confessional perspectives, but rather see religious development as the interaction, friendly or hostile, of many different groups, Protestant and Catholic, Christian and Jewish.[1]

Nevertheless, there is more to the story of the religious experience of the American peoples than that of their formal institutions and expression. Americans—or those who were to become Americans—continually broke the bounds of their traditional modes of expression and organization, and gave rise to new symbols through which they hoped to come to terms with the problematic character of life in a universe whose pattern and meaning seemed continually to be shifting and eluding their grasp. In the New World, all bets were off: anything might happen, and often seemingly did. The limitless possibilities of an uncharted continent, the unprecedented intermingling of peoples from all parts of the globe, a new beginning in political organization on a massive scale, the rapidity of social and technological change, all necessitated continual reappraisals of ways of interpreting the relationship of both individuals and groups not only to the world around them but to the whole cosmos as well. Organized religion, to be sure, underwent change enough, sometimes adapting and at other times withdrawing from the give and take of "Freedom's Ferment." But organized religion could do only so much.

In the gaps and interstices that emerged among the various traditional religious communities, whether Catholic, Protestant, Jewish, or Native American, new movements began to form—sometimes fairly systematic and organized, more often inchoate and unformed—which at least temporarily helped to bridge the gap between the experience of chaos and its symbolic resolution into order. Some of these movements developed structures and formal organizations and endured, while others disappeared or continued to exist loosely at the fringes of the "official" churches and religious communities. They included faith healing, witch hunting, expectations of the imminent end of the world, charismatic leaders claiming to be divine, and exotic myths compounded of elements from widely different cultures. Many of them had little influence on anyone except a small band of dedicated followers, and thus slipped through the nets of historians concerned with the broadly representative and influential. Others eluded notice by students of religion because they did not seem religious in a strict or conventional sense of the term. What they all had in common, though, was that they could not easily be classified according to traditional categories.

What we ordinarily understand by the term "popular religion" can best be treated as a particular category of a wider variety of religious phenomena and movements which we might call "extra-ecclesiastical."[2] *Ecclesia,* the Latin word for "church," refers to religion specifically in its organized, or formal social, aspects. For most people, religion has meant participation in these formal structures, whether they are the whole of a small society in its religious aspects or a more specialized set of social structures distinguished and set apart from the broader society. In certain situations, though—especially where cultural change, conflict, or disintegration is involved—religious movements arise outside these structures. It is this broad set of phenomena, which we might rather awkwardly designate as "extra-ecclesiastical religion," that we take as our subject—the study of what happens to religion outside the churches, or, more comprehensively, outside its organized social forms. Although "extra-ecclesiastical" is more precise, we might for the sake of simplicity and euphony classify this whole range of religious phenomena as "popular"—that is, coming from and belonging to the "people" rather than the "elite" specialists specifically trained in religious functions.

POPULAR RELIGION AND ACADEMIC STUDY

Popular religion provides an interesting case study in the sociology of knowledge.[3] The emergence of popular culture as a field of serious study is of quite recent origin, and is still taking place. A cursory glance at some of the journal articles and convention programs in the area is instructive.[4] Such a glance reveals a decidedly mixed picture, in which some work of very high quality finds itself in the company of contributions that suggest deliberate self-parody. It is, in short, a field that is still "finding itself."

However, all the fault does not lie with its occasionally erratic practitioners. Literary scholars have generally operated in an ethos of high seriousness and a genuine concern with aesthetic integrity which have worked against a detailed examination of subliterary genres. Political historians have often focused on decisions made at the higher levels of command, and have maintained insufficient contact with anthropologists to be sufficiently aware of the meaning of the "mass movements" they chronicle. Reactions to this "elitist" historiography often are grounded on ideological premises which aim at social change rather than at an understanding of the cultures of the poor and oppressed whose conditions they propose to alleviate, or submerged in statistical analyses which, however useful they may be in some ways, do little to illuminate internal cultural dynamics.[5]

Another aspect of the problem emerges from the social situation of American academics themselves. The academic profession in America has never enjoyed anything approaching the prestige accorded its European counterpart, and often has met with outright hostility, especially from congressional investigating committees and recalcitrant state legislatures charged with appropriating funds for higher education. Academics have therefore often tended to study the artifacts produced by their own kind—literary, theological, and philosophical works—and have been inclined to idealize the intellectual enterprise itself as particularly worthy of study. It has been suggested that the preoccupation with the Puritans that has emerged in American historical and religious scholarship during the past few decades is an unconscious reaction to the general public hostility or indifference towards "eggheads" and a corresponding glorification of one of the few periods in the American experience during which intellectuals actually enjoyed both prestige and a very real power.[6]

An additional corollary emerges from the problematical position of American scholars vis-à-vis their European counterparts. Emerson was among the first to articulate the cultural "inferiority complex" of Americans toward England and the Continent, and American scholars from his time on have been concerned (at times, even obsessed) with demonstrating that Americans have in fact produced a high culture worthy of being taken seriously.[7] A perhaps disproportionate amount of energy has therefore been devoted to first the rehabilitation and then the minute editing and interpretation of the work of religious intellectuals.

American religious scholarship has also been influenced substantially by the theological presuppositions of its practitioners. The Neo-Orthodox movement in religious thought and ethics has stressed the importance of Christian involvement in the historical and political arenas, and has correspondingly lent itself to a particular, even exaggerated, interest in the interrelationships of religion and the political sphere.[8] Popular religion, from this normative standpoint, emerges as at best irrelevant and at worst reprehensible. Correspondingly, religious movements and phenomena that have regarded political activity as indifferent or negative have received rather short shrift.

This is not to attack traditional scholarship in itself. Rather, it is to suggest that cultural presuppositions and hidden agenda in considerable measure shape the paths which scholarly investigation pursues. More constructively, it is an effort to note in the following pages some phenomena which have not come in for their proper share of attention, and some ways in which they might now be revealed as a hitherto largely unsuspected source of illumination of the American—and, more broadly, the human—experience.

RELIGION, CULTURE, SYMBOLS, AND SOCIETY

Much of the interpretation that follows draws heavily not only on the work of historians but also on that of behavioral scientists, particularly anthropologists. This is not accidental. In the first place, the fortunes of the study of religion as an independent subject—*Religionswissenschaft*—have been tied intimately to the rise of the social and behavioral sciences as academic disciplines.[9] The nineteenth-century pioneers in these realms—Freud, Marx, Tylor, Frazer, Weber, Durkheim—all found themselves obliged to encounter head-on the problem of religion, whether they were sympathetic, hostile, or indifferent to its contemporary manifestations. Primitive cultures were irretrievably suffused with often baffling symbolic behavior, and could not even be approached by an interpreter without a direct confrontation of that behavior. Sociologists contemplating the "dilemma of modern man" equally had to note the correlation of the emergence of that dilemma with the gradual or rapid erosion of "sacrality" and the onset of "secularization" brought about by the political, social, and technological upheavals of their time.[10] Both religion and its absence were radically problematic, and had to be dealt with directly.

Anthropology's great and basic contribution to the study of religion in general (and of popular religion in particular) is the extraordinarily rich concept of *culture*.[11] "Culture" is almost as difficult to define as is "religion"; nevertheless, we can make a few preliminary observations about the relationships between the two. First, the notion of culture involves the interrelatedness of all realms of human activity. It suggests that there are no independent variables in collective life, and that, in particular, symbolic activity correlates with other aspects of social and cultural experience. Religion, in short, cannot be dealt with in a vacuum. Although it may possess its own unique structures and institutions, their particular manifestations reflect and in turn influence all other aspects of culture.

Secondly, the study of culture—especially when accompanied by its corollary, cultural relativism—relativizes not only the value of one people's experience compared with that of another but also the importance of the various components of a particular culture. All of a culture's aspects become significant, since each holds a place in a matrix that is indissolubly linked up with all the others. Each aspect potentially implies all the rest. A culture therefore consists not simply of the aggregate of its individual parts but also of the interrelationships among those parts and the patterns or principles that govern those interrelationships. Nothing, then, is trivial; no detail, however humble, is without its value as a clue to the grander pattern. Theologizing and shoe-tying are both worthy of attention and respect.

Religion is part of the continuum of the symbolic activity every culture carries on. However, it is rather difficult to say exactly which part it constitutes, where it begins, and where it leaves off. Symbolic activity is the attribution of power or significance that cannot be empirically measured or verified to persons, places, things, times, events, or situations. Worshipping a god, saluting a flag, or avoiding a broken mirror are all therefore types of symbolic activity by this definition.

However, it is intuitively clear that all these activities are not identical in their meaning or significance. The first, we sense, is without question religious, while the third is probably not. The second case is somewhat more difficult to label, and we shall return to it and similar acts later (in the context of "Civil Religion"). Part of the distinction between religious and other sorts of symbolic action lies in the particularity of an act and its consequences and implications. A broken mirror may bring bad luck, but such misfortune is probably of limited force and not cosmic in its potential significance. We are intuitively inclined to designate this sort of reaction as "superstition" rather than religion, and with good reason.

A symbolic act comes to be "religious" when it is interpreted as part of a wider system of meaning. Superstitions, if they are in fact survivals from pre-Christian belief systems, may once have made sense as part of such a larger framework. However, this structure is now disintegrated. Breaking a mirror or spilling salt no longer has reference to any comprehensive, metaphysical interpretation of the presence of evil or misfortune in the universe; rather, it is a vestigial form of behavior which resembles more closely neurosis than what we commonly mean by religion. (This raises the interesting but not immediately relevant larger issue of Freud's interpretation of religion as a collective neurosis. Let us simply observe at this point that the utility of labeling any culturally prevalent pattern of behavior as "neurotic" is questionable.)[12]

Religion, then, may be tentatively defined as a system of symbolic beliefs and actions—myths, rituals, and creeds and their supporting social structures—which provides its adherents with a coherent interpretation of their universe. Religion is a process of cosmos-construction: it creates order out of chaos, and informs its constituency with a sense of meaning, purpose and significance that would otherwise be lacking. Religion creates order, an order which, ideally, is exhaustive and personally satisfying.

Religion is, moreover, a social phenomenon. The occasional mystic and the contemporary cult of the quest for individual meaning and fulfillment stand, in the larger pattern of human experience, as atypical and eccentric. Even the notion of religious pluralism—of the individual as free to choose among a number of competing religious or ideological options (or none whatever)—is a rather recent development, and has attained wide acceptance only in the context of the American experience.[13]

Much more typical of human experience in the long range has been the coexistence and coextensiveness of belief and social systems. Every known human society (at least until recently) has possessed not only some form of social organization but also some integrated system of myth and symbol through which its sense of cosmic order and purpose has been articulated. The drive for order and security in both the political and conceptual spheres comes close to being as universal and constant as the family and the incest taboo. The varieties of this expression have, of course, varied greatly, and have moreover varied in consonance with broader changes in cultural and social organization. Still, we can assert with some confidence that through most of human experience, the drive toward both social and symbolic order has been nearly irresistible.

RELIGIOUS EXPRESSION AND SOCIAL CONTEXT

Sociologists such as Max Weber, Ferdinand Toennies, Robert Redfield, and Robert Bellah constitute one loosely connected school of the study of social phenomena which has provided a useful schema for the investigation of popular religion in its social context. Using the models or paradigms of social organization these theorists have provided, we can construct a framework through which we can classify a number of types or strains of extra-ecclesiastical (or, loosely, "popular") religion.

The notion of popular religion makes no sense in the context of homogeneous and undifferentiated societies, such as those of most peoples called "primitive." To belong to such a group is *ipso facto* to accept its constructions and interpretations of the universe. It is with increasing differentiation within a society, and more especially with the variety of options presented when complex societies come into contact and conflict with one another and with simpler groups, that the possibility of religious differentiation emerges. It is at this point in social development (or degeneration, if you prefer) that we may first begin to speak of popular religion.[14]

The first "strain" of popular religion which arises in this framework might be called "demotic" religion (from the Greek δῆμος, "people"). The increasingly complex societies that began to emerge in Meso-America, southern and eastern Asia, the ancient Near East, and the Mediterranean worlds in what we call "historic" time all represented consolidations of numbers of different tribes and peoples with varying traditions and cultures. Although these newly amalgamated societies generated their own homogeneous cultural systems, they were usually characterized by increasing internal complexity and differentiation. A military aristocracy, a court bureaucracy, and a caste of religious specialists (priests) emerged as the higher social echelons, and a much larger mass of peasants and soldiers provided a broad base of economic and military support.

On the one hand, these varying groups partook of a common cultural and belief system. On the other, religion, as well as other aspects of culture, began to differentiate in correspondence with the varying classes or castes that emerged in the social sphere. The official cult of the society was maintained, interpreted, and gradually altered by its official guardians, the priestly caste. However, not surprisingly, the official interpretation did not always coincide with that of the people, whose view of the cosmos was inevitably permeated with their own perception of their condition, destiny, needs, and wants. As a result, the "Great Tradition" of the priests, scholars, and aristocrats found a counterpoint in the "Little Tradition" of the people.[15]

The "Little Tradition," then, is the first form of religion we might call authentically popular, in the sense that is of the people rather than the elite. This sort of demotic religion runs through most of the history of Catholicism. It finds its fullest manifestation there in the syncretistic beliefs and practices of peasant peoples—that is, agriculturalists maintaining a traditional and largely isolated way of life, but still living in a symbiotic relationship with the more diverse and sophisticated cultures of the cities (or, perhaps for a time, monasteries). The (at least nominally) Catholic peoples of southern and eastern Europe, of parts of French Canada, and of Mexico are the most significant examples of

Catholic little traditions for our purposes, and we will return to them later.[16] The problem of the little tradition in speaking of Jewish and Protestant peoples is more complex, and we shall deal with it also in due course.

A little tradition is the product of time. It grows slowly as social differentiation emerges in a hierarchically organized society, or as a simpler culture is absorbed into one more powerful. It finds its coherence not only in the experience of the small group but also in the sophisticated tradition in which it at least nominally participates. Therefore, it is not sharply focused on a broad scale, and consists of the aggregate of many often quite differentiated local traditions which all partake of and work variations on the universal themes and symbols provided by the more remote great tradition.

In contrast to the slow nurture of the little tradition, a number of religious movements which develop (and often subside) much more suddenly may also be called popular. In this category fall such relatively recent phenomena as millenarianism, "cargo cults," and revitalization movements such as the Ghost Dance of the Plains Indians in the late nineteenth century. These movements arise in times of cultural crisis, when the traditional ways of a heretofore isolated people come into rapid and disruptive contact with an aggressive and technologically more advanced culture. Typically, part of the symbolic vocabulary of the new order is appropriated (somewhat ironically) into a call for the restoration of the old ways, authenticated by prophecies, revelations, and visions of the victory of the forces of tribal tradition. Such movements almost inevitably fail in their ostensible purpose, and this collapse often paves the way for a new, syncretistic belief system which may be the first stage in the formation of a new little tradition.[17]

A third strain of popular religion also arises out of cultural conflict, but in this case from the confusion that arises out of the internal dislocation brought about by rapid change within a culture. The history of the West since the discovery of America can be seen as a whole chain of often dramatic upheavals, predicated on a technology advancing with geometrical acceleration, and affecting all aspects of human experience. Traditional ways of life were first disrupted on a major scale in Tudor England through the enclosure of common grazing lands, the confiscation of monastic properties, and the repudiation of papal authority. These dramatic strokes, however, had been preceded by a gradual erosion of both the substance and the symbolic legitimation of the traditional, agriculturally based feudal order that had dominated Europe for centuries. Urbanization and later industrialization brought in their wake a chain reaction of social dislocations and a corresponding need for cosmological reorientation which has not yet stopped or been resolved.

A key concept we should introduce at this point is encapsulated in the term *modernization.* This concept, which has its roots in the thought of Max Weber, refers to the broad process through which societies emerge from a traditionalistic orientation toward all aspects of communal life—authority, social organization, knowledge, economy, and so on—and move instead toward a rationalized, centralized, empirical, and efficiency-oriented cultural system. Societies have abetted or resisted the modernization process in varying degrees, but England and the United States have been the nations in which modernization achieved its earliest and in many ways most dramatic consequences.[18]

Modernization is in many ways a secularizing process, and generally results in what we might call the "desacralization" of the world.[19] Scientific, empirical, and pragmatic means of investigation displace authority, tradition, and myth as sources of knowledge and orientation toward the universe. This does not necessarily mean that religion is thereby discredited or displaced completely. It does mean, however, that religious belief and practice tend to become abstract and rationalized, and that certain kinds of symbolic behavior which were typical of premodern forms of religion become increasingly relegated to the interstices of society—that is, they come to constitute "popular religion."

Modernized religion can perhaps best be described as "desupernaturalized"—the role of the supernatural as a direct, tangible force is downplayed considerably. Religious liberalism, in such forms as Unitarianism and the Social Gospel, is a direct response to the modernization process. It downplays the supernatural aspects of Jesus, and stresses rather the continuity of all aspects of the cosmos and the role of ethics as the best way in which religious concern should be displayed. Neo-Orthodoxy, the theological movement which achieved widespread popularity in "elite" circles during the earlier twentieth century, criticized liberalism for its underestimation of human sinfulness, but did not return to a literalistic reading of scripture or a rigid notion of human depravity. It too stressed the importance of ethical conduct, especially in the political realm, but postulated a God totally removed from the realm of the human and finite. This God, who was a far cry from the gentle, human Jesus of the liberals, was nevertheless equally remote from the evangelical God who tended to intervene directly in human affairs, whether individual or collective. Rather, he at times approached the Great Watchmaker of the Enlightenment thinkers in remoteness, and left only his Word as a guide for daily affairs which finite humans could attempt to interpret and apply as best as their meager resources might allow.

Although the rise of Protestantism has correlated significantly with the modernization of the United States and the nations of northwestern

Europe (especially Britain), Protestantism is such a vast movement—or loosely interconnected system of movements—that this harmony has by no means always been the case. The supernatural, which modernization would discredit and discard, by no means disappeared, and divine agency or the intrusion of divine power into the mundane world has been a frequent characteristic of American Protestant belief, especially at the popular level. Miraculous healings, expectations of the imminent return of Christ, seizures of individuals with the power of the Spirit, all have been manifestations of direct appearances of the divine—*hierophanies*—into the realm of the ordinary. This intensely concrete, vivid, and personal kind of religious belief, practice, or experience may be said to characterize popular Protestantism in the United States.

The concept of modernization (and the uneven rates at which it proceeds) in any large society is thus a useful framework for understanding the changes in symbolic or religious life which take place in a society undergoing this process. Religious expression usually correlates with and derives its imagery from the experience of everyday life. A society that is predominantly agricultural will tend to formulate its religious symbols in terms drawn from the natural world; a warlike society will have warrior gods; a feudal society will depict its gods as feudal lords.

A society that is experiencing an increasing depersonalization of social relationships, however, will tend to depict its gods as increasingly remote and depersonalized. At least, this will be the case with those who benefit from and feel at home with the modernization process in its cosmological aspects. Those who are fearful of or impatient with the removal of the supernatural from the realm of history, nature, and the everyday will often embrace religious expression that affirms the supernaturalism that modernistic creeds such as liberalism, Neo-Orthodoxy, or conservative Protestant scholasticism deny. Thus, one way in which contemporary popular religion can be seen is in its aspect as a countermodernization movement, a clinging to or resurrection of supernaturalism in an increasingly desacralized world.

Another theoretical framework that helps to illuminate the phenomena we are classifying as "popular" comes from the thought of the great French sociologist Emile Durkheim.[20] Durkheim postulated that religious experience is ultimately derived from social experience, and that sense of the "holy" or the "sacred" is in fact an emotion derived from the sensation of losing one's self in common participation in the life of a group. Religiosity is thus the symbolic expression of tribalism—that is, of the implicit sense that transcendence attaches itself to or is derived from the social collectivity. For Durkheim, in short, society quite literally is god.

One does not have to accept such a bald-faced formulation of the issue to recognize the suggestiveness of Durkheim's work for investigating the relationship between religious expression and social experience. Social relationships are so integral a part of the human condition that it seems plausible that they should help to shape the expression of "ultimate concern"—that is, religion. Within a culture, people who have known nothing but stable and highly structured relationships with one another are likely to have a different attitude toward the universe than people who have known continual instability, and are likely to express that attitude in correspondingly different symbols. While a theologian would be concerned with sorting out the transient from the permanent validity of these different symbols, it is our concern here simply to examine some of the ways in which social experience helps to mold and shape religious expression.

Mary Douglas and Victor Turner are two contemporary social anthropologists who have attempted to translate Durkheim's fundamental insights into theories applicable not only to primitive tribes but to modernized societies such as our own. We will encounter these theories in more detail later. We might mention at this point, however, that each has provided a useful set of formulations for dealing with the relationship between symbolic expression and various sorts of social dislocation. For example, Turner's notion of the dialectic between "structure" and "anti-structure" provides an interesting way of viewing such highly disparate movements as the early Franciscans and the Hippies of the 1960s in terms of common social experience.[21] Similarly, Mary Douglas has delineated a number of common factors that seem to underlie most situations—whether in tribal Africa or Puritan New England—in which accusations of witchcraft proliferate.[22] Both Douglas and Turner, in short, are concerned with identifying certain types of symbolic or religious expression which correlate consistently with certain types of social experience.

The sociologist Robert Bellah has also built upon Durkheim's fundamental theoretical insights to formulate the richly suggestive notion of "civil religion."[23] Although neither the phrase nor the idea is entirely new with Bellah, he nevertheless has given a definitive formulation to the kind of symbolic activity that takes place when a political unit, such as the modern nation-state, is accorded what amounts to religious reverence. Such a civil religion may include, but is not simply equivalent to, religious nationalism, since it also encompasses some very basic processes of socialization that take place in the public schools. It may be looked upon as the form of tribalism characteristic of modernized societies, and a contemporary manifestation of the basic impulse to worship society which Durkheim saw lying at the very core of religion itself.

We have now mentioned three broad types of social organization which generate significantly different varieties of extra-ecclesiastical religions or symbolic expression which we have called "popular." Sociologists have also recently recognized yet another broad paradigm, which is derived from their reflection on the state of our own society today. In many ways contemporary American society has completed the modernization process. It is heavily urbanized and industrialized, but has moved beyond the "consciousness" or personality type associated with the state of achieving those conditions. Rugged individualism and laissez-faire capitalism are now honored more in the breach than in the observance, and the bureaucrat has displaced the entrepreneur as the typical member of this "post-industrial society" (as it has been designated by the sociologist Daniel Bell).[24]

Some features of this new society especially relevant to the realm of religious and symbolic expression are its emphasis on consumption and enjoyment rather than production and discipline; the all-pervasiveness of media for rapid transportation and communication; the displacement of individual operations by massive, centrally controlled organizations, whether governmental, educational, commercial, or labor; and an increasing freedom from anxiety regarding physical and financial security. As a result, some of the roles organized religion had previously played in providing a buffer against a hostile environment or in providing incentives toward achieving the self-discipline necessary for worldly success have become less and less relevant. Although institutional religion shows no sign of disappearing, and even experiences periodic resurgences, it has come increasingly to share some of its previous functions with other agencies.

Popular religion in post-modern society may be described as diffuse, fragmented, and privatized (not necessarily all at the same time). "Civil religion" is one example of diffuse religiosity, in the sense that such behavior is not systematically codified into a formally prescribed set of myths and rituals that are enacted at times and places specifically designated as religious. Rather, it is *diffused* through the culture at large, and pops up in such occasions as football games, school assemblies, and Memorial Day picnics.[25]

The fragmentation of popular religion is well illustrated in some of the examples given at the very opening of this introduction. Such mass-media features as religious radio or television broadcasts, advice or opinion columns in the newspapers, and even billboards and bumper stickers only loosely cohere into anything resembling a formal structure. Rather, it is possible for an individual or family to be inundated with religious (especially evangelical) stimuli while never attending a service or participating actively in an organization. Religious expression and information, in short, exists in some measure apart from its institutional structures, and one can feel "religious" without ever going to church.

Finally, popular religion has frequently resulted from a process that may be called "privatization." For many people, the experience of the integration of the self with the cosmos, or the achievement of a sense of internal harmony, has been achieved (or approximated) not in the context of formal institutions but rather by the self or in the small group. This experience of integration may take the form of knowledge, experience, or action, but if it is shared at all it is usually with a small group of devotees who either reject the dominant society or are widely scattered throughout that society. While in some ways this pattern resembles that of the religious sects, from the Rhineland Anabaptists to the Jehovah's Witnesses, it is significantly different in one major way: many of these newer groups do not perceive or label themselves as specifically religious. Whether their aim is the transformation of the self or the transformation of society, the impact they have on the individual participant resembles very closely that which has traditionally been the province of religion. Thus, the quest for "ultimate meaning" not only becomes privatized but also, at least ostensibly, "secularized" as well.

In summary, we have described (along a continuum of development derived from the thought of Max Weber) four different types of societies: "primitive," "peasant," "modernizing," and "post-modern." Each of these types of society has generated (or had generated for it) its "official" religion, with beliefs and practices prescribed in most cases by religious specialists operating in the context of institutions. "Popular" religion is generated when these different types of societies come into conflict with one another; when the "official" religion proves inadequate for the purposes of those for whom it is prescribed; or when social confusion reaches such a point that no institutionalized religion is adequate to interpret the ultimate relation of the group or the individual to the cosmos. It is to all of these loosely related forms of "unofficial" or "extra-ecclesiastical" religion that we refer when we invoke the term "popular."

In dealing with these various forms of popular religion, our attention will focus primarily on the relationship of their symbolic expression with the social experience of the groups that generate them. It will be our premise that symbolic expression correlates—if at times only obliquely—with social experience, and we will expect to find that certain types of social structure are congenial to certain types of religiosity. More particularly, we will look to American society, both contemporary and historical, as a virtual laboratory for social and symbolic expression, and try to correlate the rich variety of religious life that has occurred therein with the continual ferment generated by peoples variously affected by the modernization process coming into abrupt and often rather disconcerting contact with one another.

POPULAR RELIGION: TOWARD A WORKING DEFINITION

As this brief survey of the scope of this work suggests, the term "popular religion" is being used to cover a multitude of sins. Despite the radical differences between, say, an American Indian millenarian movement and Catholic Pentecostalism, all the movements that are dealt with in these pages have been selected according to the following principles:

1. In terms of *social structure,* all these movements exist apart from or in tension with established religious groups with regular patterns of organization and leadership. Some of the movements have lasted for a brief period and then evaporated. Others have gone on to develop organizations, but their development no longer concerns us after that point. Still others are loosely organized movements at the fringes of the established churches and denominations, and serve as supplementary sources of religious expression, sometimes encouraged, at other times tolerated or frowned upon by the established groups.
2. In terms of *sociology of knowledge,* the beliefs and lore of these movements are transmitted through channels other than the official seminaries or oral traditions of established religious communities, whether tribal or modernized. This may take the form of new revelation before it receives definitive codification and commentary, or else becomes discredited and discarded; of word-of-mouth transmission after such traditional communication has been largely displaced by the written word; or of mass-circulation paperbacks which convey "how-to-do-it" techniques not explicitly sanctioned (but not necessarily condemned) by established denominations. The relationship of this sort of knowledge to that of the established groups is problematical: it may be tacitly welcomed as a relatively harmless channeling of religious energies and emotions with which the "official" church is unwilling or unable to deal.
3. In terms of *symbolism, expression,* and *behavior*, "official" religion tends to take on characteristics consonant with the broad sociological process called "modernization." It usually is routinized and bureaucratic, and views with suspicion expression and behavior disruptive of its routine. Among conservative groups, theology tends to harden into scholasticism—that is, the codification of revelation into specific propositions and the working of increasingly detailed commentary upon those propositions. Among liberals and the "Neo-Orthodox," God tends

> to become either very human (such as the Unitarian Jesus, who is not really God at all), or else very abstract, and the theological concern is focused largely on social ethics.
>
> Popular movements, in contrast, generally look for signs of divine intervention or manifestation in the realm of everyday experience. This may take the form of possession by the Holy Spirit; of the expectation of an imminent millennium; or miraculous healings or other providential intervention into the natural or social realm; of new revelation from on high; or, conversely, of the demonic disruption of everyday life in the form of witchcraft. Elements of symbolism or behavior of this kind may become the basis of a new movement or may become incorporated into an established cultus; when this happens, however, such behavior tends to become routinized, its immediacy and spontaneity overshadowed by its almost mechanical implementation through the pressure of cultural expectation.

Not all the movements or phenomena included in the following pages conform rigorously to all three of these criteria, though most meet at least two of them. I have thought it advisable to include some movements which might be classified as "sects" or "cults" because of their resistance to routinization and the radical character of their departure from the norms of the "established" churches and sects. (Here we might cite the Father Divine Peace Mission Movement.) On the other hand, much popular religious literature of the last century or so lacks any hint of supernatural intervention into the realm of the everyday, but has certainly been popular both in its extra-ecclesiastical character and in its widespread acceptance among large numbers of people from a wide variety of organized traditions. (Charles M. Sheldon's *In His Steps* and Norman Vincent Peale's *The Power of Positive Thinking* are good examples of this latter category.)

In short, we should always keep in mind as we attempt to study popular religion that it is by no means a rigorous, scientific category of classification. Much of the specialized literature of the sociology of religion concerns itself with questions about the adequacy of by now traditional terms such as "sect," "church," "cult," or "denomination." The fact that such terms are artificial constructs which in the final analysis bear an only approximate relationship to the particularity of social reality should be clear from the briefest perusal of this literature. On the other hand, understanding finally comes only through the continual interplay in the mind between abstractions and specifics. Such terms, in short, are too useful to be dispensed with, whatever their inadequacies. Similarly, "popular religion" is too useful as an heuristic, if not a classificatory, device to be done away with. It points to a whole range of phenomena which, because they have heretofore not been recognized as worthy of serious attention or as constituting a realm of data which bear at least a "family resemblance" to one another, have not received the attention they deserve. What follows is an attempt to begin to focus that attention.

NOTES

1. AHLSTROM'S *Religious History of the American People* (New Haven: Yale University Press, 1972) perhaps represents the fullest development of this irenic, comprehensive approach.
2. The term "popular religion" has to my knowledge only appeared once in the title of a serious academic study—that of LOUIS SCHNEIDER and SANFORD M. DORNBUSCH, *Popular Religion: Inspirational Books in America* (Chicago: University of Chicago Press, 1958/73).* See Chapter 4 for a discussion of its contents.
3. A good introduction to this field by authors who have also written extensively on the sociology of religion is PETER L. BERGER and THOMAS LUCKMANN, *The Social Construction of Reality: A Treatise in the Sociology of Knowledge* (Garden City, N.Y.: Doubleday, 1967).*
4. The Popular Culture Association has been holding annual conventions for several years, and publishes the *Journal of Popular Culture.* Some general works in the area include HERBERT J. GANS, *Popular Culture and High Culture: An Analysis and Evaluation of Taste* (New York: Basic Books, 1974); BERNARD ROSENBERG and DAVID M. WHITE, eds., *Mass Culture: The Popular Arts in America* (Glencoe, Ill.: Free Press, 1957); and GEORGE H. LEWIS, ed., *Side Saddle on the Golden Calf: Social Structure and Popular Culture in America* (Pacific Palisades, Calif.: Goodyear, 1972). Occasional papers and essays on popular religion appear at these conventions and in these journals and anthologies.
5. A good discussion of this phenomenon in the specific context of the study of American religions can be found in MARTIN E. MARTY, *A Nation of Behavers* (Chicago: University of Chicago Press, 1976), Chap. 2 ("History and Religious Social Behavior").
6. This observation was made during the session on "Puritan Studies" at the 1969 annual meeting of the American Historical Association. To the best of my recollection, PROFESSOR JOHN M. BUMSTEAD was its source.
7. See RALPH WALDO EMERSON, "The American Scholar," in ROBERT E. SPILLER, ed., *The American Literary Revolution, 1783-1837* (Garden City, N.Y.: Doubleday Anchor, 1967).* The entire volume is concerned with the phenomenon of American literary nationalism.
8. REINHOLD NIEBUHR was the best-known American spokesman for this position.
9. For the history of this discipline, see JOSEPH M. KITAGAWA, "The History of Religions in America," in MIRCEA ELIADE and JOSEPH M. KITAGAWA, eds., *The History of Religions: Essays in Methodology* (Chicago: University of Chicago Press, 1959);* JACQUES WAARDENBURG, *Classical Approaches to the Study of Religion* (The Hague: Mouton, 1973); MIRCEA ELIADE, "The His-

tory of Religions in Retrospect: 1912 and After," in *The Quest: History and Meaning in Religion* (Chicago: University of Chicago Press, 1969);* and E. E. EVANS-PRITCHARD, *Theories of Primitive Religion* (Oxford: Clarendon Press, 1966).*

10. For a discussion of interpretations of religion in classical sociological theory, see ROBERT A. NISBET, *The Sociological Tradition* (New York: Basic Books, 1966),* Chap. 6 ("The Sacred").
11. For discussions of the development of the concept of culture, see FREDERICK M. BARNARD, "Culture and Civilization in Modern Times," in *Dictionary of the History of Ideas* (New York: Scribner's, 1968/73), I, 613–21; and A. L. KROEBER and CLYDE KLUCKHOHN, *Culture: A Critical Review of Concepts and Definitions* (Cambridge, Mass.: Peabody Museum, 1952).
12. SIGMUND FREUD, *The Future of an Illusion,* ed. JAMES STRACHEY (Garden City, N.Y.: Doubleday Anchor, 1927/64).*
13. It is interesting to note, however, that sociologists of religion are of late beginning to rediscover ERNST TROELTSCH's third category of "mysticism"—in addition to "church" and "sect"—to categorize and interpret recent, extra-ecclesiastical and cultic religious phenomena. See for example, COLIN CAMPBELL, "The Secret Religion of the Educated Classes," in *Sociological Analysis* 39, 2 (Summer 1978), 146–156, as well as the entire Fall 1975 (36, 3) issue of the same journal ("Church, Sect, Mysticism").
14. Much of the following discussion is based on the theoretical framework developed by MAX WEBER in *The Sociology of Religion,* trans. EPHRAIM FISCHOFF (Boston: Beacon, 1922/64).* See also ROBERT N. BELLAH, "Religious Evolution," in WILLIAM A. LESSA and EVON Z. VOGT, eds., *Reader in Comparative Religions: An Anthropological Approach,* 3rd ed. (New York: Harper & Row, 1972).* The LESSA and VOGT volume contains a considerable number of influential articles and essays on our general theme.
15. The terms "Great Tradition" and "Little Tradition" were developed by ROBERT REDFIELD in *Peasant Society and Culture* (Chicago: University of Chicago Press, 1956).* See also WEBER, "Religion of Non-Privileged Classes," *Sociology of Religion,* Chap. VII.
16. ROBERT REDFIELD was a pioneer in studies of this kind. See his *Tepoztlan: A Mexican Village* (Chicago: University of Chicago Press, 1930/73),* and *Chan Kom: A Maya Village* (with ALFONSO VILLA ROJAS) (Chicago: University of Chicago Press, 1934/62).* See also the work of REDFIELD's student, HORACE MINER, *St. Denis: A French-Canadian Parish* (Chicago: University of Chicago Press, 1939/63).* We will return to all these studies in Chapter 2.
17. We will deal with these phenomena in Chapter 1; the footnotes there will contain relevant bibliography.
18. The best introduction for our purposes to the idea of modernization is RICHARD D. BROWN, *Modernization: The Transformation of American Life 1600–1865* (New York: Hill and Wang, 1976).* BROWN provides both a succinct summary of the concept and a provocative application to the development of American society (and, to a lesser extent, England as well).
19. HARVEY COX provides a handy summary of these ideas in his controversial *The Secular City* (New York: Macmillan, 1965).*
20. On DURKHEIM, see especially ROBERT NISBET, *The Sociology of Emile Durkheim* (New York: Oxford University Press, 1974),* and ERNEST E.

WALLWORK, *Durkheim: Morality and Milieu* (Cambridge, Mass.: Harvard University Press, 1972).

21. VICTOR TURNER, *The Ritual Process: Structure and Anti-Structure* (Chicago: Aldine, 1969),* Chap. 4.
22. See Chapter 3, notes 125 and 135.
23. ROBERT N. BELLAH, "Civil Religion in America," in WILLIAM G. MCLOUGHLIN and ROBERT N. BELLAH, eds., *Religion in America* (Boston: Beacon, 1968).*
24. See Chapter 4, note 1. Chapter 4 deals more fully with religion in the "post-Modern era."
25. A theoretical framework for discussing the diffusion of religious functions into other aspects of culture is provided in THOMAS LUCKMANN, *The Invisible Religion* (New York and London: Macmillan/Collier, 1963/67/70).*

1

Traditional Religions and the Clash of Cultures

PRELIMINARY OBSERVATIONS

The rise to public attention of the sufferings endured by black and aboriginal peoples in the United States has made it clear that their historical experience with the forces of modernization has been less than happy. The once coherent and vital cultures of these peoples were violently disrupted as they were systematically displaced from their homelands by kidnapping and sale into slavery or by forcible displacement into reservations. We do not need to rehearse here the causes, the history, or the deplorable character of these melancholy events; these tasks have already been accomplished. It is rather for us to note the consequences of this process of social dislocation in the symbolic and religious lives of these peoples.

Over the centuries, many blacks and Native Americans have chosen a course of acculturation to, if not total assimilation into, the culture and religion of the dominant whites. Black denominations parallel to the Baptists, Methodists, and Pentecostals have arisen and thrived, and other blacks and Indians have joined the Roman Catholic Church and the various Protestant denominations with a greater or lesser degree of acceptance. However interesting these developments might be to an historian or sociologist of religion, however, they are not of direct concern to us.

What does interest us are those phenomena and movements which arose to fill the vacuum created by the cultural disintegration that was the result of the impingement of aggressively modernizing Western cultures on the traditional societies of Africa and North America. Some, like the Ghost Dance and the Father Divine Peace Mission Movement, proved evanescent, and did not survive such shocks as the death of their founder or a disastrous military encounter. Others, such as the Peyote Cult and the Nation of Islam (Black Muslims) have endured beyond their initial phases, and have modified considerably their original emphases in the direction of accommodation with the broader American society. It is these movements in their initial stages—those periods pregnant with the generation of new symbols—which are our concern.

How we interpret these new symbolic clusters depends in considerable measure on our vested interests and point of view. An orthodox Christian theologian might see some of the movements we are about to examine as consisting of some shreds of Christian truth irreparably compromised by the debris of paganism that surrounds them. This is not a viewpoint that is profitable for our purposes. Neither is its converse—namely, the liberal theological position that they contain germs of truth only somewhat obscured by lack of opportunity to emerge into complete fruition. Whether either of these viewpoints is true from the standpoint of theology is here irrelevant; neither, in short, is *useful* in achieving the sort of clarification we are after.

An historian operating simply *qua* historian would approach these movements by seeking the earliest manifestations of their essential parts, and then tracing the development of those parts over time. The results of this enterprise are indispensable building blocks for our undertaking, but they are not themselves part of that undertaking. Similarly, the "functionalist" sociologist would look upon these symbolic activities as finally aimed at the achievement of certain very this-worldly goals—social reintegration, protection from the hostile outside world, the attainment of material success—rather than the ostensibly supernatural aims which most religious movements claim as their overt ends. This sort of analysis is also ancillary to our purposes here, since it undeniably contributes to the number of plausible angles of interpretation that must finally converge to provide a full and satisfactory complex of explanations.

Our major concern here is to note that in many cases there seems to be a distinct relationship between the social experience undergone by a people—in our cases, mostly that of cultural dislocation—and the kinds of symbols that arise to form the centers of new movements generated by or responding to changes in social experience. This is not to explain religious movements by reducing them to a set of historical roots or latent functions. Rather, it is simply to point out that certain types of social experience are frequently accompanied by corresponding types of symbolic expression and activity. No final and irreducible formulae can be derived to express these relationships or to predict what might happen in future, similar situations. What we can do, however, is to look back and observe the significant (though hardly inevitable) congruences between experience and expression.

The Amerind and Afro-American movements we are about to examine in some detail may all be seen as responses to cultural and social dislocation through the erosion or rupture of cultures which had until the modern period evolved through interaction with their environment and with similar societies. Although they may have been "primitive" from the standpoint of technological sophistication, their languages, mythologies, and kinship systems were much more complex than those of the "advanced" societies of today. Nevertheless, they proved unable to generate more than a temporarily successful resistance to the encroachments of the modernizing societies of Western Europe and, later, the United States. The result was genocide, enslavement, or reduction to a half-life on reservations or urban ghettos on the fringes of the mainstream of American life.

For those who were unable to cling to the traditional myths and rituals of their tribal religions but who were simultaneously unwilling to adopt the religion of the more powerful interlopers, a symbolic vacuum arose that was not long in being filled. The new movements that arose in these contexts were usually *syncretistic* in their symbolism—they borrowed elements from other, newer systems and grafted them onto the base of tradition, or they combined elements from two or more different cultural systems to form a new synthesis. Such movements in their initial, "effervescent" stages were usually unstable. Either they spent themselves quickly in futile military endeavor or millenarian expectation or they came more and more to resemble the religions of the dominant culture as they achieved greater stability and routinization.

It is these effervescent moments particularly that are of interest to us as students of extra-ecclesiastical religion. In the first place, the rapid emergence of a new religious movement takes us out of the realm of the established structures, whether traditional or bureaucratic, through which ritual is organized and myth is perpetuated and interpreted. These movements take shape when established social structures lose their compelling quality for a significant number of believers, and a new system of worship, belief, and—often most dramatically—behavior and action is sought.

Secondly, the kind of symbolic expression and action that is usually generated by such movements is conspicuous in the modern world for its overt supernaturalism. Whether this takes the form of millenarian expectation, adoration of a deified human being, or the cultivation of mystical or visionary experiences, the result is that those conditioned to think in terms of God working (if at all) through the orders of nature and society often regard such "fringe" movements as at best weird and at worst threatening. Similarly, the appeal to mythic modes of explanation, the invocation of immediate revelation for legitimacy, and the juxtaposition of seemingly incongruous or illogically related symbols all give offense to the pattern of discursive thought and empirical cognition that seems to be a peculiarly Western characteristic.

The typology that best describes the phenomena in which we are interested is "movement," a term self-chosen by some leaders such as Father Divine for his enterprise. "Movement," which is hardly a technical term, is extremely useful in its suggestion of fluidity, lack of formal structure, and freedom from traditional modes and sanctions. Some of these movements go on to become "sects" or "cults," terms which imply a greater fixity and stability of self-conception and organization, but which are also difficult to define precisely. What follows are descriptions and interpretations of a number of quite different movements among the black and Amerind populations of North America, with emphasis on their "effervescent" stages. That consideration is given in some cases to their emergence into more permanent organizations points to the difficulty of deciding exactly when a "movement" changes into a "sect" (or, in some cases, a "church"). In addition, it simply rounds out stories that might otherwise be left dangling.

NATIVE AMERICAN (AMERIND) MOVEMENTS

The story of the inexorable and often violent pushing back of the American Indians from a position of dominance over the entire continent into a handful of barren reservations is now common knowledge. By the late nineteenth century, armed resistance occurred only occasionally, and most Amerinds realized that they were vastly overpowered in technological capability by their white adversaries. The result was not only loss of political and military power but also an increasing sense that culturally and cosmologically, in John Donne's phrase, all coherence was gone.

Not surprisingly, the violent disruption of the traditional patterns of Indian life had major consequences for their religious expression. Before discussing these consequences, however, we should note first that tribal life had been anything but static. The history of the American Indians from the time of their migration across the Bering Strait into the New World was a story of endless wanderings and intercultural contacts among themselves. A great diversity of cultures thus arose, ranging from the simple food-gatherers of California to the complex high civilizations of the Aztecs and Mayas of Meso-America. After the Spanish conquest those Indians who had maintained their independence readily incorporated many elements of European culture into their own. The stereotype of the Indian on horseback hunting bison on the plains is in many ways accurate, but only for the period after which the horse and rifle had been introduced by the Spaniards.[1]

The traditional religions of the American Indians were similarly open to modification through cultural contacts. Although each tribal unit had its own particular complex of myths and rituals, new circumstances made possible the incorporation of novel elements either through borrowings from other tribes or through the elaboration of new visions received by shamans. Supernatural power was not usually concentrated in a high god or pantheon so much as it was diffused throughout all nature. When new manifestations of power made themselves felt through contact with other cultures—including, finally, the European—the symbols of that power could be assimilated syncretistically into a complex of myths and rituals and result in a modification rather than the total overthrow of one religious system in favor of another. This pattern of selective modification through a combination of borrowings on the one hand and the introduction of new, indigenous visions on the other is characteristic of the movements inspired by white contacts which we are about to discuss.[2]

Responses to a more powerful culture which attempts conquest or domination can take place in a number of ways. Before it was apparent that the Indians must necessarily succumb to the superior military force of the whites, much of their response was pragmatic: force would be pitted against force. More usually, however, such military movements would draw on supernatural legitimation of a prophetic sort.[3] The "conspiracy of Pontiac" in 1763 and the attempts of Tecumseh, with the aid of his visionary brother Tenskwatawa, to establish an intertribal alliance against the Americans in the first decade of the nineteenth century were both examples of movements in which pragmatic and supernatural elements combined to result in anti-white militancy.[4] Since most important Indian undertakings had traditionally drawn on supernatural assistance, these responses in themselves were not particularly novel.

As the nineteenth century progressed, it became increasingly apparent that even supernaturally assisted military force was inadequate to the radical challenge the imperialistic ambitions of the whites posed to Indian hegemony. Two major patterns of response, each based primarily on supernatural as opposed to pragmatic force, emerged during the course of that century. The more dramatic of these was the expectation that a "millennial" cataclysm would take place in which the intruders would be destroyed and the aboriginal peoples restored to power. This was the underlying pattern of the Ghost Dance. The other, less dramatic but more durable in the long run, is illustrated in the teachings of Handsome Lake among the Seneca and in the peyote religion which achieved a great popularity among a considerable number of tribes during the twentieth century. This latter type of movement, often called "accommodationist," involves a radical transformation of individual lifestyle, so that adjustment to the new order is achieved while elements of traditional identity are also retained. In the remainder of this section, we will consider these three movements in chronological order.[5]

The Seneca of western New York among whom Handsome Lake

began his movement were members of the powerful but loose confederation of tribes known collectively as the Iroquois.[6] Seneca men were hunters and ferocious warriors; the women, though more sedentary, carried on the tribe's agriculture and played an important role in the political life of this matrilineal and matrilocal people. During most of the eighteenth century, the Iroquois had managed to maintain a good deal of autonomy by successfully playing off the French and British against one another. When they later tried the same game with the British and the Americans, however, they met with considerably less success, and were obliged to come to terms with the armies and government of the victorious new nation.

Fortunately for the Seneca, the years in which they negotiated with the newly formed American government were ones of change from a policy of treatment of Indians as a conquered people to a policy that at least attempted to do them justice and to provide programs of technological assistance and instruction to aid them in adjusting to a new way of life. Nevertheless, the Seneca fell prey to unscrupulous land speculators, and had been so unsettled by their military defeats and the erosion of their traditional power that they fell into a state of collective demoralization. Their numbers had been decimated not only through military losses but also through crop destruction, famine, and epidemics of diseases introduced by the whites. Alcoholism and an increase in witchcraft accusations betokened a disintegrating society, and the Seneca were reduced to a squalid life in what Anthony F. C. Wallace has described as "slums in the wilderness."[7]

The military powerlessness of the Seneca, together with their proximity to white settlers, made it unlikely that they would turn to supernatural hopes of millenarian upheavals as a way of coping with their situation. If a movement of revitalization were to arise, it was much more likely to take the form of a supernaturally sanctioned accommodation with white society instead. That, in fact, is precisely what happened through the message of the warrior turned drunkard turned prophet, Handsome Lake. From a state of nearly total demoralization during the last years of the eighteenth century, the Seneca underwent what Wallace has described as their "death and rebirth." They emerged no longer a completely independent group following traditional ways, but rather a reconstituted people, very much Indians, but having adopted a sufficient portion of white ways and values to be able to survive in the world that had been thrust upon them.

The acculturation of the Seneca was facilitated by two related external factors. On the one hand, the new national government was willing to abrogate its old policy of suppression and to provide territorial assurances and some measure of technical assistance. Secondly and more important, a number of Quakers arrived from Philadelphia to work among the Seneca and to try to help them without imposing their own brand of Christianity through coercion. These people were warmly received by most of the Indians, though their arrival polarized to some degree the dominant faction that was receptive to assimilation and the hostile minority committed to resistance of any white influence or interference. The Quakers began a school, set up a model farm to demonstrate agricultural techniques, and in a low-key fashion went about setting an example of sobriety and hard work which the Seneca might take or leave as they liked. This approach of "friendly persuasion" proved remarkably effective in the long run in contrast to the "hard-sell" techniques of other Protestant missionaries, even though the eventual religious realignment of the Indians took an unforeseen turn through the influence of Handsome Lake.

Handsome Lake had once been a powerful warrior and leader among the Seneca but, with many of his fellows, had fallen upon bad times. He had succumbed to the curse of the Indian, whiskey. His health was poor, and he did not expect to live very long. However, in June of 1799, he experienced the first of a series of visions which would radically transform not only his own life but ultimately the lives of his whole people as well.

The supernatural vision was nothing new among American Indians. In many tribes, shamans were expected to make trance voyages into the world beyond from time to time, and young men often underwent similar experiences during their initiation into manhood. The Seneca had placed special emphasis on dream visions, in which messages were conveyed to the dreamer by supernatural beings. These were sometimes intended to be conveyed to the whole tribe as well. According to Wallace, the Seneca also placed great value on another sort of dream, in which the unconscious wishes of the dreamer's soul were expressed. Once interpreted, these had to be satisfied either literally or symbolically before the tribe could rest content again.[8]

Dream visions in which a supernaturally derived program of revitalization for a whole people were revealed also had precedent in the experience of the Indians of the Northeast. In the years 1762 and 1763, the "Delaware Prophet" had appeared on the Cuyahoga River near Lake Erie and proclaimed the results of his own journey to the Other World. He had gone to heaven in search of the Master of Life, who, when found, proceeded to deliver a series of instructions for the Indians. They were to be temperate and monogamous, and to maintain peace among themselves. These basically European virtues, however, were counterpointed with an injunction to drive out the very whites from which these values had been acquired. If the Indians succeeded in this program and rejected white ways (or those which they perceived to be such), they would be restored to their former happy state. His program, though presented as a movement of restoration, was in fact highly syncretistic, and incorporated such European concepts as a high creator god as well as the white values already mentioned. It was this movement to which Pontiac became a convert, and which he utilized as an ideological grounding for his anti-European military campaign.

The visions of Handsome Lake, then, did not take place in a vacuum. They had general precedents in tribal experience and more specific models in the messages of the Delaware Prophet and other Indian messiahs. However, their specific content was molded both by the particular circumstances of the Seneca and by the personality of Handsome Lake himself. The Seneca were too down and out to respond to any call to arms against the whites. Rather, any message that could serve as a basis for their regeneration had to be one that could accommodate their own situation realistically if it was to have any staying power. This is exactly what Handsome Lake provided for them.

In his first vision, three angelic visitors (perhaps metamorphoses of his Quaker benefactors) appeared to Handsome Lake and delivered a series of injunctions which the Seneca were to obey if they were to prosper.[9] On the one hand, they were to retain many of their old customs, especially the traditional Strawberry Festival. On the other, they were to abstain from the practices that were symptomatic of the social breakdown of their community, such as drunkenness, witchcraft, love magic, and abortion. The visitors also prescribed a ritual for confession.

Another vision followed, in which a fourth "angel" conducted the prophet on a tour of the other world while he remained in a trance. There he saw, as had Dante, the plan of heaven and hell, and learned how the faithful were rewarded and the miscreants punished. (The latter, as in the *Inferno,* were subjected to retribution appropriate to their offences. Drunkards, for example, had molten metals poured down their throats.) In the Indian version of the *Paradiso,* Handsome Lake was introduced to both George Washington and Jesus, and learned how the latter had also been betrayed by the whites.

The gospel Handsome Lake derived from these visions and began to preach to his people was apocalyptic. After three generations, the earth would be enveloped in flames in which the wicked would perish. Those, however, who followed the ethical teachings—the *Gaiwiio*—which had now been revealed, would be eligible for eternal residence in the Indian version of heaven. It is worth noting here that this map of the cosmos which Handsome Lake had been given by his divine visitors bore little resemblance to traditional Indian conceptions of the afterlife, which were usually of a rather vague and ethnocentric sort. A clearly delineated heaven and hell were Christian ideas, and their appearance in this context illustrates how syncretistic the whole program of Handsome Lake had been from the start.

Beginning in 1801 and continuing till his death in 1815, Handsome Lake's preaching of the *Gaiwiio* shifted in its emphasis. Where the earlier version had been primarily eschatological, the second and more enduring body of teaching was ethical. Again, the borrowings from Christianity and especially from the Quakers is evident. He advocated temperance, peace, social unity and, in distinction from the Delaware Prophet, living on good terms with the whites. Quaker schooling was good as long as it did not interfere with the observance of the *Gaiwiio*. Similarly, Handsome Lake endorsed the white example of a sedentary agricultural life, with the provision that crops were to be grown for intratribal consumption rather than for competitive sale in white markets. The rest of his program consisted of moralistic prohibitions similar to those of Evangelical Protestantism—gambling, dancing, and, of course, alcohol—together with a series of injunctions emphasizing domestic harmony and the primacy of the nuclear family on the white model.

Handsome Lake's influence as a political leader rose and at times rather abruptly fell during the remaining years of his life, but the *Gaiwiio* was enthusiastically accepted by the Seneca from the beginning. Some opposed any acculturation whatever and others became fully Christianized, but in the main the way of Handsome Lake prevailed. After his death the movement became institutionalized by his followers and descendants, and it continues to this day as the religion of several thousand Seneca Indians.

The appropriateness of Handsome Lake's message for the Seneca should be clear enough. On the one hand, it was a way of maintaining identity through the retention of many of the old ways (several important traditional ceremonies were incorporated into the ritual). On the other, it provided an ideological framework for a change to a way of life that was similar to but not identical with that of the surrounding dominant culture. Anthropologists have called this sort of movement "accommodationist," "introversionist," or "redemptive," according to which of its features they have chosen to emphasize. As we shall see, the Peyote religion of the twentieth century is similar to that of Handsome Lake in many respects. However, in order to provide some context for Peyotism, we must now turn in chronological sequence to a movement of a very different sort.

For Handsome Lake, it was obvious that the whites were in such firm control of the situation that there was no real hope for their military overthrow. However, the situation on the western frontier during the middle and later nineteenth century was not nearly so clear-cut. White settlement had been slower and more dispersed than in the East for simple geographical reasons, and the Indians had been left with considerably more physical and psychological space in which to maneuver. Contact with whites had been less systematic and more violent than had been the case with the Iroquois, and the influences of such acculturative agents as missionaries and government agents had been less potent. As it became clearer to the Indians that their destiny was to be confinement to the reservations (which often consisted of land rejected by whites as unsuitable for settlement), they began to express their frustrations in supernaturalistic modes very different from those of the Seneca.

The basic experience of all of these Indians was similar. The old way of life was vanishing. The buffalo herds that had been the basis for both material and ceremonial life were disappearing from the plains, and a prestige system based on warfare was now unworkable under white supervision. It was also clear enough who was responsible for these conditions. Since armed conflict against the whites was becoming increasingly problematical and unattractive, an even stronger force had to arise on the behalf of the Indians if the enemy was to be overcome. This power could only be supernatural.

Both the Delaware Prophet and Tecumseh's brother Tenskwatawa seem to have preached that if the Indians gave up white ways and returned to the purity of their traditional practices, the whites would be driven out. In the former case, the Indians themselves were to have grown powerful enough to accomplish the task for themselves. The case of Tenskwatawa is less clear, but probably involved a combination of direct action and a supernaturally induced cataclysm in which the Indian dead would return to life and the whites would be destroyed. In the 1870s and 1880s, a series of prophets arose among some of the western tribes. These prophets predicted destruction of the whites and, at times, the return of ancestors as well. These desiderata were to be brought about through varying combinations of direct action and supernatural intervention.[10]

The tribes of the Northwest also possessed a tradition of an expected cosmic cataclysm and a subsequent return of the dead which antedated contact with whites. With the advent of white encroachment, however, these beliefs were combined both with Christian millenarian elements and with the prediction that the whites would be annihilated in the apocalyptic event. This message was first articulated in compelling form by Smohalla, a member of the Wanapum of eastern Washington. Smohalla had attended Catholic schools as a youth and also had experienced visions at an early age.[11] After traveling in the Southwest, he returned to claim that he had visited the Spirit World, and had learned of the Great Chief's anger at those Indians who were abandoning traditional ways for those of the usurping whites. To save themselves from divine wrath, Smohalla preached that the Indians should adopt a new syncretistic ritual that had been revealed to him. In additon, they were hereafter to live on the spontaneous produce of Mother Nature rather than disturb her through the use of the plow and the hoe. Although the whites were to be annihilated by divine action at the end of time, Smohalla's pacifistic message was transformed by some neighboring tribes into a call for militant action. The results, not surprisingly, were not to their liking.

A similar movement among other western tribes which may have been influenced by the teaching of Smohalla was the Ghost Dance, which took place in two phases. The earlier dance was revealed by the Paviotso prophet Wodziwub in western Nevada around 1870.[12] His message was similar to that of Smohalla: if the new dance were carried out, the dead would return, the whites would be supernaturally destroyed, and the Indians would live forever in an earthly paradise. The movement did not advocate overt aggression, and faded soon after it became clear that no cosmic cataclysm was imminent.

The Ghost Dance that is best remembered today began in the same region of Nevada in 1889 through the prophecies of Wovoka (Jack Wilson), the immediate heir of the tradition of Wodziwub.[13] Like Smohalla and Handsome Lake, Wovoka experienced a vision in which he too visited the world of spirits. There he beheld a land filled with game and inhabited by all the Indians who had died in the past. The instructions he received were of a pacifistic sort. The Indians were to abstain from warfare and live peaceably with one another. If they obeyed these commandments they would be united with the dead and would live forever in health and prosperity.

The Ghost Dance of Wovoka achieved an immediate and extraordinary popularity among Indians of a wide variety of different tribes. Envoys came from all directions to receive the message directly from Wovoka. Local elaborations and variations were worked on the basic themes in the different tribal contexts. Although the Dance itself was not intended to engender militant movements, it took on an activistic dimension in some areas. The temptation to direct military action was enhanced as well by the innovation called the "Ghost Shirt," which was supposedly (but, alas, not actually) efficacious in providing invulnerability against the bullets of the whites.

The Ghost Dance came to a tragic climax among the Sioux. Recently confined to reservations in the Dakotas, many of them still relished the memory of the recent defeat they had inflicted on General Custer and his troops at the battle of the Little Big Horn.[14] Many of the younger men especially were reluctant to abandon their warlike traditions for a sedentary agricultural life on marginal lands. As had been the experience of most of the Plains tribes, the Sioux had been continually engaged in frustrating negotiations with the American government over the terms of settlement by which they had agreed to reservation life. They had been forced to deal with a succession of Indian agents, military men, and various governmental bodies in Washington whose integrity and capacity for dealing with the Indians varied considerably. In their frustration, many Indians eagerly turned to the Ghost Dance as an appeal for supernatural relief. Unfortunately, many whites interpreted this strange new activity as a manifestation of potential violence. A long succession of misunderstandings ensued, culminating in the massacre at Wounded Knee on 29 December 1890. Scores of women and children as well as Indian men were killed by the American troops, and the latter suffered numerous casualties as well. The combination of this disaster and the inefficacy of the Ghost Dance in bringing help from the world beyond marked the end of the Sioux as a proud and independent people.

Although the Ghost Dance was as doomed to failure as are all millenarian movements through their very nature, it had been conspicuously successful as a forerunner of the pan-Indian movements that would characterize much of American Indian religion and culture during the twentieth century.[15] Earlier movements such as that of Tenskwatawa had succeeded temporarily in allying several tribes in common beliefs and endeavors, but none had achieved the extraordinary popularity which the Ghost Dance received among the Plains Indians. It was indicative of a new consciousness that was arising among American Indians of all sorts. No longer could they live as small, localized groups which could interpret their experience in terms of traditional indigenous mythologies. Now they had become a people who found a common identity in their negative experiences with and differences from the whites. Some, of course, chose to reject any traditionalistic identity, and aggressively pursued a course of acculturation. Others rejected any innovation, and attempted to cling to what was left of their individual tribal heritages. For a significant number, however, a new identity, neither entirely traditional nor fully assimilationist, seemed to be the answer. The Peyote religion was the most successful manifestation of this new impulse.

Peyote, or *Lophophora williamsii,* is a small cactus whose dried flesh resembles a button.[16] Its active ingredients are nine alkaloids, the most important of which is mescaline. When ingested, peyote acts as an hallucinogen. Its effects are not pleasant: it is bitter to the taste and produces nausea, anxiety, and depression. Once the unpleasantness subsides, however, it leaves the user in a state of euphoria, and produces alterations in perception and consciousness which are highly valued by its proponents. It is neither a narcotic nor addictive. Those aspects of the external world which users perceive under the influence of peyote seem to contain a personal meaning, giving them a feeling that they are communicating with a universe that has something important to reveal to them about themselves.

The use of peyote for prophecy and curing was common in Mexico for some centuries before it became incorporated into the ritual of the Native American Church (the loose organization of Indian Peyotists founded in the twentieth century).[17] It was also utilized by the Mescalero Apache around 1870, but their ceremonies lacked the syncretistic Christian elements which were later introduced by most of its practitioners. The Kiowa, Comanche, and Caddo were the first tribes to use the cactus in rituals that were to form the basis of the contemporary cult. The movement spread rapidly from these southwestern tribes, and eventually reached as far north as Wisconsin and British Columbia. Today its adherents are probably the most numerous of any exclusively Indian religious group.[18]

In some tribes Peyotism filled a void that had been left in the wake of the failure of the Ghost Dance. Although its origins had been pacifistic, its militaristic transformations had left tribes like the Sioux with little except a sense of frustration and defeat. It was becoming increasingly clear not only that the whites were there to stay but also that they were the sole possessors of real worldly power. The only serious alternatives were withdrawal and in-turning or an effort at assimilation. Peyotism provided a combination of both of these responses, which appealed primarily to those who had already undergone some degree of acculturation but were reluctant or unable to carry the process of Americanization to its dubious conclusion.[19]

Although the details of ritual and belief vary somewhat among the considerable number of tribes that practice Peyotism, a standard form has emerged as a basic ceremony.[20] The participants assemble in a tipi around a fire and a crescent-moon-shaped mound of earth. The fixed part of the rite is conducted in English, while the rest of the ceremony consists of spontaneous prayers in the native language. The ceremony begins on Saturday evening and continues through the night until the meeting is dispersed for a Sunday-morning meal and a period of sociability in which women are also included. (Only men are allowed to participate in the ceremony proper.) The central feature of the ritual is the passing around of the peyote buttons, which are then eaten in various quantities. Much of the time is spent in individual meditation and indulgence in visions inspired by the peyote. As in a traditional Catholic mass, the worshippers divide their activity between social participation in the ceremonial rites and isolated individual contemplation, so that contact with the divine is simultaneously mediated and immediate.

This individual encounter with the Peyote Spirit through the use of peyote lies at the heart of the religion, although the ritual context is a *sine qua non* for a successful encounter. The traditional Indian cosmos was filled with power, and the goal of any religion was to come into contact with its manifestations and to channel it to one's individual or a tribe's collective purposes. This was not simply a magical transaction in which the correct performance of certain rites would automatically bring specified results. Rather, the worshipper had to have first attained purity of heart, so that he was spiritually prepared to encounter the otherness which the powers pervading the universe represented. Only then could he take the power unto himself.

Peyotism has been given theological expression in which various Christian symbols such as the Trinity and its members are reinterpreted in terms of Indian thought patterns.[21] Formal doctrine, however, is really beside the point. What really matters is the encounter of the individual with powers beyond himself through the mediating agency of peyote. In this way the individual gains an insight that cannot be derived through empirical or logical processes. He instead attains to a psychological state in which external truth perceived in its immediacy becomes relevant to his own existential situation, and he is thus enabled to come to terms with himself and his situation in the world. The day-to-day concerns of life thus become relativized and placed in a perspective through which their exigency is diminished. The acquisition of power is thus expressed not so much in terms of force that can be utilized to change external circumstances, but in terms of a state of internal harmony that renders the frustration of living in a white world less problematical.

Although doctrine is subordinate to experience, ethics, in the broad sense of orientation toward others as well as specific rules of conduct, plays an important role among the more acculturated of the Peyotists.[22] The ethic is called "Peyote Road," and consists of a combination of emphases derived both from tradition and from Christianity. It is similar in many ways to the teaching of Handsome Lake, and stresses abstinence from alcohol, brotherly love, care of family, marital fidelity, and self-reliance. It is a practical and workable set of injunctions and attitudes, adapted specifically to the needs of a traditionalistic people who are no longer able to function in the old ways and need simultaneously to deal with the white world while protecting themselves from the special dangers that world holds out to Indians.

Like the Ghost Dance (and unlike the Handsome Lake movement), Peyotism is a pan-Indian movement that has gained adherents among highly diverse tribes. Especially among peoples like the Navaho, where hostility to the movement is strong and its members constitute a fairly small minority of the entire community, identification tends to be more with other Peyotists regardless of tribe rather than with fellow tribe members of differing religious attachments.[23] While not rejecting Christianity and, in fact, incorporating a number of Christian elements into their symbol system, Peyotists regard the institutional forms of Catholicism and Protestantism as a white person's faith, appropriate for whites but not meant for Indians. Instead, they conceive of themselves as relating to the same god through a different mediator. The Peyote Spirit encountered in the ritual is sometimes identified with Jesus or the Holy Spirit, and serves the same mediating functions as do the Christian figures. It is the spiritual means through which divine power comes into contact with and can be assimilated by human beings. In the pluralistic spiritual universe of Indian traditional religions, no contradiction is involved. All spiritual power is ultimately one, but its manifestations are modified according to the situation of the individuals or groups who seek to encounter it.

Finally, a word is in order on the organization of Peyotism[24]. The notion of a formal, rationalized organization is as foreign to unacculturated Indians as it is to all traditional peoples. However, the hostility expressed by whites toward Peyotism—especially by the powerful Bureau of Indian Affairs before the administration of the sympathetic anthropologist John Collier—made some sort of structure necessary for self-defense and representation to the outside world. Beginning in the first decade of the twentieth century, a series of organized groups came into being and eventually culminated in the founding of the Native American Church of the United States in 1944. ("United States" was changed to "North America" in 1955 to acknowledge the Canadian component of the movement.) The role of the organization, however. was confined to the handling of external affairs (primarily legal) rather than doctrinal formulation or internal supervision. The localistic character of traditional Indian religiosity was thus preserved, while the exigencies of dealing with hostile whites was simultaneously acknowledged. This approach to organization is characteristic of Peyotism in general: it accommodates a modified traditionalistic approach to religion with the acoutrements of white society necessary to live at the same time in two worlds.

To summarize, each of the new movements that arose among the American Indians during the period when their relationship with the increasingly dominant whites was being worked out was an attempt to bring about a new relationship through social reorganization legitimated by supernatural sanctions. In each case a new mandate for action, organization, and behavior was mediated by supernatural revelation, often through the agency of a prophet other than the usual shaman or medicine man who was the source of religious knowledge in more stable situations. The replacement of tribal identity by that provided by participation in a pan-Indian, intertribal movement involved extensive social reorganization, some sort of which was in any case necessary as the realities of white encroachment became all too evident. The emphasis on dream visions as a source of knowledge—whether unique as in the cases of the prophets Handsome Lake and Wovoka, or common, as among the Peyotists—stands in contrast to the relegation of immediate revelation to a remote historical event that is characteristic of the religions of more completely modernized societies. As the Handsome Lake and Peyote cults established themselves over the years, however, they have predictably become routinized, and tend to resemble such "cultic" religions on the borderline of traditional Christianity such as Mormonism.[25]

RELIGIOUS SYNCRETISM AND INNOVATION IN THE BLACK COMMUNITY

Like the American Indians, the black Africans who came to the New World were confronted with a complex of Western institutions and life patterns that were thoroughly alien to the traditionalistic cultures in which they and their ancestors had lived for centuries. Unlike the Indians, however, the blacks were simultaneously and abruptly enslaved and deracinated, rather than undergoing, as did the Indians, decades or even centuries of gradual contact, conflict, and a final more or less unsatisfactory accommodation. Virtually all the Africans who came to America during the Colonial period were brought here by force, and most were systematically deprived of their traditional cultural baggage upon arrival. Little of the old ways consequently remained after the first generation or two of American residence. This was the context within which popular religions developed among American blacks during the nineteenth and twentieth centuries.[26]

The black experience in the United States actually represents one extreme of a continuum of African cultural transformation in the New World.[27] In South America groups of Africans from the same tribe often remained together, and thus were able to carry on their linguistic, religious, and other cultural patterns without the devastating disruptions that resulted from the American policy of systematically mixing slaves from different tribes. Those living in urban areas usually developed new syncretistic cultures. These included religions which incorporated both traditional African elements and extensive borrowings from Catholicism. Those who were sent to plantations in the interior, however, lived in much greater isolation and retained their African heritage in even greater measure. One group that successfully revolted and escaped into the interior of Surinam has lived to this day in a manner in many ways identical with that of their African forebears.[28]

The retention of at least some elements of traditional culture was facilitated in several ways by the Roman Catholic religious hegemony in the Latin countries. Catholicism itself, with its hierarchy of saints and angels, was much closer in its symbolic structure to the polytheistic religions of Africa than was the dominant monotheistic Protestantism of North America. Thus it was easy enough to associate particular African divinities with Catholic saints, and the Church itself was reasonably tolerant of such blendings as long as they did not interfere with institutional loyalties. Latin American attitudes toward race were similarly much more permissive than were those of North Americans, and intermarriage among Europeans, Indians, and blacks in various combinations was common enough. The result was a highly diversified culture in which Africanisms were not only preserved but blended in any number of fashions with elements from both indigenous and European traditions.

The only even approximate parallels to this syncretism in the United States took place in Catholic Louisiana, where the Haitian cult of Vodun expressed itself in the form of Voodoo, and on some of the sea islands off the coast of Georgia, where isolation helped to preserve native traditions much more fully than was possible on the mainland.[29] In general, however, a combination of circumstance and design precluded very much of traditional African culture being preserved in the American South. On the one hand, the Protestant attitude toward evangelization emphasized the necessity for wiping out all traces of "heathenism": on the other, slave-holders thought it expedient to deprive blacks of any opportunity for using a common heritage as a rallying point for insurrection by systematically mixing slaves from different tribal backgrounds together. The fact that whites greatly outnumbered blacks in the American South, which was not the case on many of the plantations of the Latin American interior, further worked toward the elimination of any possibility that either successful revolts or the maintenance of traditional culture could be accomplished.

During much of the Colonial period, Christianization of slaves was opposed by their masters on the grounds that the promises of liberation contained in the New Testament might be taken too literally in a political sense. Any evangelization that did take place was conducted mainly by members of the Anglican Society for the Propagation of the Gospel in

Foreign Parts (SPG). Its work was largely unsuccessful owing both to the ineptness of many of its missionaries and the lack of appeal of a staid and decorous religion to most of its prospective converts. The Great Awakening of the 1740s, however, unleashed a religious force of much greater power and swept up both black and white in its wake. The Methodists and Baptists who harvested the fruits of the new enthusiasm appealed to Southerners of both races, and initial opposition to slavery, especially on the part of Methodists, soon yielded to an accommodation with regional mores.[30]

Some slaves attended services conducted by white preachers during the antebellum period, but they were usually supervised closely by their masters and relegated to separate galleries. However, an "invisible institution" was arising among the blacks at the same time, a genuine folk religion composed of Christian elements given a particular twist by its new practitioners.[31] Much of this worship was conducted surreptitiously, since slave-owners believed it inexpedient to let blacks congregate by themselves even for ostensibly religious purposes. The attraction of the new religion was too strong, though, and many masters were finally forced to look the other way when their charges sneaked off for a covert worship service.

Considerable ink has been spilled already over the question of whether African elements did in fact survive the Atlantic crossing and become incorporated into the religious and other cultural practices of American blacks. The anthropologist Melville Herskovits argued in 1941 that certain specific themes, such as baptism by immersion and burial practices, were in fact direct survivals from the indigenous religious practices of African tribes.[32] Black sociologist E. Franklin Frazier countered with the argument that the extirpation of traditional cultures by the white policy of separation of tribal members was so devastatingly effective that such supposed evidences of continuity were merely coincidental.[33] During the 1960s this scholarly debate took on ideological overtones in the context of the new quest for black identity.

It is probably impossible to settle conclusively the question of whether there has been a continuity of specific practices in most cases. However, the recent study of American slavery by the historian Eugene Genovese suggests that another, more fruitful approach is possible. The question now becomes not whether specific practices survived, but rather whether certain patterns of behavior and outlook which are more typical of a traditional rather than a Western world view persisted in the consciousness of American blacks.[34] The evidence that this has indeed been the case is extremely persuasive.

The traditional cultures of Africa were as varied as those of the American Indians, and it is impossible to make accurate generalizations that would hold true in all cases.[35] However, certain underlying motifs which are in fact very similar to those of American Indian and other traditional cultures are characteristic of many indigenous African religions. Many of these traits can be subsumed under the rubric of "pluralistic continuity." Western cultures generally postulate radical distinctions between God and man, man and nature, past and present, present and future. These modes of perceiving the world are simply irrelevant to traditional peoples. For them, divine power is not usually concentrated in a high god, but rather is diffused throughout nature in any number of personifications and guises. Similarly, temporal sequences are not linear. Instead, past, present, and future coexist simultaneously, and what has been interpreted by Europeans as "ancestor worship" in fact represents the necessity for all generations to remain in direct communication with one another.[36] The natural and supernatural, moreover, stand in continuity rather than disjunction. Divine power is manifested in the natural realm, and it is difficult to say where (or if) one leaves off and another begins. The resemblances to various aspects of American Indian religious attitudes discussed earlier should be apparent.

In addition to these radical differences in outlook on the world, African religion, again like that of other traditional peoples, was characterized by a greater emphasis on action than on conceptualization. No theology as such existed, and myths functioned in the context of ritual rather than as isolated explanatory stories. Thought, expression and action were not separable; rather, they constituted a whole, the individual components of which were meaningless when divorced from their relative situation in a complex of elements. Particularly important in African ritual was the dance, which usually took place to the accompaniment of drums. Spirit possession and communication with supernatural powers were only possible in the context established by such a rhythmic, ritual setting.

Finally, African religions were characterized by the blend of magical practices characteristic of most traditional peoples. These practices were usually thaumaturgical or oriented to the counteraction of the effects of witchcraft. As with the American Indians, illness was not attributed to natural causes, but perhaps even more emphatically in Africa was thought to be the work of malevolent witchcraft. Magical curing did in fact survive in the American South, and "hoodoo" (a variant of Voodoo or Vodun) was practiced by black conjure-men for white as well as black clients.[37]

The blurring of categoreal distinctions characteristic of the old cultures seems to have survived, in general form if not in specific content, in the new American environment. The version of Christianity that developed among the slaves was indeed different in highly significant aspects from that of the whites, and these differences can be accounted for in many ways through this phenomenon. The subtleties of Christian theology were far too abstract to be comprehensible or relevant; rather, what was important was the experience of religious power that was encountered during worship. Preaching was more incantatory than discursive, and the call-response pattern characteristic of African ceremonies found a new expression in the active participation of slave congregations while they were being exhorted by their own preachers.

Similarly, white notions of divinity, of the relationship between nature and supernature, and of the redemptive process all underwent significant metamorphoses in early black Christianity. Moses and Jesus merged together into one undifferentiated bringer of deliverance, and the two were joined in this messianic role by Lincoln during the time of the Civil War. Also, as Genovese points out, the question of whether black spirituals that spoke of other-worldly salvation were not in fact coded messages of political liberation is not meaningful when posed in terms of a clear-cut dichotomy. This world and the next did not stand in opposition, but rather formed a continuum of possibilities. Liberation was liberation, and was not interpreted as a choice between immediate political freedom and "pie in the sky by and by when you die.[38]

Sin, in the sense of the radical alienation of the individual from the divine, was also not a significant category in the religion of the slave community. This notion also involved a discontinuity which found no counterpart in the Afro-American cosmos. Slavery was not a punishment for sin but rather was due to bad luck. The Christian promise of deliverance was welcomed not as an absolution from individual guilt, but instead as a release from earthly tribulations which were the result of misfortune rather than of evil deeds or a consciousness not in harmony with the divine will.[39] The collection of slave conversion narratives entitled *God Struck Me Dead* is notable for the absence of many specifically Christian elements in these accounts.[40] Conversion seems to have been an intense emotional experience, but one that often took place in the context of a very diffuse and unfocused frame of symbolic reference.

During the antebellum period in the North, and throughout the nation after the Civil War, free blacks began to organize themselves into specific Christian denominations based on white models.[41] The Methodists and Baptists had early obtained a near-monopoly on black allegiance, in large measure owing to the appealing emotional and demonstrative character of their worship. Since blacks were often allowed to participate in white churches only on a segregated basis, many preferred to establish parallel churches of their own. The African Methodist Episcopal and A.M.E. Zion Churches were early examples of this adoption of white models, and the National Baptist Church later took its place alongside the American and Southern Baptists. Some of the more assimilated urban blacks preferred to join white middle-class denominations such as the Presbyterians instead, but the majority found that their own structures offered both a more appropriate form of worship and an autonomy denied them on the basis of numbers if not of overt discrimination in the predominantly white churches. What had of necessity been extra-ecclesiastical religion during the period of slavery was now becoming organized into social structures and beliefs characteristic of a modernizing society.

The combination of Jim Crow laws and lack of economic opportunity in the rural South resulted in a massive exodus of southern blacks to the urban centers of the North following the First World War; this has continued to the present day. The resulting sense of cultural displacement created a religious vacuum among the in-migrant blacks which was rapidly filled by the proliferation of store-front churches, usually of the Pentecostal-Holiness variety, and of a series of "urban cults" which were often beyond the confines of Christianity itself.[42] As we shall see in more detail in a later chapter, Pentecostalism was a movement that was panracial during its beginnings in the late nineteenth century.[43] Its unstructured worship and emphasis on speaking in an unintelligible flow was well suited to the expressive character of black religion in general and, more specifically, was an apt symbolic vehicle for the alienation from social structures that was characteristic of those who suddenly had found themselves adrift in a hostile and forbidding environment. The friendliness and sense of community these churches provided—and continue to provide to this day—made them especially attractive to people who had been deprived of the comforts of family, friends, and familiar surroundings.

Many blacks, however, were not comfortable with Christianity itself. As did many American Indians, they regarded it as a "white man's religion." Unlike the Indians, however, they lacked any coherent memory of their traditional religions to which they might turn as an alternative, and were so far removed from Africa in time and space that their ancestral past probably did not remain even as a dim memory. Instead, a series of urban movements arose, usually around charismatic figures of obscure origin, which provided new non- or anti-Christian ideologies that could serve as a basis for racial identity and pride. Among these were the Father Divine Peace Mission Movement and the Nation of Islam. The rest of this section will be concerned mainly with these two movements.

Father Divine was the most successful of a number of similar figures who emerged from purposely obscured origins to found movements which were based on personal charisma, and which provided a refuge, especially during the Depression, for countless alienated and dispossessed blacks for whom mere survival was a pressing concern.[44] Father Divine was born George Baker, probably around 1880, on a rice plantation in South Carolina. Officially, however, he "was combusted one day in 1900 on the corner of Seventh Avenue and 134th Street in Harlem."[45] After an early career as an itinerant gardener and preacher, he arrived in New York City in 1915 and gradually began to acquire a following. After various successes and reverses, his movement crystallized into the Father Divine Peace Mission Movement, and his followers began to include well-to-do whites as well as the poor blacks who had initially responded to the lavish banquets he offered them for little or nothing. Legal battles finally forced him to abandon New York in favor of Philadelphia, but he remained the undisputed leader of an extraordinarily successful (and well-endowed) movement until his death in 1965.

Father Divine cannot be called modest. He claimed to be God and he lived in a correspondingly appropriate style. To the everlasting frustration of the Internal Revenue Service, however, he was never proven to have possessed any personal wealth. He lived instead on the largesse of his followers and in and through the considerable chain of cooperative restaurants, lodging houses, and other enterprises which the Movement held in the followers' names. He demanded total loyalty and obedience from his disciples, and received it in an extraordinary measure. After his death the Movement, as might have been predicted, lost its mass appeal and settled into a small group of older and devoted followers of both races who lived on in the knowledge that Father's spirit continued in their midst.[46]

The Father Divine Peace Mission Movement resembled less a Protestant denomination than the "total institutions" such as Catholic monastic orders analyzed by Erving Goffman in his *Asylums.*[47] The Peace Mission was in fact an "asylum" for many of all races and social classes who sought refuge from a world in which, for one reason or another, they were unable to find comfort or serenity. Many of his white followers had previously been religious "seekers," drifting from Unity to Christian Science through a variety of "cultic" groups until they finally found peace with Father. The price for this peace, however, was total commitment. Followers willingly renounced all ties with the outside world and all continuity with their previous lives. If they had families, they either brought them into the Movement with them or else renounced them completely. (Within the Movement ties of kinship were not acknowledged. Relatives regarded one another simply as sisters and brothers, even if they were in fact mothers and sons.)[48] All income was turned over to or invested in the Movement. Members received in turn a modest allowance which provided room and board in the Movement's lodging houses and restaurants and a few dollars in addition for other expenses. As in Catholic religious orders, they received new "spiritual" names such as "Sweet Angel," "Beautiful Peace," or (perhaps less plausibly) "Universal Vocabulary."[49]

A preoccupation with the importance of words was also exhibited in Father Divine's ban on negative thinking or speaking (a link, perhaps, with Christian Science and Mind Cure.) Followers were never to use words with negative meanings or connotations, even when they incidentally formed parts of other, innocuous words. Thus, "Hello" was avoided since it contained a reference to the infernal regions, and "Peace" was ordinarily substituted as a greeting. When its use was unavoidable, a rather awkward euphemism was provided in "the-other-place-o." Similarly, Harlem followers would refer to taking the bus down "Amsterbless Avenue."[50] Although there is clearly no direct genetic link, it is tempting to speculate that this form of avoidance behavior may have counterparts in the practices of African and other traditional peoples.

Another peculiarity of the Movement that has evoked confusion or ridicule from outsiders was Father Divine's claim to be God. To those accustomed to thinking in the categories of Western logic, this claim was patently absurd and self-contradictory. To some extent, Divine did attempt to present himself in these categories, and claimed that he could bring down violent retribution upon those who opposed the Movement. (Some of these claims were buttressed by remarkable coincidences in which his opponents did in fact die shortly after receiving his maledictions.) The clear limitations to his temporal power, however, never seemed to constitute a stumbling block for his disciples.

The frame of reference provided by appeal to a traditional rather than a modern world picture helps to clarify this problem of how his extravagant and contradictory claims could be accepted unquestioningly by so many residents of twentieth-century America. In the cosmologies of traditional peoples, gods are plural rather than singular: they are manifestations of an underlying power which expresses itself in diffuse, diverse, contradictory and highly particularistic ways. Father Divine's ability to work seeming "miracles" in his provision of food and security for the unemployed and comfort to the emotionally dispossessed was potent confirmation of his divine power in immediately tangible fashion. Such universalistic conceptions of the deity as omnipotent and omniscient were of little relevance to those who wanted particular action in the immediacy of the here and now. For them, Father Divine's lavish banquets and his day-to-day provision of more modest sustenance was proof enough of his divine power. His thaumaturgical healings of everything from cancer to acne were further compelling instances of his supernatural abilities.

Another source of bewilderment and scandal surrounding the person of Father Divine was that of his two marriages and his accompanying battery of extremely attractive young secretaries of both races.[51] (These latter seemed to many to be very like a harem.) It is not clear whether he actually indulged in overt sexual activities with any of the women, but it seemed to the skeptical that such a course of action was not only probable but irresistible. Since his disciples were all required to lead lives of complete celibacy, his alleged behavior seemed even more contradictory and outrageous. And, in the context of Western Christian notions of religious thought and behavior, it was.

However, it is inappropriate to think in those categories if we are to understand the Movement's internal logic. In pre-modern societies, behavior that is inappropriate to everyday life or for ordinary mortals attains a reversed significance when practiced in a cultic setting and/or by sacred figures.[52] In the ancient Near East, for example, cult prostitution was a highly esteemed form of religious observance, as was incestuous marriage between royal brothers and sisters. What is forbidden behavior in the profane sphere becomes sacred and obligatory conduct when its practitioners are divine or operating in the realm of the holy. Even if Father Divine had in fact been wallowing in orgies of promiscuity (which is doubtful), he may still be said to have been following a code of conduct appropriate for a god.

In many ways, then, the Father Divine Peace Mission Movement represented a withdrawal from the logic and mores of everyday American life into a separate world governed by a communistic economy, a regimen of asceticism, and a leader whose behavior stood in dramatic contradiction to the expectations of conventional Christianity. In another way, however, the Movement represented a more comprehensible political protest against the ways of white America. One of the major teachings of its leader was the unreality of racial distinctions, and his followers included a considerable number of well-to-do whites. The Movement was in fact a powerful (if eccentric) protest against white racism, and the life of its members in interracial community was a literal expression of the "kingdom beyond caste." As in many radical communitarian groups, the social boundaries of profane life were dissolved to result in what the anthropologist Victor Turner has called "communitas."[53] The tensions this racial mixing and general communal living might have generated at the sexual level were dealt with effectively if extremely through a total prohibition on erotic activity. Although the alien character of the Movement's symbolic expression and organizational forms precluded its ever becoming an effective vehicle for alleviating racial tensions in America on a significant scale, it did in fact reflect and attempt to deal practically with the massive fact of racial discrimination that has always plagued American blacks.

The appeal of Father Divine was thus presented in universalistic terms, even though it was highly particularistic in many ways. Through his denial of the reality of race (just as Mary Baker Eddy had denied the reality of sickness and death), he aimed at and received white as well as black converts, and proclaimed a deracialized America as his goal. Other groups that were emerging in the ghettos of America's larger cities around the same time, however, were choosing a very different symbolic strategy as a response to urban *anomie* compounded by hard times and racial discrimination. They chose instead to create a mythological ancestry for black peoples based on a rejection of their adopted country and an espousal of exotic cultures of the Middle East and Northern Africa from which their actual line of descent was at best tenuous. Among these were the Black Jews of Harlem, whose worship was carefully rooted in traditional Jewish practice, and the Moorish Science Temple of Noble Drew Ali.[54]

Another movement of the 1920s which looked to the Old World rather than the New for its inspiration was the Universal Negro Improvement Association of Marcus Garvey.[55] Garvey was a widely traveled Jamaican who, like Father Divine, eventually arrived in New York City and settled upon it as the most appropriate place to foster a wide-scale black movement. His program called for a literal rather than a mythological return to the African homeland, and he self-consciously borrowed the Jewish interpretation of a people in diaspora awaiting a return to their rightful origins. An elaborate apparatus which included a theology and church, a series of business enterprises including an ill-fated steamship ("the Black Star") line, and a group of fraternal organizations all helped to recruit a considerable following, but Garvey's own managerial ineptness led finally to his imprisonment and the dissipation of the movement's energies and resources. His doctrine of pan-Africanism (in many ways like the pan-Indianism of the Ghost Dance and the Peyote religion) and his program of black-owned businesses, however, helped to arouse an interest in black independence which has continued to the present day.

A more durable movement which drew on several of these earlier expressions of black nationalism for its inspiration arose in Detroit during the 1930s, when a silk peddler of obscure origins who called himself W. D. Fard began to make himself known.[56] Fard himself does not seem to have gone very far in organizing a movement, but his self-proclaimed messenger Elijah Muhammed went on to build the Nation of Islam, or "Black Muslims," on the foundation Fard had erected. Thus arose what was to become probably the most controversial of all black religious movements, one that has overcome even the death of its (actual) founder, Elijah Muhammed, to endure as a major force in black life.[57]

In some ways, the Nation of Islam resembles in origin and function the Father Divine Peace Mission Movement. Both Divine and Fard emerged out of a (perhaps deliberately created) obscurity to found a new faith, although Fard rapidly faded out of the picture. Each appealed to alienated and unemployed urban blacks and stressed that they should develop pride in themselves, although the Muslims made this appeal specifically racial rather than Father Divine's universalistic type of appeal. Each repudiated explicitly or implictly the teachings of Christianity, and substituted instead an exotic mythology and rigorous set of behavioral practices. Each also developed a successful network of cooperative business institutions which provided the movements with financial support, and each required its followers to repudiate their former lives and to confine their associations solely within the context of the movement. These similarities are important. However, as the following discussion should demonstrate, the Nation of Islam charted a course that was to take it in a very different direction from that of the Peace Mission Movement. This course was made possible by the historical and social context in which each gained its momentum and grew from a small collection of zealots into a significant force in American life.

The most vivid introduction to the Black Muslims is the *Autobiography of Malcolm X,* the life story of the movement's fiery spokesman who eventually met his death at the hands of men who had probably once been his fellow devotees. Malcolm X began his life as Malcolm Little near Lansing, Michigan. As he grew up, he saw his father killed for his unwillingness to accept a position of racial inferiority (he had at one time been a Garveyite) and his mother put away as "crazy" as she watched her family disintegrate. He subsequently journeyed to Boston, where he became part of the jazz subculture, and then to Harlem, where he lived as a hustler and pusher till he found that his life was in immediate danger. The story of his career through this phase is one of progressive disintegration and of Malcolm's loss of a personal center in the midst of societies which themselves seemed to lack any center. He lost all sense of himself as a social being, and lived only for the evanescent pleasures of sex, alcohol, and drugs until he finally came to the end of this particular road.[58]

After returning to Boston, Malcolm was finally arrested for masterminding a burglary ring and sent to prison. While in confinement he began a program of self-education, and also began to learn about Elijah Muhammed's movement. He was accepted into the Nation of Islam, and went after his release from prison first to Detroit and then to Chicago to become the movement's most visible spokesman. He became disillusioned after his leader was taken in adultery and he himself was subjected to disciplinary action for expressing outrage at this betrayal. He left to found a group of his own based more strictly on the traditional Islam he had observed in the Middle East. Shortly afterward he was assassinated, probably by vengeful Muslims whom he had repudiated. The story he left behind him remains gripping, and also provides a great deal of insight into the original movement.

The designation "Islam" which the movement chose for itself was based more on a desire for symbolic identification with an exotic non-Western religion and culture that was in some way related to the African continent than on a substantive espousal of its traditional doctrines. The real mythology of the Nation of Islam is revealed in the story of Mr. Yacub which Malcolm X recounts in his *Autobiography.*[59] It is an authentic myth of the age of technology, and incorporates themes derived from the dominant culture into a traditional symbolic structure which provides the movement with a history, an eschatology, and a general orientation toward the world. It is at once explanatory and a program for action.

In brief, the myth teaches that the original inhabitants of the earth were black. As a result of various schisms, a "big-headed scientist" named Mr. Yacub arose, and attracted a large following which was sent with him into exile. In revenge he created, through scientific breeding, "a bleached-out white race of people" who were innately susceptible to "wickedness and evil" as a result of their inferior genetic structure. After wandering about Europe in a half-bestial condition for some time, they were civilized by Moses, and then enabled to enslave some of the original blacks so that the latter might better learn the true depravity of the "white devils" at first hand. However, the bondage of these latter people—the black Americans of today—had a terminus. After the white race had ruled the world for six thousand years, "the black original race would give birth to one whose wisdom, knowledge, and power would be infinite.[60] The present time was that in which the end was drawing near, and the prophet of the overthrow of the whites and the return of the Blacks to pristine glory was W. D. Fard.

This myth is at the same time etiological and millenarian. It explains the origins of the universe, of a particular people, and of evil, ironically in an idiom borrowed from the rationalistic science that is so much a product of the culture of the "white devil." (On the other hand, the prophesied overthrow of the products of science by supernatural action is authentically antirational.) Like the Christian myth, it promises an end to the fruits of that evil, and at the same time a prophet through which that promised consummation can now be known by the elect. In other ways it resembles Judaism more than Christianity, since its appeal is to an ethnically distinct people now held in bondage whose deliverance is to be this-worldly. Like the revitalization myth of the Ghost Dance, moreover, it attributes evil to the presence of a specific alien people and predicts that, after the transgressors are destroyed in a supernaturally induced cataclysm, the true heirs of the Kingdom will be restored to their rightful place, and will live in peace and plenty forever.[61]

The syncretistic character of Muslim belief should by now be apparent. Its mythology, though nominally Islamic, is in fact a pastiche of both secular and sacred elements drawn from a variety of sources, and its general structure and function are very similar to those of the nativistic movements among American Indians which we discussed earlier. There are other aspects of the movement, however, which demonstrate its similarities both with the traditional patterns of thought which it has repudiated in an attempt to identify with a "high religion" (i.e., Islam) and with the mainstream Christianity from which it so vehemently distances itself.

This latter similarity is best illustrated in the movement's sectarian character. In many ways it conforms to Ernst Troeltsch's classic definition of a sect.[62] It is exclusivistic and in fact openly hostile to outsiders; membership is voluntary (at least for the first generation); it practices vicinal segregation to some degree by creating enclaves within urban areas and calling for a territory of its own; it imposes a rigid code of behavior on its members, and exerts sanctions to insure that the code is observed. Unlike other black sects, however, it eschews emotional demonstrativeness, and its worship consists primarily of lectures aimed at inculcating group loyalty and fastidious observance of the group ethic.

The ethic of the Muslims is interesting again as an example of the group's tendency toward syncretism. On the one hand, its code of conduct can only be described as rigidly puritanical. Laziness, uncleanliness, lying, stealing, gambling, alcohol, and sexual irregularities are all condemned, as are such offenses against boundary maintenance as socializing with outsiders or showing disrespect to superiors within the movement.[63] Many of these regulations are aimed specifically at the kinds of behavior that have been characteristic of transplanted southern blacks who have sought refuge from the hardships of urban life in escape (primarily through alcohol and drugs) and who have demonstrated socially pathological behavior in marital irresponsibility. The orientation to be attained through this resocialization, however, can best be described as a rigorous adherence to the Protestant ethic. The goal of the movement is to create a disciplined corps of workers and managers who can "beat Whitey at his own game" through success in business. Economic activity is collective rather than individualistic, but the basic personal qualities necessary for success are identical with those of the capitalistic order the Muslims so vociferously reject. Although the movement substitutes revealed for experiential knowledge, its ethic also resembles in some ways the "Peyote Road," another syncretistic ethic (although a less militant one) which is also aimed at accommodation to the white world through the selective adoption of its rules of conduct and its goal orientations.

Another aspect of Muslim syncretism can be found in its extensive list of dietary prohibitions. This list contains a wide variety both of recommended and prohibited foods which at first glance seems to have been put together rather haphazardly.[64] (A relevant discussion of Jewish dietary prohibitions can be found in Chapter 2.) Some of the prohibited foods are in fact those contained in the "abominations of Leviticus" such as pork (which is polluting for orthodox as well as Black Muslims) and shellfish of various sorts. Once these borrowings are set aside, however, a clearer pattern begins to emerge. Among the forbidden items are black-eyed peas, cornbread, possum, coon, catfish, and carp. All of these of course are "soul food," the traditional diet of southern blacks. (Pork can be included in this category as well.) "Clean foods" listed in a parallel column have nothing especially in common with one another except that they are all staples of a well-balanced middle-class diet. (Whole wheat is recommended instead of cornbread, but chicken is given only a rather grudging approval.) With the exception of a few arbitrarily included items from an alien tradition, the list represents a clear attempt to resocialize poor urban in-migrant blacks away from their traditional cultural patterns (those of the rural South) into a new way of life ironically modeled on that of the white bourgeoisie for whom they express so much contempt.

A major aspect of resocialization is also indicated in the very name of the author we have been citing: Malcolm X. Upon entering the movement as full members, Muslims do precisely what the followers of Father Divine and entrants into Roman Catholic religious orders do as well. They repudiate their old, "worldly" identity by taking on a new name. The new designations—which are all the letter "X" or a numerical modification thereof—have a simple ideological rationale. All slaves were alienated from their authentic identities when they came to America and took on Western names (usually those of their masters) instead. Since their real names are irrecoverable, the "X" serves as a convenient substitute, and also provides a ready way of distinguishing members from outsiders. (First names are retained—e.g., "Malcolm"—presumably for convenience.) As in the case of the dietary prohibitions, the purpose here seems to be totally functional, with little of the admixture of word magic that characterized the followers of Father Divine.

One possibly magical element that has crept into Muslim usage, however, is a fascination with numbers. As in the rather eccentric numerological speculations of some white millennialists, the story of Mr. Yacub alludes continually to the mystical quality of specific numbers. Another example is contained in the argument that helped draw Malcolm X to the movement while he was in prison. It was pointed out to him that while the Masons, who were guided by the Devil, had only thirty-three degrees of knowledge, God possessed the full three hundred and sixty.[65] On the surface, this story makes no sense whatever. However, the occult fascination which numbers exert is by no means confined to primitive peoples. (It is probably alien to them, in fact.) It is rather characteristic of such highly sophisticated speculators as the medieval Jewish Cabbalists. I can offer no explanation for the phenomenon in general except to observe that it may be a sort of gnosticism, a taking refuge in the occult as an escape from the frustrations of the mundane. Since so much of the rest of the novement is reality-oriented, however, it is probably just another aspect of a fascination with the exotic that is also present in the movement's identification with Islam. In many ways these exotic borrowings are similar to the elaborate paraphernalia of both white and black fraternal orders (e.g., the Shriners and those Masons whom the Muslims detest so thoroughly.) Such fraternal and benevolent organizations play an important role in the associational life of American blacks, and the Muslims are very much in continuity with this tradition.[66]

In short, while the practices of the Nation of Islam bear some important resemblances to those of the Father Divine Peace Mission Movement, the differences are also striking. Where Father Divine relied on occult means and personal charisma (as well as economic activity) to weld his followers into a stance of defiance of white expectations, the Muslims represent a much more rationalized and militant strategy for achieving the same ends. Although a certain amount of exoticism characterizes its mythology and practices, the Nation is primarily neither magical nor thaumaturgical. It can best be characterized as millenarian, militant, and nativistic. It predicts a violent supernaturally induced cataclysm that will destroy the usurping oppressors and restore the chosen people to a condition of earthly bliss; it advocates organized activity often couched in rather threatening language to achieve its proximate goals of resocialization and economic organization; and its appeal is to a specific ethnic group that has temporarily fallen from the power of its earliest, mythological state to a new state of rightful dominance. It is also syncretistic to a great degree, and combines a few exotic elements with a nearly wholesale adoption of the society it rejects and by which it has been rejected. The Nation of Islam in many ways is the black person's version of both the Ghost Dance and the Peyote Cult.

NOTES

1. Most of my general remarks about American Indian religion and culture follow RUTH UNDERHILL, *Red Man's America* (Chicago: University of Chicago Press, 1971)* and *Red Man's Religion* (Chicago: University of Chicago Press, 1965).*
2. On the general phenomenon of syncretism, see J. D. Y. PEEL, "Syncretism and Religious Change," in *Comparative Studies in Society and History,* 10 (1967-68), 121-41.
3. On militant movements, see BRYAN R. WILSON, *Magic and the Millennium: A Sociological Study of Religious Movements of Protest Among Tribal and Third-World Peoples* (London: Heinemann, 1973), Chap. 8 ("Religious Responses and Military Enterprise").
4. On the Delaware Prophet, see WILSON, ibid., pp. 224-29; on Tecumseh and Tenskwatawa, ibid., pp. 229-36.
5. Discussions of typologies of such movements include Wilson, ibid., Chaps. 1-2 and *passim*; DAVID F. ABERLE, "A Classification of Social Movements," Chap. 19 of *The Peyote Religion Among the Navaho* (Chicago: Aldine, 1966); RALPH LINTON, "Nativistic Movements," in WILLIAM A. LESSA and EVON Z. VOGT, eds., *Reader in Comparative Religion: An Anthropological Approach,* 3rd ed. (New York: Harper & Row, 1972);* ANTHONY F. C. WALLACE, "Revitalization Movements," ibid.; BERNARD BARBER, "Acculturation and Messianic Movements," ibid.
6. The following discussion of Handsome Lake is based on ANTHONY F. C. WALLACE, *The Death and Rebirth of the Seneca* (New York: Knopf, 1970).*
7. Ibid., Chap. 7.
8. On Seneca attitudes toward dreams, see ibid., pp. 59-75.
9. On Handsome Lake's visions, ibid., pp. 239-48.
10. On these early movements, see WILSON, *Magic and Millennium,* pp. 274-78; VITTORIO LANTERNARI, *The Religions of the Oppressed* (New York: New American Library/Mentor, 1963),* Chap. III ("Other Prophetic Movements in North America"); and HOMER G. BARNETT, *Indian Shakers: A Messianic Cult of the Pacific Northwest* (Carbondale, Ill.: Southern Illinois University Press, 1957). Further detailed and specialized bibliography on all the American Indian movements discussed here can be found in Wilson's chapter notes.
11. On Smohalla, see WILSON, pp. 278-83; and LANTERNARI, pp. 110-13.
12. On the first Ghost Dance, see WILSON, pp. 283-87; LANTERNARI, pp. 113-16; and CORA DU BOIS, "The 1870 Ghost Dance," *Anthropological Records* 3, 1, 1-151 (Berkeley: University of California Press, 1939).
13. The classic study of the Ghost Dance is JAMES MOONEY, *The Ghost-Dance Religion and the Sioux Outbreak of 1890* (Chicago: University of Chicago Press, 1965),* edited and abridged by ANTHONY F. C. WALLACE (original edition 1896). For more recent accounts, see ROBERT M. UTLEY, *Last Days of the Sioux Nation* (New Haven: Yale University Press, 1963);* LANTERNARI, pp. 128-32; WILSON, pp. 292-306 (probably the best brief interpretive treatment); and DAVID HUMPHREYS MILLER, *Ghost Dance* (New York: Duell, Sloan and Pearce, 1959), a less authoritative account. For a first-hand ac-

count by an Indian participant, see JOHN G. NEIHARDT, *Black Elk Speaks* (New York: Pocket Books, 1972),* especially Chaps. XXI-XXIV.

14. This paragraph is based on UTLEY, *Last Days*.
15. On pan-Indian nationalism, see J. S. SLOTKIN, *The Peyote Religion: A Study in Indian-White Relations* (Glencoe, Ill.: Free Press, 1956),* Chapter I ("A Theory of Nationalism"). Slotkin's work is an excellent condensed treatment of the Peyote religion from theoretical and factual standpoints.
16. For a discussion of the ethnobotanical aspects of peyote, see WESTON LABARRE, *The Peyote Cult* (New York: Schocken, 1969).* See also SLOTKIN, p. 22, and DAVID F. ABERLE, *The Peyote Religion Among the Navaho* (Chicago: Aldine, 1956), pp. 5-11.
17. On the forerunners of Peyotism, see SLOTKIN, Chaps. III and IV, and LABARRE, pp. 23-56.
18. In addition to the sources already cited, discussions of Peyotism can be found in LANTERNARI, *Religions of the Oppressed,* Chap. II, and BRYAN WILSON, *Magic and the Millennium,* Chap. 13. WILSON's notes and SLOTKIN's bibliography are good sources for detailed and specialized studies.
19. SLOTKIN, p. 20; WILSON, 426-29.
20. SLOTKIN, Chap. III, contains a detailed account of the basic ritual. ABERLE discusses the Navaho versions in his Chaps. 9 and 10.
21. For Peyotist theology, see SLOTKIN, pp. 68-71.
22. SLOTKIN, p. 71. See also ABERLE, Chap. 11.
23. See ABERLE, Chap. 13.
24. For Peyotist organization, see SLOTKIN, Chap. VI.
25. The most recent twist in the story of Amerind uses of hallucinogens for religious purposes is the phenomenal success attained by the writings of the popular anthropologist CARLOS CASTANEDA during the decade of the 1970's. (The volumes of his encounters with Don Juan, a Yaqui Indian *brujo* or sorcerer, include *The Teachings of Don Juan: A Yaqui Way of Knowledge* [1968]; *A Separate Reality* [1971]; *Journey to Ixtlan* [1974]; *Tales of Power* [1974]; and *The Second Ring of Power* [1978].) These writings have been extremely controversial, and their authenticity has been repeatedly questioned, although some writers have chosen a middle course of praising them as clever adventures into metaphysical fiction. (See DANIEL C. NOEL, ed., *Seeing Castaneda: Reaction to the "Don Juan" Writings of Carlos Castaneda* [New York: Putnam, 1976], and RICHARD DE MILLE, *Castaneda's journey: The Power and the Allegory* [Santa Barbara, Calif.: Capra Press, 1976], for a variety of responses.) What is indubitable, however, is the popularity of these works, originally among the "counter-cultural" young people of the late sixties and earlier seventies, and later among a much wider readership. If taken seriously, whether intellectually or existentially, Castaneda's claims to have experienced a perceptual reality radically different from that of the modern West presents a major challenge to American patterns of thought and behavior. However, with the subsiding of the drug culture, it seems more probable that the reading of Castaneda on a large scale is more an example of a fashionable primitivism which has little resonance for most in the actual interpretation of reality and everyday living patterns. (One unsympathetic reviewer in the *New York Times* dismissed *The Second Ring of Power* as fiction, giving "capitalist college kids what they want—fantasies of gaining power without becoming more compassionate or more honest."

[See *New York Times Book Review,* 22 April 1979.]) For a good summary of Castaneda's work from a religious studies perspective, see STEPHEN J. RENO, "Castaneda and Don Juan: Some Preliminary Observations," *Religious Studies* 11 (12-75), 449-65.

26. Good general treatments of slavery and its backgrounds are DAVID BRION DAVIS, *The Problem of Slavery in Western Culture* (Ithaca, New York: Cornell University Press, 1966)* and *The Problem of Slavery in the Age of Revolution: 1770-1823* (Ithaca: Cornell University Press, 1976);* KENNETH STAMPP, *The Peculiar Institution* (New York: Random/Vintage, 1964);* JOHN BLASSINGAME, *The Slave Community* (New York: Oxford University Press, 1972);* and EUGENE D. GENOVESE, *Roll, Jordan, Roll: The World the Slaves Made* (New York: Random/Pantheon, c. 1972/74).* For the slave trade in particular, see BASIL DAVIDSON, *The African Slave Trade* (Boston: Atlantic-Little, Brown, 1961).* ALBERT J. RABOTEAU'S *Slave Religion: The "Invisible Institution" in The Antebellum South* (New York: Oxford University Press, 1978) is a fine synthetic work on religion in the slave community.

27. On black religion and culture in other parts of the New World, see ROGER BASTIDE, *African Civilizations in the New World* (New York: Harper Torchbooks, 1972);* GENOVESE, "Slave Religion in Hemispheric Perspective"; LEONARD E. BARRETT, *Soul-Force: African Heritage in Afro-American Religion* (Garden City, N.Y.: Doubleday Anchor, 1974);* and RABOTEAU, pp. 16-42.

28. "The First Rebels," *Time,* July 12, 1976, p. 34.

29. On Voodoo, see ALFRED METRAUX, *Voodoo in Haiti* (New York: Schocken, 1972);* GENOVESE, pp. 174-76, pp. 220-23, and *passim;* RABOTEAU, pp. 75-80 and *passim.*

30. On Christianity among slaves during the colonial period, see GENOVESE, pp. 169-71, pp. 183-93, pp. 202-209; E. FRANKLIN FRAZIER, *The Negro Church in America* (New York: Schocken, 1964),* pp. 6-12; AHLSTROM, *Religious History,* pp. 698-705; and, most fully, RABOTEAU, Sec. II.

31. See FRAZIER, pp. 12-19, GENOVESE, pp. 209-85, and RABOTEAU, *passim.*

32. MELVILLE J. HERSKOVITS, *The Myth of the Negro Past* (Boston: Beacon, 1971/58).* For a good summary of the Frazier-Herskovits debate, see RABOTEAU, Chap. 2 ("Death of the Gods").

33. FRAZIER, *Negro Church,* pp. 1-6.

34. GENOVESE, "Origins of the Folk Religion," in *Roll, Jordan, Roll.* GENOVESE himself argues for a mediating position between FRAZIER and HERSKOVITS. A comparison with RABOTEAU's position is instructive.

35. For African religions, see GEOFFREY PARRINDER, *African Traditional Religion* (New York: Harper & Row, 1962);* BENJAMIN C. RAY, *African Religions: Symbol, Ritual, and Community* (Englewood Cliffs, N.J.: Prentice-Hall Studies in Religion Series, 1976);* and NEWELL S. BOOTH, JR., *African Religions: A Symposium* (New York: NOK, 1977).* A good brief summary of elements of the traditional worldview of African peoples can be found in BARRETT, *Soul-Force,* pp. 17-39. Much of the following discussion is based on BARRETT. See also RABOTEAU, Chap. 1.

36. On early European reaction to African religions, see RAY, pp. 2-5.

37. GENOVESE, pp. 220-28.

38. Ibid., "The Gospel in the Quarters," pp. 232-55. See also RABOTEAU, pp. 243-66, and LAWRENCE W. LEVINE, *Black Culture and Black Consciousness*

(New York: Oxford University Press, 1977), Chap. I ("The Sacred World of Black Slaves").

39. GENOVESE, pp. 243–47, and LEVINE, p. 39.
40. CLIFTON H. JOHNSON et al., *God Struck Me Dead: Religious Conversion Experiences and Autobiographies of Ex-Slaves* (Philadelphia and Boston: Pilgrim, 1969).* See also RABOTEAU, pp. 266–75.
41. On the development of free black churches, see FRAZIER, *Negro Church,* Chap. 2 ("The Institutional Church of the Free Negroes"); CAROL V. R. GEORGE, *Segregated Sabbaths: Richard Allen and the Rise of Independent Black Churches, 1760–1840* (New York: Oxford University Press, 1973);* and AHLSTROM, *Religious History,* Chapter 42 ("The Rise of the Black Churches").
42. These groups are dealt with by ARTHUR HUFF FAUSET in *Black Gods of the Metropolis: Negro Religious Cults in the Urban North* (Philadelphia: University of Pennsylvania Press, 1944/71)* and HOWARD M. BROTZ, *The Black Jews of Harlem* (New York: Schocken, 1964/70).*
43. A recent study of Pentecostalism among blacks is MELVIN D. WILLIAMS, *Community in a Black Pentecostal Church: An Anthropological Study* (Pittsburgh: University of Pittsburgh Press, 1974). On its origins, see W. J. HOLLENWEGER, *The Pentecostals* (Minneapolis: Augsburg, 1972), pp. 22–24, and JOHN THOMAS NICHOL, *Pentecostalism* (New York: Harper & Row, 1966), pp. 32–37.
44. The following discussion is based primarily on the materials in SARA HARRIS, *Father Divine* (New York: Collier, 1971).* See also FRAZIER, *Negro Church,* pp. 57–60; FAUSET, *Black Gods,* Chap. VI ("Father Divine Peace Mission Movement"); KENNETH E. BURNHAM, *God Comes to America: Father Divine and the Peace Mission Movement* (Boston: Lambeth Press, 1978); and KEITH V. ERICKSON, "Black Messiah: The Father Divine Peace Mission Movement," *Quarterly Journal of Speech,* 63 (December 1977), 428–38.
45. HARRIS, *Father Divine,* pp. 4–5.
46. For the story of the movement after Father Divine's death, see HARRIS, pp. 353–67.
47. ERVING GOFFMAN, *Asylums: Essays on the Social Situation of Mental Patients and Other Inmates* (Garden City, N.Y.: Doubleday Anchor, 1961).*
48. This elimination of kinship distinctions is a good example of VICTOR TURNER's concept of "communitas," which we will discuss in Chapter 3.
49. See HARRIS, *Father Divine, passim* for numerous examples of such naming.
50. Ibid., pp. 131–32.
51. Ibid., Chap. 20 ("—Rosebuds of My Heart") pp. 319–30.
52. See VICTOR TURNER's discussion of "liminality" in *The Ritual Process: Structure and Anti-Structure* (Chicago: Aldine, 1969),* pp. 166–68 and *passim.*
53. Ibid., Chaps. 3 and 4.
54. See BROTZ, *Black Jews;* FAUSET, *Black Gods,* Chaps. IV and V; E. E. ESSIEN-UDOM, *Black Nationalism: A Search for an Identity in America* (Chicago: University of Chicago Press, 1962), pp. 44–48.
55. On Garvey, see E. DAVID CRONON, *Black Moses: The Story of Marcus Garvey and the Universal Negro Improvement Association* (Madison: University of Wisconsin Press, 1955),* and AMY JACQUES-GARVEY, ed., *Philosophy and Opinions of Marcus Garvey* (New York: Atheneum, 1970).*

56. The two best accounts of the Black Muslims (Nation of Islam) are ESSIEN-UDOM, *Black Nationalism*, and C. ERIC LINCOLN, *The Black Muslims in America* (Boston: Beacon, 1961).* Considerable descriptive and historical material is also contained in ALEX HALEY, ed., *The **Autobiography** of Malcolm X* (New York: Grove, 1966).* On Fard, see ESSIEN-UDOM, pp. 56-57 and *passim.*
57. Since the death of Elijah Muhammed, the movement, under the direction of his son Wallace, has backed away from its doctrines of extreme racial separation, and is now accepting white members. See KENNETH L. WOODWARD (with NOLAN DAVIS), " 'Second Resurrection,' " *Newsweek,* August 22, 1977, p. 67.
58. See *Autobiography of Malcolm X* for the extremely engaging narrative, edited by Alex Haley, from which this brief biographical summary is derived.
59. Ibid., pp. 164-67.
60. Ibid., p. 167.
61. See JAMES H. LAUE, "A Contemporary Revitalization Movement in American Race Relations: The 'Black Muslims,'" in Nelsen, Yokley, and Nelsen, eds., *The Black Church in America* (New York: Basic Books, 1971).
62. ERNST TROELTSCH, *The Social Teaching of the Christian Churches,* 2 vols. (New York: Harper Torchbooks, 1960) I, Chap. 2, sec. 9. On sectarianism and sect theory in general, see BRYAN WILSON, *Religious Sects* (New York: McGraw-Hill, 1970).
63. ESSIEN-UDOM, *Black Nationalism,* p. 228.
64. Ibid., pp. 226-27.
65. *Autobiography of Malcolm X,* pp. 158-59.
66. On fraternal organizations, see FRAZIER, *Negro Church,* pp. 36-38, and JOHN HOPE FRANKLIN, *From Slavery to Freedom: A History of Negro Americans* (New York: Knopf, 1967),* pp. 226-27 and pp. 406-407.

2

American Folk Religions and Their Transformations

FOLK RELIGION AND THE "LITTLE TRADITION"

The modernization process involves a movement of society, gradually or suddenly, from one "ideal type of social order" to another. One end of this continuum is often characterized (perhaps unfortunately) by the term "primitive," while the other, our own society, is known as "modern" (or sometimes "mass" culture).[1] Robert Redfield, the anthropologist who has contributed most to the notion of this continuum of development, describes these two types succinctly in *The Primitive World and Its Transformations:*

> We may say that a society is civilized insofar as the community is no longer small, isolated, homogeneous and self-sufficient; as the division of labor is no longer simple; as impersonal relationships come to take the place of personal relationships; as familial connections come to be modified or supplanted by those of political affiliation of contract; and as thinking has become reflective and systematic.[2]

Societies seldom embody fully one or the other of these sets of characteristics; rather, they are in process, moving from one to the other, but often pausing at a certain point in the course of development if circumstances are propitious. It is difficult for any contemporary society to escape completely from the inexorable logic of modernization. However, some peoples try their best to escape its implications if not its outward trappings, and the course of modern history provides a host of examples of cultures in various stages of tension between one pole and the other.

The stage of social organization called "primitive" is really outside our sphere of concern. In order to label a culture or religion as "popular," some element of contrast must at least implicitly be present. A culture that is homogeneous—one that has not experienced the process of differentiation which distinguishes the "people" from the "elite"—interests us only as a potential example for contrast or comparison with "mixed" types of society, those in which this process of differentiation has at least begun.

It is the symbolic expression of these mixed societies, as they are found on the North American continent and in those cultures that were transplanted to these shores, that is the subject of this chapter. In them, a small group of religious specialists has already begun the process of reflective thought, the systematic arrangement of the culture's traditional lore into a set of discursive propositions. Judaism's rabbinical schools, the theological faculties of the great medieval universities, and, in a rather different context, the divinity schools and seminaries of contemporary America, are all examples of such institutionalized speculation. Although such work is largely inaccessible to non-specialists, especially those who lack literacy or formal education, it nevertheless provides a point of reference for the organized religious expression of the society in which it takes place.

In any society in which literacy and education are less than universal, however, a counterpoint to this "elitist" speculation will survive and adapt itself to the sophisticated teachings of the "Great Tradition."[3] For our purposes, we may call such religiosity that of the "Little Tradition"—"folk religion." Folk religion, in our sense of the term, is invariably syncretistic—it incorporates elements from the great tradition into a body of pre-existent beliefs and practices which have been handed down for countless generations among those who had been isolated from the influence of the "high culture." Folk religion, then, involves an implicit tension, and may be viewed as a dialectic between two opposed forces which those who are caught between them attempt to reconcile into an uneasy equilibrium.

The degree to which a folk religion adapts itself to the great tradition emanating from the urban centers of civilization depends a great deal on the degree of both physical and psychological isolation a rural people want or are able to maintain. Some Mexican villages situated high in the mountains or far in the remote regions of the Yucatan managed for a long while to resist assimilation into the larger Mexican culture, whether in its feudal or revolutionary aspects.[4] Christianity was often a thin veneer adapted to traditional customs, or else existed as an alternative to those traditions, to be invoked when pressures for conformity ran high or when invocation of the old gods proved inefficacious. Similarly, the voluntary isolation of such groups as the Hutterites in the Canadian prairies has made possible the preservation of many of the features of life and worship that characterized the group in Luther's time. In such cases, religion acts as a conservative influence. As long as it can provide a coherent and functional interpretation of the universe for its adherents, as long as it is not too far removed from the realities of social organization, a traditional worldview can provide a stimulant for the resistance of the psychological implications of whatever "new ways" may have been introduced. It will fail when the traditional social structure has disintegrated beyond repair; on the other hand, it can go far in providing a framework for resistance to such disintegration, particularly if the external culture is perceived as hostile and the will to adhere to the old ways is thus reinforced.

Each cultural and religious system has a logic of its own. That of our own technological culture, against whose standards we are often unfortunately tempted to judge those of others, is inductive and empirical. In other words, it is "scientific"—it surveys a range of phenomena, arrives at abstract principles which govern their relationships, and tests its conclusions by applying them to specific problems. Functional applicability and performance are the ultimate tests: if the bridge does not collapse, if the plane gets off the ground, if the patient feels better—the theory is valid, the logic is good.

The logic of hierarchical societies tends to be rationalistic. First premises or principles are supplied through tradition or revelation; from them, all needful knowledge can be deduced syllogistically through the correct application of the principles of reasoning. Logic, in this way, tends to reflect social structure. While our own president fills a largely functional office, and is judged (at least theoretically) on his effectiveness as a problem-solver, the kings, emperors, and popes of feudal cultures do not require such empirical legitimation.[5] Their office, and with it their charisma, is inherited and/or divinely ordained. Their edicts, similarly, are not subject to the canons of logical consistency or empirical verification; however, they are *implemented* in a consistent and rational fashion, and are as effective as the king is powerful and as his bureaucracy and army are efficient. When first premises are overthrown through the erosion of the power of revelation or by the downfall of a dynasty, the rest collapses like a house of cards. Scholasticism and royalty are only as good as their first terms.

The logic of primitive cultures is again distinct from either of these models. Perhaps surprisingly, it is more complex than that of either of the varieties we have already considered. First, its appeal is to tradition: "We have always done it this way" is perhaps the most characteristic justification for any given action or belief. Any significant action is theoretically modeled on that performed by the gods at the creation of the world, during the "strong time" when paradigms for all aspects of human activity were provided.[6] Secondly, it is a logic not of abstract terms and their relationships but of specific, "condensed" symbols. Reasoning is conducted through the juxtaposition of images into congruent patterns which, when properly arranged, provide solutions to the problematic aspects of existence. Such a universe has a genuine consistency, but its coherence is plural. Just as power is diffused among the members of a tribe that has only a minimally centralized structure and leadership, so is the symbolic world composed of a wide variety of powers, forces, and beings which exist simultaneously and in their full individual particularity.

When a primitive people is incorporated into the social and political orbit of a more highly differentiated society, a folk culture or little tradition generally results as long as the process of assimilation remains incomplete.[7] (A modernized society generally promotes complete assimilation and homogenization of all its members; a feudal society, on the other hand, usually strives to maintain a hierarchical structure in which the differentiation of classes or castes is enforced.) The resultant folk culture continues to manifest many of the characteristics of the logic of primitive societies. In the great tradition, individuality and originality, whether expressed in the continuity of an ongoing tradition (e.g., the work of Dante and Aquinas) or as deliberate departures from tradition (Wordsworth, Baudelaire, Joyce) are highly valued. In folk culture, however, individuality is at best eccentric and at worst dangerous. Anonymity is a greater hallmark of value and authenticity than is "creative" expression; what is true is that which is timeless, which has always and everywhere been believed by everyone.

One important characteristic of folk tradition is its formulaic quality.[8] This literature is transmitted orally rather than in writing, and its continuity depends on its being memorized easily. Therefore, "singers of tales" such as Homer composed not with the aim of continuous originality of expression, but rather in easily remembered formulae which could be inserted frequently to develop a basic narrative theme as it was told and retold. A recent study has pointed up the formulaic character of much of the preaching in black American churches, in which the sermon becomes a chant of interchangeable units which flesh out a central theme.[9]

Before going on to discuss folk religion and its various manifestations in the American context, we should pause to note some of the difficulties which make a precise division of subject matter nearly impossible. The United States has not been very hospitable to the survival of folk culture in its "pure" form—that is, as carried on in a preliterate society which has only tangential relationships with the great tradition. In the first place, especially since the closing of the frontier, the highly developed character of American technology and communications have made effective geographical isolation of a folk people difficult. Some, like the Hutterites, have sought isolation voluntarily; others, like the Mormons, had it thrust upon them; still others, like the Appalachian and Ozark "hillbilly" enclaves, have maintained a considerable degree of isolation through the combination of choice and physical circumstances. The first two examples, however, are both characterized by a considerable degree of literacy, which in itself tends to work against the maintenance of a folk tradition. The mountain peoples have similarly not been exempt from the forces of modernization. In fact, they are descended from English and Scotch-Irish stock which at the time of their settlement in America had already been affected by the new culture that was emerging in the wake of the Reformation.

The Reformation itself had a powerful impact on the erosion of folk culture. In the first place, Protestantism in its most rigorous forms was not hospitable to the symbolic character of folk expression. Secondly, the high premium placed on literacy by Puritans as a prerequisitive for the direct encounter of the individual with the Word of God revealed in Scripture provided a powerful incentive for educational as well as religious evangelization. The transfer in emphasis from religious to political literacy which began with the Enlightenment gave a further impetus to the goal of universal literacy, an ideal from which only the black slaves were excepted (a significant exception, to be sure). In any case, few enclaves of illiteracy were left in white America, and the resultant quality of cultural expression was affected in great measure by the pursuit and reasonably complete achievement of this goal.

The remainder of this chapter will concern itself, perhaps a bit arbitrarily, with the development of folk religion in the context of those groups which remained for some time, before or after their transplantation to the New World, in greater isolation from the forces of modernization than did the mainstream of American Protestantism. I have chosen to deal here with Roman Catholicism especially as a totality, even though its development in urban America retained only a few of the characteristics of folk religion in a meaningful sense, and in many of its aspects it can best be described as "clerico-popular." Also, I have decided to treat only those "Protestant" groups which have more or less voluntarily withdrawn themselves from the mainstream of that tradition's development, and chosen an isolated and in some measure communitarian life remote from the encroachments of modernization. A discussion of the "folk" aspects of such denominations as Methodism will be deferred to a later chapter, even though many of its elements are similar to some of the phenomena discussed below.

SOME CHARACTERISTICS OF FOLK RELIGION

Folk religion is part of folklore, but is distinguished from other forms, such as the folktale, by its greater degree of syncretism. Folk religion is the center of the little tradition in its full sense in that it represents the development of popular interpretations, elaborations, and variations around the themes provided for it by the great tradition. Folk Catholicism, for instance, accepts as true the central teachings of the universal Catholic Church. What it does with those teachings, however, is rather different from the theology of a Thomas Aquinas or a Karl Rahner. While the folktale exists as a literary form independent of the teachings of the academy or the practice of the urban writer, folk religion is by its nature involved in a larger enterprise, and must work its way carefully between the demands of the remote centers of authority and the needs and wishes of the local constituency. In this sense, it is more like political and economic institutions than those, such as art, music, and literature, which we identify more readily as "cultural." It is of necessity implicated in the crucial activities of the broader society, but it is not content to accept them as given. It is the adaptation of these givens to the local situation and its traditions that results in folk religion.

The core of folk religion exists in the dialectical tension between the abstract, universalistic, and often historically grounded teachings of a great tradition and the more immediate, ahistorical, and particularistic worldview of primitive religions. This occurs especially when the missionary or other representative of the great tradition is unable to translate its doctrines into immediately comprehensible and relevant terms, or is so much a part of the folk culture himself that he is as much its own agent as that of the great tradition. Also, the religious aspects of the great tradition are not easily implanted with any firmness unless other aspects of the culture within which it developed have been successfully grafted as well. A remote, agricultural people are not likely to be willing or able to think immediately in the universalistic, rational, historical categories that developed through centuries of cosmopolitan, urban experience. The resulting gap, when the great tradition cannot be ignored, is filled by folk religion.

Folk religion can be divided into three parts. The first, which we need deal with only in passing, is the core of symbols provided for it by a great tradition. Secondly,and at its heart, is the system of elaborations and interpretations which it works on these themes. Third, there exists around the edge of these concentric rings a third circle, which consists of a broad collection of beliefs and practices which once made sense as part of the greater unity of an earlier primitive religious system, but which are now incompatible with the new synthesis. Instead, they live a half-life as a collection of magical practices, folk cures, and "superstitions" which still retain a power and fascination.

The traditional religions of the peoples of North America, Europe, and Africa were characterized by a much greater plurality and diffusion of supernatural power throughout the various aspects of the universe than is the case in the "high religions." This power was sometimes personified in gods or legendary heroes, and in other cases was perceived as immanent in aspects of nature and social situations. Most particularly, religious significance and power were experienced in the here and now. Such power pervaded all aspects of human existence, and had to be dealt with in every important situation, ordinary or exceptional, of daily life. Catholicism and Judaism both, in rather different ways, recognized the importance of these symbol-generating situations, and in more rationalized fashion attempted to provide ways of dealing with them without compromising the transcendence of the one God they postulated. Protestantism eliminated these modes of accommodation, and left an even greater vacuum which often had to be filled piecemeal. We shall deal with all three of these situations in due course.

Folk religion can therefore be seen as a process of retaining and dealing symbolically with the problematic situations of daily life for which the great traditions provide no immediately compelling solution. Where possible, it adapts the symbolism of the great tradition to fill these gaps; where the symbols are insusceptible to satisfactory manipulation and reinterpretation, or when the agents of the great tradition protest too strongly against such adaptations, the "third circle" mentioned above takes on a greater fullness to help fill the perceived void.

Compilations of folk beliefs and practices, regardless of source or locale, reveal a striking uniformity. (Whether this is due to cultural contact or spontaneous simultaneous activity is not a matter with which we need concern ourselves here, and is probably not resolvable.) A rough typology may help us to perceive the general pattern:[10]

1. Beliefs and practices about food at all stages of cultivation, preparation, and serving. Elaborate rules regarding food are also present in "high religions," especially Orthodox Judaism.
2. Beliefs and practices about *health* and *sickness.* Before the advent of modern medicine, the art of the healer and the priest were often closely intertwined, and the tribal medicine man often occupied a religious office. Even in technologically advanced societies, organized medicine is beginning (if rather grudgingly) to acknowledge the interconnectedness of mind and matter, and to admit that the practices of folk healers may be efficacious when more scientific methods fail.
3. Beliefs and practices about the *life cycle.* Birth, puberty, marriage and death have never been easy times for anyone, and have been facilitated in traditional cultures by elaborate processes for symbolic mediation. Many of the problems connected with childbirth and puberty are also physiological in character, and this category overlaps with the general area of health and sickness as well.
4. Beliefs and practices about *the dead.* This is an obvious continuation of the previous category, and isolates the aspect of life—its termination and what, if anything, lies beyond—that has been most resistant to the impact of modernization (for what are probably obvious reasons).

Heaven, hell, purgatory, ghosts, and other symbolic representations of life beyond the grave almost inevitably constitute a major preoccupation of folk religion.

5. Beliefs and practices about the *prediction of the future*. A glance at any tabloid available at one's local supermarket checkout counter will reveal immediately that interest in what is yet to come is hardly confined to preliterate cultures. The future is, almost by definition, unknowable through empirical means, and is often provocative of any number of anxieties (its connection with death is also worth noting). Astrology reached the state of high art among the Babylonians and other sophisticated peoples, and is still with us today. Omens, the interpretation of dreams, and various other indicators of the course of future events constitute a sizable component of folk beliefs.
6. Beliefs and practices about *evil* and *misfortune*. Theodicy has traditionally been one of the most vexing and problematic tasks of the theologian, and it is not surprising that other than orthodox explanations of human suffering should continue to proliferate. *Witchcraft,* in the sense of "black magic," is the trafficking of antisocial individuals with supernatural powers for the purpose of achieving immediate effects, often malevolent, in the mundane realm.[11] The belief in (and often the practice of) witchcraft has been remarkably prevalent in all sorts of societies, particularly those undergoing acute disruption. The *evil eye* is a variant on the same theme found in many folk cultures, and is represented in the United States among both Chicanos and Sicilians.[12] (The preoccupation of Mary Baker Eddy, the founder of Christian Science, with "malicious animal magnetism" may be attributed to paranoia, but is perhaps more accurately explicable as the persistence of this type of symbolic behavior in what Sydney Ahlstrom has characterized as a boarding-house subculture.[13] The hysteria generated both at Salem in the 1690s and in Washington in the 1950s is indicative of witchcraft belief in societies which can only metaphorically (or morally) be characterized as "primitive."

In addition to these categories, we should note two other realms of folk belief which do not fall into parallel with those listed above. First is the notion of *taboo*—that is, the avoidance of certain objects, practices, people, or situations which, when performed or encountered directly, bring automatic defilement or retribution.[14] Taboos may arise in connection with most of the above categories, as well as with others. A rough converse of the notion of taboo is the attribution of good results to the performance of certain acts or contact with certain persons or things (the recent repudiation of St. Christopher medals by the Catholic Church is an example of the divorce of great and little traditions after a long conjunction). Charms, amulets, and the like are all illustrations of this sort of "taboo in reverse."

Another characteristic of folk culture is a tendency to attribute preternatural powers to specific individuals. Witchcraft is an example of this practice in the realm of maleficent power, and is incorporated into little traditions through the notion of the possibility of trafficking with the Devil. (Such dealings often have heavy sexual aspects, and Satanic cults with erotic overtones have persisted into contemporary America.) Witches and sorcerers, however, are seldom remembered or celebrated in their individuality. On the other hand, persons possessed of the power to do good works through magic or spiritual means achieve a lasting place in the folk pantheon, even though their individuality often tends to become blurred in the formulaic accounts of their lives and careers which rise up after their deaths (or transfigurations).

The proliferation of angels (and, to a lesser extent, demons) in the extra-biblical Jewish and Catholic traditions is one example of this tendency to attribute miraculous powers to beings with distinct personalities. However, angels have always been a bit too remote to provide great satisfaction or immediate results. Particularly wise and holy men have attained legendary stature among the Jews from time to time, but the historical bias of that tradition has generally held those worthies fairly close to factual ground. The most conspicuous example of this phenomenon in the little traditions of the West has been the Roman Catholic cult of the saints. The most powerful and popular of these have usually been the Holy Family: Mary, Joseph, the Infant Jesus (who always seems more human than divine in this particular manifestation), and occasionally Saint Anne (who is especially popular in French Canada).[15]

The great tradition of Roman Catholicism has generally been tolerant and often supportive of the veneration of saints, but has always tried to hold the tendency toward their apotheosis under control through careful theological distinctions and an elaborate procedure of historical investigation (conducted especially by the Bollandist order) before risking definitive canonization. Nevertheless, the saints have often led a life of their own within the little traditions of Catholicism. Their intercession has been sought in almost every aspect of personal life, especially in the particularly problematic categories outlined above. (Saint Anthony, for instance, has been widely believed to be useful in the recovery of lost articles, another area of difficulty in the course of everyday activity.)[16]

Patron saints have also provided legitimation to the popular desire for local identity and recognition. The Shrine of the Immaculate Conception in Washington, D.C., is dedicated to the Virgin Mary, and has to either side of the main altar a series of smaller shrines, many of which are dedicated to a particular national or ethnic avatar of the central figure.[17] (Poles, Mexicans, and Lithuanians are among the groups thus distinguished.) Saint George of England and Saint James (*Santiago*) of Spain are other saints who have become specifically associated with a nation or people.

Even more specific identification occurs throughout Latin America, where individual villages each honor a specific patron.[18] The tension between a centripetal monotheism and an implicit centrifugal polytheism has often proved embarrassing to the maintainers of the great tradition, since aspersions cast on the historical authenticity of a particular saint or the quantity of piety directed thereto can easily be interpreted as an ethnic aspersion.

In general, the patterns of symbolic activity that form the undergirding and dynamics of folk religion (and other sorts of popular religion as well, as we shall see) may be categorized in two areas. First, they are intimately connected with the problem areas of everyday life. They especially accrue to those processes of life which involve a *transition* from one state to another. Symbolic mediation is often invoked in passing from one state of life to another (or into and out of life), in moving from one place to another, at critical times of the year (e.g., the harvest), or on other occasions when the outcome of an event of great importance is uncertain. (Arnold Van Gennep and Victor Turner have pointed to the *liminal* character of these times—that is, their situation as a *limen* or threshold between one state or condition and another).[19]

Secondly, symbolic activity is often invoked to provide legitimacy and protection for a particular social group. Emile Durkheim has postulated that religion itself arises out of a people's symbolic projection of their own collective sense of self onto a totem or, eventually, a god.[20] Whatever the limitations of this theory, it is certainly suggestive in the context of such phenomena as patron saints. This kind of activity also becomes important in other forms of popular religion such as the "Civil Religion," with which we will deal in a later chapter.

FOLK, DEVOTIONAL, AND "CLERICO-POPULAR" STRAINS IN ROMAN CATHOLIC SYMBOLISM

The Roman Catholic Church has been the primary *locus* of folk religion in the development of the Western world. Before discussing its specifically American manifestations, it seems worthwhile at this point to take a brief historical glance at the development of folk religion in the broader Catholic context in order to examine some of the variations that can take place in such a historically prolonged and geographically diverse cultural experience. An examination of Buddhism and Hinduism would almost certainly produce some illuminating parallels, but such a project is far beyond our present scope.

We should also note at this point that the symbolic repertory of American Catholicism is an extraordinarily complex amalgam of elements accumulated over a long period of time. It reflects the historical and ethnic diversity of Catholicism and its capacity to blend syncretistically symbols generated during widely different historical periods and in highly divergent cultural and social situations. For this reason, it is extremely difficult to isolate "folk," "popular," and "official" strains of Catholicism, since these elements tend to blend together in America to form a unique synthesis. The recent impetus to rationalize these complex and even conflicting elements has led to considerable congnitive confusion and anxiety since Vatican II. In any case, we will attempt to deal with American Catholicism as a whole, with a few addenda included in Chapter 4.

Christianity in its earliest phases was without question a popular religion. Judaism had become divided into a number of sects and parties, and the members of those which especially appealed to the educated and socially successful were somewhat less than keen about their new rival. The earliest followers of Jesus did not number themselves among the elite, however diverse they may have been in other respects. This very diversity, however, was also significant. From almost the beginning Christianity presented itself as a universalistic religion: in Christ there was neither Jew nor Greek. Tribalism and ethnic particularity had been definitively repudiated. Whatever else may have been required of the newly converted, geography and ancestry were ruled out of the picture.

As the centuries progressed, however, the inevitable process of "the routinization of charisma" worked its effects. Instead of remaining a persecuted minority and a witness against the established structures of society, Christianity had establishment thrust upon it with the Constantinian settlement. With the subsequent collapse of the Western Empire, the responsibility for the maintenance of a whole (if rather precarious) social system devolved upon the successors to a once despised band of fanatic sectarians. The Catholic Church, with its leadership now firmly established at the ancient seat of the Empire, progressively grew to imitate that Empire in its structures and its ambitions.

The ensuing centuries, once cavalierly dismissed as the "Dark Ages," witnessed the spread of the (now-not-so) new faith over the European continent. In some cases, individuals or small groups of missionaries gained adherents on a voluntary basis. More often, however, newly Christianized groups of barbarians promoted further conversions by force, so that whole tribes of "pagans" streamed into the arms of the Church willy-nilly. Even though the medieval Church achieved seeming miracles of organization and administration, it is not particularly surprising that it was unable to provide adequate clerical guidance to large areas of its new Empire, and that those especially who lived in the more far-flung corners of Christendom retained, perhaps *faute de mieux,* a considerable attachment to the religious ways of their forebears.

Although the medieval Church expended considerable energy in attempting to impose an orthodox understanding of Christian teaching on its constituents, the flow of religious interpretation was not entirely one-sided. From its earliest days, Catholicism embraced a dialectical interchange between its great and little traditions, so that official theology often represented an incorporation and rationalization of what had begun as popular piety. Much of its official teaching (now as well as then) has appeared to those of Protestant (or generally skeptical) inclinations to bear only the most tenuous resemblance to anything contained in canonical Scripture. Consequently, those in the Reformation and the Puritan movement saw themselves as an attempt to return to the pristine simplicity of primitive Christian teaching and practice, and to purge Christianity of the pagan accretions that had adhered to it like barnacles over the intervening centuries.

During the High Middle Ages, Catholicism flourished at a number of different levels, which simultaneously supported and checked one another.[21] The realistic doctrine of the Eucharist, which taught that the symbolic bread and wine of the Mass were literally transformed into the Body and Blood of Christ through priestly agency, was the theoretical underpinning for a vast range of symbolic behavior that regarded the sacred as manifest in the material world. The other sacraments provided potent symbolic support for the difficult times of transition encountered in all lives, and were not so far in conception from primitive *rites de passage* that the message was entirely lost on the less well instructed. The cathedrals contained a wealth of highly vivid and tangible iconography, which encompassed all aspects of life and history, and which provided legitimation for all sorts and conditions of men and women.[22] The anointing of kings, a sort of sacrament in itself, gave the political order an ontological grounding, even though the universal Empire had presumably replaced particular tribes as the locus of significance.[23] This universalism was offset, however, by the abundance of patron saints of all descriptions which we encountered earlier.

The cult of saints reached its fullness as part of both great and little traditions during this time. Pilgrimages, such as that rather skeptically described by Chaucer in the *Canterbury Tales,* were highly regarded means of obtaining grace through vicarious contact with the holiest of the company of the spiritually elite, and perhaps offset the implicit particularism of the cult with a cosmopolitanism engendered by geographical movement.[24] Jesus at times seemed to take his place as *primus inter pares* among them, and occasionally fell into the danger of being overshadowed in importance by his mother.

Henry Adams, though perhaps not the most reliable of guides to this period, offers some interesting speculations as to the power of the Marian cult in particular in his brilliant *tour de force, Mont-Saint-Michel and Chartres.*[25] Adams saw the Gothic cathedrals of France, and particularly that at Chartres, as popular repudiations of the officially sanctioned cultus which attained such power that the agents of the great tradition could only look the other way. The Trinity represented the power, judgment, and impersonality of the institutional Church and its ally, the State. As peasants of all times and periods have felt, such institutions were more to be suspected than loved, even though their necessity may have been acknowledged. The Trinity was an abstraction: it could bring punishment and perhaps a rather lofty justice, but it could not stand for pity and compassion. These latter qualities were instead embodied in the Virgin, whose power was sufficient to exact from the nobles and emergent bourgeoisie a grudging but nevertheless impressive financial tribute. If the Trinity was structure, Mary was antistructure. She suspended or reversed the rules, and restored the Gospel promise that the last shall be first and the first, unless they were extraordinarily circumspect in their bearing toward her and her humble adherents, would indeed be last.[26]

Adams went even further in identifying the Virgin, most suggestively, as the latest in a long succession of female goddesses including Isis, Astarte, and Demeter.[27] The architectonic theological system of Aquinas represented unity and a universalism bordering on the deterministic. The Virgin stood in contrast for radical particularity, for the intrinsic worth and claims to respect of each individual, in her roles of asserting the biological life force on the one hand and the unconditional affirmation of mother love on the other. Protestantism represented a reaction against the anarchy implicit in this latter position. In an attempt to assert (paradoxically, in view of the usual interpretations of the Reformation) their entitlement to admission to heaven through works-righteousness and social respectability, the emergent bourgeoisie was "not satisfied with abolishing [the Virgin], but sought to abolish the woman altogether as the cause of evil in heaven and on earth. The Puritans abandoned the New Testament and the Virgin in order to go back to the beginning, and renew the quarrel with Eve."[28]

Although Adams may have pushed his arguments to somewhat fanciful lengths, he was essentially correct in his perception of the implicit polytheism of popular Catholicism and in the significance of the elimination of female symbolism from the symbolic vocabulary of Protestantism. Whatever else it may have been, Puritanism was in fact the reflection of the increasing rationalization of Western life, and had little room in its orthodox formulations for embodiments of the particularistic and irrational short of the ultimate and inscrutable arbitrariness of its transcendent God. Particularistic elements would gradually creep back into Protestantism, but the institutionalized particularism of the Catholic pantheon had been at least temporarily laid to rest at Geneva, Westminster, and Massachusetts Bay.[29]

Major shifts in symbolic expression and the interaction between the great and little traditions within the Catholic Church also took place as a result of the Protestant challenge. The Council of Trent abruptly checked the increasing fragmentation of the Church, and introduced a wide range of reforms promoting centralization, rationalization, and literacy. However, the relegation of Catholicism by the post-Reformation political settlement to the sphere of the less progressively minded districts of Europe held such tendencies in check. The Enlightenment wreaked further havoc among any latent inclinations in the direction of rationalism and democracy, and the chaotic politics of the Italian peninsula transformed an initially liberal Pius IX into the promulgator of the authoritarian Syllabus of Errors.[30]

The major symbolic shift within Catholicism which occurred between the sixteenth and nineteenth centuries was a virtual reversal of attitude on the part of the great toward the little traditions. The official church of the Middle Ages had been supportive enough of pilgrimages, devotion to the saints, and the like. Still, it was careful to keep them within the bounds of orthodox interpretation lest they spill over into the heresies which kept cropping up in scattered pockets of the Empire, where the local populace was loath to surrender its traditional (and implicitly subversive) adherence to pre-Christian dualistic religions. The Incarnation symbolized, among other things, the coordination of the spiritual and material realms, and any repudiation of one or the other—as in the alarming episode of Arianism—could upset this implicit rationale for the coexistence of the temporal and ecclesiastical ruling powers. Millenarian movements represented a similar threat to the this-worldly/other-worldly balance. The Church had far less to fear from the Turk or the Hun than from internal subversion, and many of the great religious orders had their origin in this crusade to suppress heresy from within. Popular piety, in short, was all well and good, but could not be allowed to go too far.

With the increasing beleaguerment of the Church within the European power matrix, however, the primacy of the traditional symbols of Incarnation and Trinity began to be displaced by others. Although the devotionalism which emerged from the French Church of the eighteenth century may not have been popular in origin, it was certainly so in form. The cult of the Sacred Hearts of Jesus and Mary were the most conspicuous manifestations of this new piety, and were eagerly promoted by the Church and received by a public that could understand them much more readily than the intricacies of Thomistic theology.

Catholics were not alone in their inclination toward pietism during the heyday of the Enlightenment. John and Charles Wesley, who were hardly men of the people themselves, helped launch a movement of devotionalism that would become the pre-eminently popular religion of the new United States during the following century. The Wesleys, in turn, were greatly indebted to Count von Zinzendorf and the Moravian movement, whose London conventicle had provided the occasion for John Wesley's strange warmth of heart. With the Moravians, devotion to the physical person of Jesus reached extra-ordinary heights (or depths). "The Litany of the Wounds became the central source of doctrinal orthodoxy . . . the wounds of Jesus, including the side wound and even 'the unnamed and unknown wounds,' were characterized by a wealth of adjectives, such as 'worthy, beloved, miraculous, powerful, secret, clear, sparkling, holy, purple, juicy, close, long-suffering, dainty, warm, soft, hot and eternal.' "[31] (The author goes on to explain that some of the adjectives thus employed are unintelligible even in German.)

Devotion to the persons—not to mention the internal organs—of Mary and Jesus began to assume a major role from this time within Catholicism. (Their counterparts within the evangelical Protestantism of nineteenth-century America will be dealt with in Chapter 3.) This symbolism was not accidental. The anthropologist Mary Douglas has called attention to the significance of bodily symbolism within religious expression, and has demonstrated that symbolic expressions of the physical body correlate significantly, if not always predictably, with attitudes toward the social body. The microcosm, in short, recapitulates the macrocosm.[32]

As we have seen, the early nineteenth century witnessed the culmination of a gradual process of in-turning on the part of the Catholic Church. The papacy had been weakened immeasurably by its capitulation to political demands for the suppression of the Jesuit order in 1773, by the overturning of the Church in France during the Revolution, and by the subsequent humiliation of the Pontiff at the hands of Napoleon.[33] In his defiance of the forces of social, political, and intellectual change, Pius IX reversed this course of events, but in the process turned Catholicism onto a defensive course even the *aggiornamento* of Pope John could not entirely change. The Church saw its natural constituency, the common people of Europe, increasingly lost first to Protestantism and then to the ideologies of the nineteenth century, and withdrew into a garrison of dogmatic pronouncements and denunciations of almost everything.

The kind of devotionalism represented by the cult of the Sacred Hearts was an apt expression of this withdrawal.[34] Where the imagery of the Church as the Body of Christ stood for a view of society as Christian throughout and coordinated in all its parts, the Heart of Jesus symbolized a focus on the interior of the body, isolated from exposure to the harsh and threatening elements of the external world. The accompanying preoccupation with the baby Jesus, as in the Infant of Prague, similarly represented a withdrawal from the ongoing course of worldly events into the safe and protected world of childhood. (Some parallels in the American Christmas will be noted later.) The corollary to this was an increasing emphasis on the Church as Mother and the Pope as the Holy Father, nurturing parents who, if relied upon implicitly, would defend their adored but immature and defenseless offspring from the enemy without. It is significant that the three dogmas that have been promulgated in the past two centuries have been those of papal infallibility and of the Immaculate Conception and bodily Assumption into Heaven of the Virgin Mary. Microcosm, again, recapitulates macrocosm. (One might add that it is these particular doctrines which have proved to be nearly insuperable obstacles to the ecumenical reconciliation of Catholicism and Protestantism.)

The beginnings of Roman Catholicism in the United States were of an entirely different character.[35] (We shall postpone our discussion of Catholicism in Spanish-speaking America till the following section.) Colonial Maryland was settled by the Catholic aristocrat Lord Baltimore and his family, and this cultured and educated milieu would later produce John Carroll, the first American bishop. The French Revolution made necessary a massive emigration of its Catholic clergy—its episcopacy, in particular—and the cultivated Jean Lefebvre de Cheverus charmed the elite of Boston during his residence there. In short, the beginnings of Catholicism on the East Coast were neither popular nor authoritarian in character, and priests, bishops, and even laypeople often shared genuinely in authority and decision making.

Two currents developed in American Catholicism during the nineteenth century. On the one hand, the Irish displaced the French and English as the leaders of the Church, because the latter were vastly displaced in numbers by the enormous migration that resulted from the Irish potato famine.[36] However, much of the Irish and Irish-American hierarchy that subsequently emerged remained faithful to the earlier tradition. The midwestern bishops Ireland and Spalding and, to a slightly lesser extent, Cardinal Gibbons of Baltimore, all promoted the rapid Americanization of the Church. This task was facilitated by the lack of a language barrier between Americans and Irish. American Catholics were to participate in political life, support essentially Protestant reform movements such as temperance, and at least flirt with the possibility of educating their children in public schools with released-time provisions for religious education.[37] The founding of the Catholic University in Washington, D.C., and the American order of the Paulists were both instruments in this campaign to create an indigenous style of religious life that would, in the minds of at least some, provide a model for the rest of the Church which was unfortunate enough to reside in less progressive lands.

Needless to say, this program did not precisely coincide with the outlook of the Roman hierarchy, and ironically it was the socially liberal Leo XIII whose encyclical *Testem Benevolentiae* sounded the death knell for the hopes of Ireland and Gibbons for an Americanized Church.[38] Nor was it entirely the work of Rome. Not all the Irish in America were sympathetic to such reform, since they were themselves preoccupied with keeping themselves and their culture alive (a task not made any easier by the "No Irish Need Apply" signs which proliferated in Boston during the days of the great migration). The conservative Irish found spokesmen in such bishops as John Hughes of New York and, during the liberal heyday, New York's Corrigan and McQuaid of Rochester. They were strongly supported by most German Catholics in America, who, though for the most part more secure economically than their Irish counterparts, nevertheless resented liberal attempts to force an alien language and culture onto their own customs.[39]

The tone for the subsequent development of American Catholicism was set by such bishops as O'Connell of Boston, Spellman of New York, and McIntyre of Los Angeles, who often managed to be more Catholic than the Pope in their drive to create and maintain a subculture that was at once politically loyal to the American nation and culturally distinct from the Protestant majority. In the process the great tradition, which had already been seriously modified by the Roman papacy, was further subordinated to an anti-intellectual and devotionally oriented "Ghetto Catholicism" which held sway until the early 1960s. In the sense that it was severely clerical in its orientation and control, it was not "popular" in the strict sense of originating among the "people." Rather, it was more of a *tertium quid,* an emergent "clerico-popular" culture controlled by an elite caste of celibates but aimed at and drawing broad support from a poorly educated constituency.

The most genuinely "popular" element of this "Ghetto Church" (which Garry Wills evokes brilliantly in his *Bare Ruined Choirs*) resided in the Catholic system of parish schools, which the hierarchy promoted zealously as the most effective means of rapid socialization.[40] Primary instruction in particular was largely in the hands of nuns, who were often poorly educated themselves and formed a sort of religious proletariat within the larger church structures. A genuine folk Catholicism emerged within this context in the form of a whole body of moralistic and devotional anecdotes devised and perpetuated by the sisters for the edification of their charges. Jesus, for example, was said to be the only man who was ever exactly six feet tall. (A sense of anachronism was apparently not a sisterly virtue.[41])

More particularly, many of these anecdotes were concerned with the preservation of sexual morality. One universally popular injunction was addressed to pubescent females, cautioning them against the reflective properties of patent-leather shoes.[42] Similarly, they were advised to bring telephone books with them on social engagements where crowded transportation arrangements might necessitate their sitting on the laps of their escorts. This preoccupation with virginity, which was carried to occasionally obsessive lengths by the celibate clergy and sisterhoods, was another reflection of the generally defensive posture of the Church on an international scale. Similarly, the microcosmic exaltation of sexual purity can be read easily enough as a symbolic representation of the fear of cultural penetration on the level of the social body. A defensiveness that had its origins in the genuine hostility of and economic discrimination by the dominant culture took on a life of its own, which the contemporary Catholic preoccupation with contraception and abortion continues, at least obliquely, to reflect.[43]

ETHNIC VARIATIONS IN FOLK AND POPULAR CATHOLICISM

All American Catholics, however, were not Irish, and did not always share the clericalism and sexual preoccupations of the Irish-dominated clergy and hierarchy. In many cities and towns parishes were formed along ethnic lines, and the Polish church might be located directly across the street from that of the Irish. The German Catholics, relatively well-off before emigrating, more accustomed than the Irish to a pluralistic society, and less inclined to equate religion with nationalistic feeling, produced little in the way of a distinctive style of religiosity, although they maintained the use of their language in their churches and schools as long as they possibly could. Poles, Lithuanians, and other Slavic groups shared the German concern with obtaining a measure of recognition and independence from the Irish, but were considerably more inclined than the Germans toward such nationalistically flavored devotionalism as represented in the cult of Our Lady of Czestochowa.[44]

The most distinctive alternate styles of Catholicism to that made normative by the Irish were those of the Southern Italians and the Mexicans. (An extraordinarily large percentage of Puerto Ricans who have emigrated to New York City have converted to Pentecostalism.) If the style of the Irish-American Church can best be characterized as "clerico-popular," that of the Italians was unmistakably "folk."[45] The Catholic Church in Italy was anything but united, and the great and little traditions not only developed as distinct but as openly hostile movements. In the eyes of the Sicilians, the papacy represented a different Italy that was at once elite, alien, and exploitative. The village priest was often regarded as a money-grasping intruder whose presence was barely tolerated by the *contadini*.

This anticlericalism was not left in the Old Country when Southern Italians began to migrate to the United States in large numbers in the late nineteenth century. The Irish were at first puzzled by the strangeness of the Italians, and soon came to resent their unwillingness to support the church with which they had been provided. The folk practices of the Italians, such as belief in the *malocchio* (evil eye) and the boisterous street celebrations of the *festa* of the village patron saint, offended the Celtic sense of decorum. The love of Italians (as well as that of other ethnic groups) for the Irish was conversely not greatly increased by the virtual stranglehold the Irish maintained on the hierarchy and much of the priesthood. The impasse has been only gradually resolved by the progressive Americanization of both groups.

Mexican Catholicism resembled the Italian in many ways. The Church had come to Mexico hand in hand with the Conquistadores, even though the early missionaries often took a firm stand to moderate the excesses of the military men. Although the clergy regarded the aboriginal inhabitants benevolently, their vision of an ideal society was highly paternalistic. The Indians were gathered into towns by the friars who, while generally protective of their charges, nevertheless took care that they should never rise beyond the state of ecclesiastical peonage.[46] The vast accumulation of wealth and property by the Church over the centuries resulted in a virtual recapitulation of medieval feudalism, but one based on a caste structure as well. There was little opportunity for the Indian or the *mestizo* to ascend in the ranks of either Church or State.

The religion of most Mexicans, except for the unchurched urban and rural radicals who flourished during the Revolution, is much more clearly that of the little tradition than was that of most of the Catholic enclaves in the United States.[47] There are still many remote villages in Mexico where Spanish is virtually unknown, and the ancient Nahuatl, Maya, or other Indian dialects are the only languages spoken.[48] In such areas, Catholicism has much the same status as the language and culture with which it is traditionally associated. Especially after the decimation of the ranks of the Catholic clergy during the Revolution and the subseuent anticlerical administration of Plutarco Elías Calles, priests have been rare in these areas, and services have often been conducted by any laity who may be capable of reading or memorizing a few prayers. The result, not surprisingly, is highly syncretistic, with a thin veneer of Christianity coexisting with what remain essentially the practices of pre-Columbian times.[49]

Mexican Catholicism shares with the Italian a common love of festivals and celebrations. The *fiesta* is a high point in the yearly life of each village, and separate celebrations are held by the different neighborhoods, each with its own patron saint, in the larger towns.[50] The Day of the Dead (All Souls' Day) provides the occasion for practices that seem rather macabre to the Anglo sensibility, such as the eating of candy skulls.[51] The latter points to a mood of fatalism that is characteristic of much of Mexican culture, a mixed sense of high destiny compromised by sinfulness which often leads to violence, death, and misfortune.[52] The familiarity with death also soggests the mood evoked by Huizinga in his description of the piety of the late Middle Ages in Burgundy and the Low Countries.[53]

Following the Revolution and the re-establishment of order under President Obregón, a new folklore began to arise among the poorer Mexicans, especially in the South. Emiliano Zapata, the idealistic revolutionary leader who was killed toward the end of the final power struggles, rapidly assumed legendary stature, and his exploits were celebrated in broadsides and ballads which attained great popularity. Like King Arthur, Zapata was said to be yet alive, and waiting for the appropriate time to return again. Many believed that they had seen him riding his white horse through the night. Where elitist attempts to replace Catholicism with socialist ideology had met with hostility or indifference among these people, the folk imagination succeeded in apotheosizing a new hero who represented deliverance from oppression.[54]

Catholicism among Mexican-Americans often takes on a heavily nationalistic character. As with the French-Canadians and the Irish, the encounter with the hostility of a wealthier and more fully modernized culture has led to a heightened appreciation of religion as a source of pride and identity, even though the institutional Church itself may be sluggish or indifferent toward the temporal welfare of its constituency. The cult of the Virgin of Guadalupe extends its orbit into the American Southwest, as do the cults of other saints, some of them canonized by popular acclaim rather than through the official channels of the Church.[55] Folk medicine coexists with that of the Anglo doctors and hospitals, and the folk healer often can cope with psychosomatic disorders that baffle or arouse the hostility of their more formally educated counterparts.[56]

Although their cultures are similar in many ways, the historical experience of the French-Canadians has led to a different set of variations from the Mexican on the common theme of Catholicism.[57] Where Catholicism was forcibly imposed upon the indigenous peoples of Mexico, it was transmitted to Canada from France through voluntary emigration. (Canada was much less thickly populated by aboriginal peoples because of the less hospitable climate, and most of the Eastern Indians were either exterminated or driven further west.) The conquest of the French by the British in 1760 did not, however, result in the elimination of French culture. The Quebec Act of 1774 assured the French of cultural independence in an attempt to secure their loyalty to Britain during the American Revolution. Nevertheless, Quebec became an enclave of traditionalism within a largely British culture, and resentment of British cultural imperialism has recently reached a new intensity of political expression.

The French-Canadians resemble the Irish much more nearly than the Mexicans in their attitude toward Catholicism. For both French and Irish, religion provided a vehicle for nationalistic expression against the hostile and contemptuous English, even though the French never experienced the brutality which Britain had directed toward the Irish since the time of Cromwell.[58] The Quebec hierarchy resisted social innovations such as the nascent labor movement as potentially subversive of its political hegemony, and the parish priests fostered a clerically dominated culture which advocated a traditional, agricultural way of life as divinely sanctioned. Until modern technology and communications began to prove irresistible, small villages such as the St.-Denis studied by Horace Miner in the late 1930s remained bulwarks against the encroachments of modernization.

As we mentioned earlier, the Holy Family is one of the central objects of devotion among the French-Canadians.[59] The Mexican family has often been characterized by a double standard, in which the code of *machismo* dictates that women must remain pure and docile, and men are all but required to attempt as many sexual conquests as possible. Similarly, Mexican women are the staunch supporters of organized religion and attend Mass regularly, while the men maintain a posture of indifference or respect mingled with hostility toward the Church.[60] While Mexicans exalt the Virgin of Guadalupe as their primary symbol, the Québeçois reflect their more balanced family structure in their inclusion of the entire family of Jesus in their particular devotions. Shrines are also popular among the French, and healing miracles, particularly relevant in rural areas which are at once physically remote from urban medicine and culturally removed from the equivalent of the Mexican *curandero,* are often the major themes for pilgrimages.[61]

The various and sometimes conflicting strains of Catholicism in North America provide a good illustration of the cultural variations that can be worked on a common "great tradition." Some groups are highly moralistic, others are permissive. Some are dominated by the clergy, others are overtly anticlerical. All, however, demonstrate a high level of group consciousness which they express symbolically, and all are, in a sense, highly conservative. Millenarian activity is virtually unknown in post-medieval popular Catholicism in Europe and North America, and none of its component ethnic groups have ever expressed symbolic rejection of the extant social order in dramatic militant fashion. Catholicism, in short, has been a socially stabilizing force, perhaps in some measure because of its capacity for the toleration of noncrucial differences in cultural emphasis.

FOLK AND POPULAR JUDAISM, AND SOME CATHOLIC PARALLELS

An apt place to begin a transition to a discussion of Judaism is the topic of food taboos, which have often served as the most important symbol for both Catholics and Jews in the United States in asserting particularistic identity. The whole question of Friday abstinence from meat is a useful index for distinguishing the various levels of interpretation on the great-little tradition continuum since, till the modification of the practice in recent years, all American Catholics (as well as those in other, especially mixed cultures) faced the necessity of coming to terms with and interpreting the practice to others.[62]

At the most sophisticated level of interpretation, the requirement of Friday abstinence was an exercise in moral discipline. Fasting has traditionally been part of ascetic regimens, and in many monastic orders abstinence from meat was the norm rather than the periodic exception. The goal of such practices was the achievement of spiritual strength through the deprivation of the flesh of sensual pleasures and indulgences. Other ascetic practices, such as clerical celibacy, were generally understood in similar terms. Such occasional *virtuosi* as the anchorites of the early Christian centuries and the first followers of Saint Francis carried these measures to extremes of rigor, but for the most part they were routinized aspects of the monastic life which were extended in some measure to laypeople during the days and seasons of penitence.

In what we have designated as the clerico-popular Catholicism of the American "ghetto," such practices took on new connotations. Clerical celibacy lost much of its early functional and ascetic significance, and served instead to set the clergy aside as a caste, who lived celibate but hardly ascetic lives in a subculture satirized in the novels and stories of J. F. Powers.[63] Similarly, the Friday abstinence requirement became a disciplinary ordinance through which, since its violation tended to be frequent, social control over the laity could be easily exercised in the confessional. An elaborate casuistry, developed by the Jesuits and closely resembling that of rabbinical interpretation of the Talmud, arose to deal with any number of questionable cases in which some deviance from such practices took place. (What was one to do, for instance, when served roast beef at the home of non-Catholic friends on Friday?) Such problematic cases of conscience required frequent counsel from the clergy for resolution, and this could not help but accentuate the importance of priests in guiding the less well equipped laypeople through the mazes of ritual propriety.[64]

At the level of folk Catholicism still further elaborations on the Friday practice took place. Although the rule called for abstinence from meat, the frequency with which fish was served as a substitute (possibly reinforced rather remotely by the traditional symbolic use of the fish as a symbol of Christ) often turned the eating of fish into a positive injunction. What had originated as an ascetic practice had metamorphosed into a taboo, the violation of which would incur an automatic punishment. (Exemplary stories of the unfortunate accidents that overtook those who violated the rules were favorite staples of Catholic homiletics.) Moreover, the requirement, which was viewed primarily as a nuisance by many middle-class Catholics, took on more positive significance for those who felt themselves on the defensive in areas in which nativistic tensions ran high. It was proudly asserted as a badge of individual integrity and identity. Resentment against a liberalized hierarchy which attempted to abolish or modify the requirement after the Second Vatican Council ran high among peoples such as Mary Douglas's "Bog Irish," who had little other effective symbolic means for distinguishing themselves from the hostile or indifferent Londoners among whom they found themselves living.

Similarly, the continuing problem of "Jewish identity" in America has often led to the observation of dietary restrictions even among those Jews who do not consider themselves to be particularly religious.[65] Mary Douglas speculates that, contrary to the traditional explanation of prohibitions on pork and shellfish as primitive hygienic measures, they most likely originated in the failure of not only the pig and the shrimp but also such unlikely beasts as the ostrich and the rock badger to conform to the normal criteria for inclusion among the accepted orders of animals.[66] An ostrich, for example, is a bird that cannot fly. Such a violation of the conceptual scheme is subversive of order, and such creatures must therefore not be ingested. The abominations of Leviticus, which have also been seen as arbitrary curiosities or perhaps as disciplinary measures imposed more or less at random, now take on a new logic and significance.

Although the rock badger never became an issue, the pig certainly did. The refusal of the Jews to partake of forbidden meat sacrificed on the altars of their conquerors during the time of the Maccabean revolt gave the old prohibitions a new significance as a means of witness to the integrity of the Jewish people in the face of brutal persecution.[67] In American culture, a modified version of the same metamorphosis has taken place. American Jews, many of them unsure of their traditional identity in the absence of the cultural reinforcements of the Old World ghetto and shtetl, often encountered anti-Semitic hostility in the New World, and turned to the traditional symbolic taboos as a means of asserting their identity. Since pork and shellfish are the only foods mentioned in Leviticus which commonly occur in the American diet, their avoidance has come to represent a commitment to the Jewish tradition and community, if not to other aspects of Jewish practice.

In general, the decentralized character of Judaism made it even harder to impose any uniformity of interpretation on traditional beliefs and practices.[68] This was to some extent counteracted by the presence of a learned rabbi in almost every area of Jewish settlement, and the conservative reliance on the Talmud practiced by most of these rabbis helped prevent widespread deviations of belief and practice. Nevertheless, a considerable magical lore, based on the manipulation of the names of God and on the harnessing of the angelic inhabitants of the spirit world to human ends, arose early in Jewish history and attained to a considerable elaboration during the medieval period.[69] This Jewish magic differed from the Christian *demimonde* of witchcraft and sorcery in that the former depended on the efficacy of intrinsically good powers and beings. The Devil, the source of the powers of black magic, was virtually absent as a personified force in Jewish tradition, and rabbis somewhat grudgingly acknowledged the at least marginal acceptability of occult practices on the part of Jews who had mastered the requisite esoteric lore. Since Christians were willing to pounce upon suspicious Jewish practices (which included practically everything that was conducted in Hebrew) as evidences of sorcery, an attitude of caution even toward harmless folkloric practices became a desideratum for self-protection.

The United States did not provide a particularly congenial milieu for the perpetuation of Jewish folk traditions. The fictionalized experience of David Levinsky in Abraham Cahan's novel illustrates vividly the totalistic character of the culture of the ghetto and shtetl, and the difficulty of separating the specifically religious from the other aspects of culture within Jewish life generally.[70] This inseparability of religion and culture was resolved for some in the Reform movement, which attempted to isolate a core of religious beliefs and practices as the essence of Judaism, while relegating all other aspects of life to the realm of the indifferent. For those less conditioned to Reform thought by previous exposure to such developments in Germany, socialist ideology or, in the case of Levinsky, a secularized pursuit of worldly success became alternatives. For many Jewish families of the middle class, an adherence more sentimental than religious to the traditional holiday practices formed a parallel with the attitudes of many American Christians toward Christmas. It was primarily within the less well-educated and assimilated Hasidic and Orthodox communities that both traditional religious practices and an accompanying cluster of folklore survived.[71]

Much of the latter is scarcely distinguishable from the folk customs and beliefs of other peasant peoples (although the term "peasant" is not really applicable to Jews, who were prohibited from land holding and farming in most of the Old World). Childbirth, medicine, change of location, and other of the usual problematic or liminal aspects of daily life have acquired their mediating layer of folk practices, although the nonagricultural character of Jewish experience has resulted in a lack of the usual lore about animals and food growing. The uniquely Jewish aspect of these practices is found primarily in interpretations and modifications of traditional Jewish rituals and taboos, many of which can be interpreted as originally a sort of folk religion themselves. The general pattern of practices which are now interpreted by the rabbis of the great tradition in moral terms or as symbols of traditional Jewish identity take on a magical overlay in folk practice, much as in the "fish-on-Friday" syndrome in folk Catholicism.

VOLUNTARILY SEGREGATED GROUPS

Finally, in our discussion of folk religions in America, we come to a number of groups which, while widely diverse in their beliefs and practices, have in common a voluntary or forced geographical withdrawal from the mainstream of American life. A few groups, like the Hasidic Jews of Williamsburg, managed to preserve their identity as a highly distinct people in the midst of a city, although even they are now withdrawing upstate.[72] For the most part, however, these groups—the Amish, Mennonites, Hutterites, Moravians, Doukhobors, and Mormons—preferred an agricultural way of life, whether from a belief in its essential goodness or through the desire for the greater physical isolation it provided.[73] Although all these groups were at least marginally literate, they nevertheless constituted enclaves of "folk," rejecting in some cases all technological and other cultural innovations of the "mainstream" and maintaining their peculiar traditions and beliefs as free as possible from external contamination.

The first three of these groups—Amish, Mennonites, and Hutterites—are all spiritual (and, in considerable measure, literal) descendants of the radical Anabaptists who flourished briefly in the Rhine Valley shortly after Luther's break from Rome.[74] These groups rejected the structures of both Church and State, often practiced pacifism, and on occasion gave way to dramatic millenarian expectations. Not surprisingly, they were frowned upon by the established authorities, who often executed them in particularly unpleasant fashions. Jacob Hutter's followers, who practiced communal ownership of goods, embarked on a complex series of migrations through Eastern Europe, and finally made their way to the United States during the late nineteenth century. Various other sectarians, such as the Mennonites and their close relations, the Amish, made their way to this country somewhat earlier, and settled together with the Moravians and other pietistic groups of German origin in Pennsylvania. The Doukhobors, an eighteenth-century schismatic group with roots in Russian Orthodoxy, settled on the Canadian prairies and in British Columbia early in the twentieth century.[75] There they found themselves in the company of Hutterites, who had regarded the United States as less than fully hospitable toward what seemed their eccentric or subversive practices of communal ownership and pacifism. The Mormons, a uniquely American phenomenon, are perhaps a bit uncomfortable in this company, since their way of life represents more of a selective intensification of certain aspects of the American mainstream than a voluntary withdrawal from and rejection of the dominant culture. They originated in the "Burned-Over District" of upstate New York following Joseph Smith's revelations during the 1820s, and those who would emerge as the dominant group migrated or were driven westward until, after the founder's assassination, they were forced to set up shop in the then uninhabitated lands of Utah. Their semicommunal way of life and the authentically "folk" character of much of their culture, however, link them as closely to the other groups mentioned here as to the mainline of American Protestant denominations.[76]

The Old Order Amish, who constitute the "right wing" of a continuum of groups which extend through various increasingly acculturated Mennonites, are perhaps the best known of these (excepting Mormons) because of their picturesque dress and the presence even today of their horse-drawn buggies on the highways of Pennsylvania, Ohio, and Indiana. The Amish, who broke from the Mennonites over the question of the strictness of application of the practice of the shunning (*Bann und Meidung*) of dissenters, cling the most rigidly to the maintenance of the style of life practiced by the earliest Anabaptists in the sixteenth century.[77] This is an interesting example of practices that had profane origins devoid of religious meaning taking on a sacred significance as they remained static while others changed. The meticulousness of adherence to the old ways—for example, the Amish refusal to replace the traditional hook-and-eye fasteners with buttons—recalls in many ways rabbinical tradition and its accompanying casuistry.[78] Also, as is to some degree the case in Judaism, what over the years have in fact become the distinguishing shibboleths of the group are physical objects and everyday customs and avoidances. Especially in the face of external harassment, these may take on a greater importance in the mind of the practictioner than what are supposed to be the central doctrines. Such concrete, physical symbols, however, are appropriate in both cases, since they reflect the emphasis on a this-wordly, family-oriented society which can be depicted symbolically as an integrated, complete body.

The folk character of the cultures of these groups has been carefully preserved through their self-conscious rejection of more than a functional elementary education for the children, and a militant resistance to governmental efforts to impose additional, secular schooling. Although literate, they reject "higher" learning, and their literature is confined largely to the Bible, hymns and, particularly with the Hutterites, narrative accounts of the histories and persecutions of the early Anabaptists. Many reject English as their language of daily use and perpetuate the German dialects of their ancestors, another instance of an originally secular practice taking on sacred significance.

The Doukhobors, who are less familiar to Americans, were a sectarian movement which arose in the eighteenth century within provincial Russian Orthodoxy.[79] Their theological tenets were similar to those of the early Quakers, although their isolation and peasant origins helped prevent their accommodation to worldly ways (as happened to many of the Friends in Pennsylvania). Like their Canadian neighbors, the Hutterites, they practiced pacificism and communal ownership of property. They were led, however, not by elected officials, but rather by a semihereditary line of charismatic prophets which culminated during the Canadian years in the remarkable Verigin family. A radical offshoot, the Sons of Freedom, attained considerable notoriety for the group throughout Canada by their practice of dynamiting and public nudity as protests directed toward various grievances against the group itself and the Canadian government. This nudity, like that of the early Quakers, is a rather dramatic symbolic rejection of social structures, and a call for either a return to the state of nature or the immediate proclamation of an antinomian, millennial kingdom.

The Mormons, who are much closer to standard American culture than any of these other groups, arose in the context of the revivalism, spiritualism, millenarian prophecies, and other religious excitement of the "Burned-Over District." Their founder, Joseph Smith, and the majority of his constituency arose from the ranks of the poorer, marginally educated Yankees who abandoned their stony plots in Vermont to try their luck farther west.[80] As is true of most of the other communitarian groups, the Mormon worldview is extremely this-worldly in its sanctification of the daily round of mundane activity, but is buttressed by a highly imaginative theology which extends the blessings of this life indefinitely into a future world. The now proscribed practice of polygamy, which provoked some rather salty comments from Mark Twain among others, was one of a number of features which represented a self-conscious attempt to restore the patriarchal society of ancient Israel.[81]

Mormonism from its beginnings was steeped in the possibilities of latter-day revelation and unusual supernatural occurrences. Joseph Smith's accounts of his translation of the books of Mormon through the aid of the Archangel Moroni and a set of special "spectacles" provided by that personage are not the sort of thing that is readily believed by those accustomed to rationalistic or empirical criteria of evidence or probability. His natural constituency was among those who saw the world through the categories of the folk—those to whom special providences and spectral appearances are inherently plausible. Skeptical "Gentiles" would do well to bear in mind that the interpretation of the career and significance of Jesus among his early followers was not notably different in kind from that accorded to Smith and his celestial companions.

Perhaps not surprisingly, the Mormon exodus westward was accompanied by any number of special providences, the most spectacular of which was the fortuitous appearance of a swarm of seagulls just in time to ward off the destruction of the first crop in Utah by crickets.[82] Legends about the martyred Joseph Smith, Brigham Young, and other founding heroes abounded. The difficulties inherent in the practice of polygamy gave rise to a body of anecdotes more humorous than spiritual. Perhaps the most notable aspect of Mormon folklore, however, was the story of the three Nephites. At various times, from one to three mysterious personages would providentially appear to aid a Mormon Saint in distress. Afterward, it would become apparent that the unknown helpers were actually Nephites, the pre-Columbian good people of Mormon tradition to whom Jesus had appeared in the New World. As the folklorist Richard M. Dorson points out, this legend has analogues in other folktales, the most recent of which is the story of the "phantom hitchhiker."[83]

FOLK RELIGION—CONCLUSION

In conclusion, the logic of American folk cultures tends toward pluralism, a coexistence of the material culture of the mainstream of American life with a system of symbols and values alien to that mainstream. The allure of technology is extremely difficult to resist, and only a few groups like the Old Order Amish have possessed the determination to eschew it in all its manifestations. We can assume, however, that even their consciousnesses have been affected by the daily necessity of encountering and making the effort to resist the blandishments of the new order. As we have seen among a number of widely different groups, the very necessity of strenuous effort as the price of resistance leads to an exaggerated stress on certain symbolic activities or renunciations which would probably not be characteristic of a "pure" primitive society, or even of a peasant group insulated from urban culture through geographical isolation.

The typical worldview of a group that has been exposed to technology and literacy but that has not fully comprehended or accepted their rationale and implications is a compartmentalization of existence into separate realms, "divided and distinguished worlds." On the one hand, all but a few are willing to accept elementary communication skills and labor-saving devices at the practical level, as part of the profane, symbolically indifferent realm of daily activity. (The Hutterites, for example, are extremely efficient farmers, and utilize the finest of modern mechanized equipment in their agriculture.) On the other hand, like many other groups, they have successfully rejected the cosmological implications of technological society in favor of a traditionalistic interpretation of their universe.

Groups like the Hutterites, the Mormons, and many rural French-Canadian Catholics have been able to maintain a rather graceful equilibrium between the old and the new because of their geographical and cultural isolation. Those, however, like the urban Irish Catholics in the United States, who have been forced into a defensive posture through the experience of external hostility, have exaggerated certain traditional practices—such as celibacy, Friday abstinence, or, with the Amish, hook-and-eye fasteners—into a badge of defiance of the cultural imperialism that surrounds them. An authoritarianism which serves to maintain a high state of internal discipline and tension in the service of this resistance is often a concomitant, and bears little relationship to the more relaxed and democratic ethos of the agrarian communitarian enclaves of the prairies.

This "clerico-popular" culture, however, is a product of a very specific and usually temporary state of affairs, and presupposes a situation of cultural differentiation and conflict that takes place at one remove from "authentic" folk religion. It is this folk logic that more commonly remains at the peripheries of our modernized culture, both in remote Appalachian hamlets and at the fringes of the Jewish community of Los Angeles. The logic of these cultures is antithetical to that of urbanized, industrial society, and applies to those areas of life which have remained impervious to the logic of modernity.

The logic of folk culture returns us to the quotation from Robert Redfield with which we began this chapter. Where "modernism" is universalistic, folk culture stresses the particular. Where a scientific worldview operates on a theory of cause and effect derived from empirical observation and subsequent generalization, folk notions of causality include the intervention of personal, highly particularistic forces into the operation of natural and social events. Where the scientific community values direct, controlled observation as necessary for proof, folk perception is shaped by broader notions of the range of the possible, and folk communication tends to fit these perceptions into standardized formulae. Both cultures generate canons of probability and possibility, but those canons differ greatly in what they include and exclude. Where the one world is governed by impersonal, predictable rules, the other provides for the specific, the personal, and the "miraculous." Where one utilizes the abstractions of words and numbers, the other prefers concrete and pictorial symbols as its units of thought. And while the first universe is ultimately one, the other is many, containing a plurality of powers and forces which a modern observer may dismiss as logically contradictory and incompatible.

Nevertheless, the logic of folk culture has not yet been finally defeated by that of modernity. Such "primitivistic" movements as the "counterculture" of the 1960s have recognized the folk world's deeper sense of the unity of the human race with the rest of the natural order.[84] Its symbolic grappling with the problems of death and sexuality have proven more relevant to some moderns than the statistics of Kinsey or the manipulationism of Masters and Johnson. Joan Baez, Alan Lomax, and others have revived the Old English and Appalachian ballads, with their preoccupation with death and uncanny beings. Modern medicine is beginning to rediscover the wisdom of folk healing, with its firmer sense of the interrelatedness of mind and body. Theoretical physicists also are less inclined today to preach a deterministic monism, and acknowledge the possibility that the universe, as Henry Adams suspected, may be fundamentally plural in its essence after all. Whether a modernized culture can appropriate these elements in their integrity without a lapse into sentimentality and wishful thinking is another matter. Nevertheless, the world of folk continues to resist defeat and, in our more uncertain moments, to return periodically to haunt us.

NOTES

1. Actually, a society that has completed the modernization process is now generally referred to as "post-modern." See Chapter 4.
2. ROBERT REDFIELD, *The Primitive World and Its Transformations* (Ithaca, N.Y.: Cornell University Press, 1967),* p. 22.
3. REDFIELD developed the terms "Great Tradition" and "Little Tradition" in his *Peasant Society and Culture* (Chicago: University of Chicago Press, 1956).*
4. REDFIELD, again, was a pioneer in the study of these communities. For a treatment of the folk culture of the Yucatan, see his *Chan Kom: A Maya Village* (with ALFONSO VILLA ROJAS; Chicago: University of Chicago Press, 1934/62);* *The Folk Culture of Yucatan* (Chicago: University of Chicago Press, 1941); and *The Village That Chose Progress: Chan Kom Revisited* (Chicago: University of Chicago Press, 1950).
5. See, however, the discussion of "Civil Religion" in Chapter 3.
6. This interpretation of the myths of primitive peoples is at the basis of all of MIRCEA ELIADE's writings. See, inter alia, his *Myth and Reality* (New York: Harper Torchbooks, 1963/68),* and *The Myth of the Eternal Return or, Cosmos and History* (Princeton, N.J.: Princeton University Press, Bollingen Series, 1954/71).*
7. This discussion is based primarily on REDFIELD.
8. See ALBERT B. LORD, *The Singer of Tales* (Cambridge, Mass.: Harvard University Press, 1960).* LORD was a pioneer in conducting field investigations of singers of traditional epics in Yugoslavia.
9. BRUCE A. ROSENBERG, *The Art of the American Folk Preacher* (New York: Oxford University Press, 1970).
10. Almost any comprehensive collection of folk beliefs will yield these categories. See, for example, RAY B. BROWNE, *Popular Beliefs and Practices from Alabama* (Berkeley and Los Angeles: University of California Press, 1958).* On religion and folklore, see also WOLFGANG BRÜCKNER, "Popular Piety in Central Europe," *Journal of the Folklore Institute,* V (1968), 158–74; FRANCIS LEE UTLEY, "The Bible of the Folk," *California Folklore Quarterly,* IV (1945), 1–17; PATRICIA K. RICKLES, "The Folklore of Sacraments and Sacramentals in South Louisiana," *Louisiana Folklore Miscellany,* 2 (1965), 27–44; and C. GRANT LOOMIS, "Folklore of the Uncorrupted Body," *Journal of American Folklore,* 48, (1935) 374–78, and "Legend and Folklore," *California Folklore Quarterly,* II (1943), 279–97. See also the notes of DONALD E.

BYRNE, JR., *No Foot of Land: Folklore of American Methodist Iterinants* (Metuchen, N.J.: Scarecrow Press and The American Theological Library Association, 1975). We shall return to the question of folklore in the Protestant context in the next chapter, with additional bibliography in the accompanying notes.

11. Witchcraft will be dealt with at some length in Chapter 3.
12. See CLARENCE MALONEY, ed., *The Evil Eye* (New York: Columbia University Press, 1976). See also BRIAN SPOONER, "The Evil Eye in the Middle East," in MARY DOUGLAS; ed., *Witchcraft Confessions and Accusations* (London: Tavistock, 1970); PHYLLIS H. WILLIAMS, *South Italian Folkways in Europe and America* (New York: Russell and Russell, 1938/69), pp. 141–44 and *passim;* JOSHUA TRACHTENBERG, *Jewish Magic and Superstition* (New York: Atheneum, 1939/70);* and the *Encyclopedia Judaica* (Jerusalem: Macmillan, 1971), 6, 998–99.
13. See SYDNEY E. AHLSTROM, "Mary Baker Eddy," in JAMES, EDWARD T., JAMES, JANET WILSON, and BOYER, PAUL S. eds., *Notable American Women,* 3 vols. (Cambridge, Mass.: Harvard University Press, 1971),* 554–55.
14. The best general discussion of the "taboo" phenomenon is MARY DOUGLAS, *Purity and Danger: An Analysis of Concepts of Pollution and Taboo* (Baltimore: Penguin, 1970.* See also FRANZ STEINER, *Taboo* (Baltimore: Penguin, 1967).*
15. On the symbolism of the Holy Family, see W. LLOYD WARNER, *The Living and the Dead: A Study of the Symbolic Life of Americans* (New Haven: Yale University Press, 1959), Chap. 11 ("Sacred Sexuality—The Mother, the Father, and the Family in Christian Symbolism"); MARINA WARNER, *Alone of All Her Sex: The Myth and the Cult of the Virgin Mary* (New York: Knopf, 1976); and HENRY ADAMS, *Mont-Saint-Michel and Chartres* (Garden City, N.Y.: Doubleday Anchor, 1913/59),* pp. 338–39.
16. On saints, see DONALD ATTWATER, *The Penguin Dictionary of Saints* (Baltimore: Penguin, 1965);* J. F. WEBB, ed., *Lives of the Saints* (Baltimore: Penguin 1965);* JACOBUS DA VORAGINE, *The Golden Legend* (New York: Arno, 1969);* JOHN M. MECKLIN, *The Passing of the Saint: The Study of a Cultural Type* (Chicago: University of Chicago Press, 1941); and MICHAEL GOODICH, "A Profile of Thirteenth Century Sainthood," in *Comparative Studies in Society and History,* 18 (October 1976), 429–37.
17. See the pamphlet *The National Shrine of the Immaculate Conception* (San Bruno, Calif./Washington, D.C., 1974) for details and illustrations.
18. See, for example, JOHN K. CARTWRIGHT, *The Catholic Shrines of Europe* (New York: McGraw-Hill, 1955); EDWIN MULLINS, *The Pilgrimage to Santiago* (London: Secker and Warburg, 1974); JACQUES LAFAYE, *Quetzalcoatl and Guadalupe: The Formation of the Mexican National Consciousness, 1531–1813* (Chicago: University of Chicago Press, 1976). None of these treatments are really adequate for our purposes, but provide useful background information. ROBERT E. QUIRK has a very good discussion of the implications of the Virgin of Guadalupe in his *The Mexican Revolution and the Catholic Church 1910–1929* (Bloomington, Ind.: Indiana University Press, 1973), pp. 3–5. See also note 24.
19. ARNOLD VAN GENNEP, *The Rites of Passage* (Chicago: University of Chicago Press, 1960),* pp. 10–11 and *passim;* VICTOR TURNER, *The Ritual Process: Structure and Anti-Structure* (Chicago: Aldine, 1969),* Chap. 3 ("Liminality and Communitas").

20. EMILE DURKHEIM, *The Elementary Forms of the Religious Life* (New York: Free Press, 1915/65).*
21. On the interaction between theological and magical elements in medieval Catholicism, see KEITH THOMAS, *Religion and the Decline of Magic* (New York: Scribner's, 1971),* Chap. 2 ("The Magic of the Medieval Church"). See also C. GRANT LOOMIS, *White Magic: An Introduction to the Folklore of Christian Legend* (Cambridge, Mass.: Mediaeval Academy of America, 1948).
22. See ADAMS, *Mont-Saint-Michel and Chartres,* and ERWIN PANOFSKY, *Gothic Architecture and Scholasticism* (Cleveland and New York: Meridian/World 1957).*
23. See KEITH THOMAS, *Religion and the Decline of Magic,* pp. 194–97.
24. On pilgrimages, see JONATHAN SUMPTION, *Pilgrimage: An Image of Mediaeval Religion* (Totowa, N.J.: Rowman and Littlefield, 1975); VICTOR TURNER, "Pilgrimages as Social Processes," Chap. 5 of *Dramas, Fields, and Metaphors: Symbolic Action in Human Society* (Ithaca, N.Y.: Cornell University Press, 1974);* and VICTOR and EDITH TURNER, *Image and Pilgrimage in Christian Culture* (New York: Columbia University Press, 1978).
25. See especially Chaps. VI ("The Virgin of Chartres"), X ("The Court of the Queen of Heaven"), and XIII ("Les Miracles de Notre Dame"). See also PETER W. WILLIAMS, "Henry Adams on Religion: An Introduction," in *Ohio Journal of Religious Studies,* 2 (1974), 57–71; and ROBERT MANE, *Henry Adams on the Road to Chartres* (Cambridge, Mass.: Harvard University Press, 1971); and note 15 above.
26. *Mont-Saint-Michel and Chartres,* pp. 278, 290.
27. Ibid., pp. 215, 292.
28. Ibid., p. 308.
29. On the re-emergence of feminine symbolism into Protestantism, see WARNER, *The Living and the Dead,* Chap. 10 ("The Protestant Revolt and Protestant Symbolism"). See also PETER W. WILLIAMS, *A Mirror for Unitarians: Catholicism and Culture in Nineteenth Century New England Literature* (doctoral dissertation, Yale University, 1970).
30. On Pius IX and the political situation of the Church in nineteenth-century Europe, see E. E. Y. HALES, *Pio Nono* (Garden City, N.Y.: Doubleday Image, 1962).*
31. GILLIAN LINDT GOLLIN, *Moravians in Two Worlds* (New York: Columbia University Press, 1967), p. 12.
32. MARY DOUGLAS, *Natural Symbols: Explorations in Cosmology* (New York: Random/Pantheon, 1970),* esp. Chap. 5 ("The Two Bodies").
33. For historical background, see E. E. Y. HALES, *Revolution and Papacy* (Notre Dame, Ind.: University of Notre Dame Press, 1966),* and *The Catholic Church in the Modern World* (Garden City, N.Y.: Doubleday Image, 1960).*
34. On Sacred Heart cults, see the following entries in the *New Catholic Encyclopedia* (New York: McGraw-Hill, 1967), Vol. XII: "Sacred Heart, Devotion to" (818–20) "Sacred Heart, Enthronement of" (820); and "Sacred Heart, Iconography of" (820).
35. A brief survey of American Catholic history is provided by JOHN TRACY ELLIS in *American Catholicism* (Chicago: University of Chicago Press, 1956/69).*

36. See Cecil Woodham-Smith, *The Great Hunger: Ireland 1845-1849* (New York: New American Library/Signet, 1962/64);* Oscar Handlin, *Boston's Immigrants 1790-1880* (New York: Atheneum, 1941/59/68);* Robert H. Lord, John E. Sexton, and Edward T. Harrington, *History of the Archdiocese of Boston,* 3 vols. (New York: Sheed and Ward, 1944); and Andrew Greeley, *That Most Distressful Nation: The Taming of the American Irish* (Chicago: Quadrangle, 1972).
37. The story of nineteenth-century attempts at accommodation with the general culture by American Catholics is told splendidly in Robert D. Cross, *The Emergence of Liberal Catholicism in America* (Cambridge, Mass.: Harvard University Press, 1967).*
38. On the events leading up to *Testem Benevolentiae,* see Thomas T. McAvoy, *The Americanist Heresy in Roman Catholicism* (Notre Dame, Ind.: University of Notre Dame Press, 1963)* (originally published under the title *The Great Crisis in American Catholic History 1895-1900*).
39. On the clash between Irish and Germans, see Colman J. Barry, *The Catholic Church and German Americans* (Milwaukee: Bruce, 1953), and Philip Gleason, *The Conservative Reformers: German-American Catholics and the Social Order* (Notre Dame, Ind., University of Notre Dame Press, 1968).
40. To date, there have been no significant scholarly studies of American Catholicism during the "Ghetto Period." Jay P. Dolan has made some good beginnings in an approach stressing social history in his *The Immigrant Church: New York's Irish and German Catholics, 1815-1865* (Baltimore: Johns Hopkins Press, 1975), but deals entirely with the nineteenth century. By far the best interpretation of the transition from the "Ghetto" period to post-conciliar Catholicism in America is Garry Wills, *Bare Ruined Choirs: Doubt, Prophecy, and Radical Religion* (Garden City, N.Y.: Doubleday, 1971).* The most comprehensive study of Catholic education is Andrew M. Greeley and Peter H. Rossi, *The Education of Catholic Americans* (Chicago: Aldine, 1966). See also James W. Sanders, *The Education of an Urban Minority: Catholics in Chicago, 1833-1965* (New York: Oxford University Press, 1977).
41. I am indebted to Prof. A. Thomas Tymoczko of Smith College for this anecdote.
42. These anecdotes, which are virtually universal in this country, remain an untapped resource for folklorists. I have heard virtually identical versions of them from a wide variety of friends and acquaintances who attended Catholic parochial schools in all parts of the United States. I do not know of any studies of this sort of oral lore.
43. This is not to argue that opposition to abortion can be reduced simply to a modality of symbolic behavior. Such opposition *may* result from, or contain a component of, the deepest fears of a subculture expressed in symbolic action. On the other hand, the whole question poses a genuine ethical dilemma that can only be resolved satisfactorily on other grounds. It is my opinion that many issues of this sort can only be confronted on their merits after the symbolic components have been sorted out as well as possible.
44. For German cultural differences, see note 39 above. On Poles and Lithuanians, see William I. Thomas and Florian Znaniecki, *The Polish Peasant in Europe and America,* 2 vols. (New York: Dover, 1918-20/58); Helena Znaniecki Lopata, *Polish Americans; Status Competition in an Ethnic Community* (Englewood Cliffs, N.J.: Prentice-Hall, 1976);* Arthur Evans Wood,

Hamtramck: A Sociological Study of a Polish-American Community (New Haven, Conn.: College and University Press, 1955);* and VICTOR GREENE, *For God and Country: The Rise of Polish and Lithuanian Ethnic Consciousness in America 1860-1910* (Madison, Wisc.: The State Historical Society of Wisconsin, 1975).

45. A pioneering study that deals with Southern Italian culture in its American setting is PHYLLIS H. WILLIAMS, *South Italian Folkways in Europe and America* (New York: Russell and Russell, 1938/69). A more recent investigation is RUDOLPH J. VECOLI, "Prelates and Peasants: Italian Immigrants and the Catholic Church," in *Journal of Social History,* 2 (Spring 1969), 217-68. VECOLI differs from WILLIAMS in his emphasis on the strained rather than harmonious relationship he perceives between South Italians and their clergy. The following discussion is based on both WILLIAMS and VECOLI, but follows the latter where they differ.

46. On the Catholic Church in the colonial period, see ROBERT RICARD, *The Spiritual Conquest of Mexico,* transl. LESLEY BYRD SIMPSON (Berkeley and Los Angeles: University of California Press, 1966). For a brief, readable survey of subsequent developments in Mexico itself, see LESLEY BYRD SIMPSON, *Many Mexicos* (University of California Press: Berkeley and Los Angeles, 1961).*

47. On the relationship of religion and revolution, see ROBERT E. QUIRK, *The Mexican Revolution and the Catholic Church 1910-1929* (Bloomington, Ind.: Indiana University Press, 1973). For a general interpretation of Catholicism in Mexico, see ALLEN SPITZER, "Religious Structure in Mexico," *Alpha Kappa Deltan,* 30 (1960), 54-58. See also PETER W. WILLIAMS, "A Journey of Personal Interest," *The Current,* 7 (December 1966), 43-55.

48. For a study of a village where Maya was the primary spoken language, see ROBERT REDFIELD and ALFONSO VILLA ROJAS, *Chan Kom: A Maya Village* (Chicago: University of Chicago Press, 1934/62).*

49. Ibid., Chap. VII and *passim.*

50. See REDFIELD, *Tepoztlan: A Mexican Village* (Chicago: University of Chicago Press, 1930/73),* pp. 64-65.

51. Ibid., pp. 92-96.

52. For a discussion of this aspect of Mexican culture, see WILLIAM MADSEN, *The Mexican-Americans of South Texas,* 2nd ed. (New York: Holt, Rinehard, & Winston, 1964/73),* pp. 17-19. This book provides a very good brief introduction to Mexican and Mexican-American culture.

53. J. HUIZINGA, *The Waning of the Middle Ages* (Garden City, N.Y.: Doubleday Anchor, 1954).*

54. On Zapata's folkloric metamorphosis, see REDFIELD, *Tepoztlan,* pp. 197-204. (For a full biography of Zapata, see JOHN WOMACK, JR., *Zapata and the Mexican Revolution* [New York: Random/Vintage, 1968/70]*). For other studies of Mexican and Central American folk religion and culture, see WILLIAM MADSEN, *Christo Paganism: A Study of Mexican Religious Syncretism* (New Orleans: Tulane University Press, 1957); MAUD OAKES, *The Two Crosses of Todos Santos: Survivals of Mayan Religious Ritual* (New York: Pantheon, 1951); WILLIAM M. HUDSON, *The Healer of Los Olmos, and Other Mexican Lore* (Austin: Texas Folklore Society, 1951); SARAH C. BLAFFER, *The Black-Man of Zinacantan, A Central American Legend* (Austin: University of Texas Press, 1972). On the Virgin of Guadalupe, see note 18 above and DONALD DE-

MAREST and COLEY TAYLOR, eds., *The Dark Virgin: The Book of Our Lady of Guadalupe* (New York and Freeport, Me.: Coley Taylor, 1956).

55. Another folk movement within Mexican-American Catholicism is that of the *Penitente* brotherhood of New Mexico, which exists within but at the fringes of official Catholicism. Best known for its rather Baroque piety, e.g., self-flagellation during Holy Week, the movement is in fact quite complex and of venerable lineage, maintaining a Franciscan devotional counterpart to a routinized official Church. On the Penitentes, see MARTA WEIGLE, *Brothers of Light, Brothers of Blood: The Penitentes of the Southwest* (Albuquerque: University of New Mexico Press, 1976); the accompanying bibliographical volume, *A Penitente Bibliography* (*ibid.*, 1976) and a collection of reprints of earlier studies of the movement, *The Penitentes of New Mexico* (New York: Arno, 1974). An interesting study by an anthropologist of the coming together of a variety of religious and symbolic cultures in the area is RONALD L. GRIMES, *Symbol and Conquest: Public Ritual and Drama in Santa Fe, New Mexico* (Ithaca and London: Cornell University Press, 1976), which deals with the Penitentes in passing.

56. MADSEN, *Mexican-Americans,* Chap. 10 and 11.

57. The following discussion of French-Canadian religion and culture is based primarily on HORACE MINER, *St.-Denis: A French-Canadian Parish* (Chicago: University of Chicago Press, 1939/63).* For a good comparative survey of the relationship between religion, nationalism, and ethnicity in several cultures, see HAROLD J. ABRAMSON, *Ethnic Diversity in Catholic America* (New York: Wiley, 1973), which includes sections on the Irish, French-Canadians, Southern Italians, Mexicans, Poles, and Germans. For general background on Canadian religion and culture, especially French Catholic, see MASON WADE, *The French Canadians 1760–1967,* 2 vols, rev. ed. (Toronto: Macmillan, 1968); the three-volume *History of the Christian Church in Canada,* ed. JOHN WEBSTER GRANT, esp. H. H. WALSH, *The Church in the French Era* (Toronto: Ryerson, 1966); KENNETH MCNAUGHT, *The Pelican History of Canada* (Baltimore: Penguin, 1969);* MARCEL RIOUX and YVES MARTIN, eds., *French-Canadian Society,* 2 vols. (Toronto and Montreal: McClelland and Stewart, 1964 [The Carleton Library]);* and, for bibliography, JEAN-PAUL MONTMINY and STEWARD CRYSDALE, *La Religion au Canada/Religion in Canada* (Downsview, Ont., and Quebec: York University Les Presses de L'Université Laval, 1974).*

58. ABRAMSON, *Ethnic Diversity,* pp. 133–36.

59. MINER, *St.-Denis,* pp. 98–100.

60. MADSEN, *Mexican Americans,* p. 50.

61. For the story of one prominent French-Canadian shrine, see ALDEN HATCH, *The Miracle of the Mountain: The Story of Brother André and the Shrine on Mount Royal* (New York: Hawthorn, 1959).

62. On the symbolic significance of Friday abstinence, see MARY DOUGLAS, *Natural Symbols,* Chap. 3 ("The Bog Irish").

63. J. F. POWERS, *Morte D'Urban: A Novel of a Priest* (Garden City, N.Y.: Doubleday Image, 1967);* *The Presence of Grace and Other Stories* (Garden City, N.Y., Doubleday Image, 1958);* *Look How the Fish Live* (New York: Ballantine, 1976).*

64. In addition to the specifically theological works that have been written on matters of religious practice, a whole genre of religious etiquette books,

especially concerning the observances of Catholics and Jews, has also arisen. See, for example, KAY FENNER, *American Catholic Etiquette* (Westminster, Md.: Christian Classics, 1965). Jewish literature of this sort often emphasizes dietary observances; e.g., SHONIE B. LEVI and SYLVIA R. KAPLAN, *Guide for the Jewish Homemaker* (New York: Schocken, 1964).*

65. The question of "Jewish identity" has been the subject of a vast literature in America during the years since World War II. See, for example, STUART E. ROSENBERG, *America is Different: The Search for Jewish Identity* (London and New York: T. Nelson, 1964).*

66. "The Abominations of Leviticus," Chap. 3 of *Purity and Danger: An Analysis of Concepts of Pollution and Taboo* (Balitmore: Penguin, 1966/70).* (Also reprinted in abridged form in LESSA and VOGT, eds., *Reader in Comparative Religion,* 3rd ed. (New York: Harper & Row, 1972), pp. 202–205.

67. See also DOUGLAS, *Natural Symbols,* 1st ed., pp. 38–41.

68. On traditional Jewish *shtetl* life in Eastern Europe, see MARK ZBOROWSKI and ELIZABETH HERZOG, *Life Is With People: The Culture of the Shtetl* (New York: Schocken, 1952/62).*

69. On this subject, see JOSHUA TRACHTENBERG, *Jewish Magic and Superstition: A Study in Folk Religion* (New York: Atheneum, 1939/70).*

70. ABRAHAM CAHAN, *The Rise of David Levinsky* (New York: Harper Colophon, 1917/60).*

71. On popular Judaism, see NORMAN L. FRIEDMAN, "Jewish Popular Culture in Contemporary America," *Judaism,* 24 (Summer 1975), 263–77. For Jewish folklore see RAPHAEL PATAI, FRANCIS LEE UTLEY, and DOV NOY, eds., *Studies in Biblical and Jewish Folklore* (Bloomington, Ind.: Indiana University Press, 1960),* especially WAYLAND S. HAND, "Jewish Popular Beliefs and Customs in Los Angeles," and BEATRICE S. WEINREICH, "The Americanization of Passover." The following discussion is based primarily on HAND.

72. SOLOMON POLL, *The Hasidic Community of Williamsburg: A Study in the Sociology of Religion* (New York: Schocken, 1962/69).*

73. BRYAN WILSON deals with such groups under the rubric "Introversionists" in Chap. 7 of *Religious Sects* (New York and Toronto: McGraw-Hill, 1970).*

74. On the Amish, see JOHN A. HOSTETLER, *Amish Society* (Baltimore: Johns Hopkins Press, 1963/68).* On Mennonites, J. C. WENGER, *The Mennonite Church in America* (Scottsdale, Pa.: Herald, 1966); HARRY LEONARD SAWATZKY, *They Sought a Country: Mennonite Colonization in Mexico* (Berkeley and Los Angeles: University of California Press, 1971); FRANK H. EPP, *Mennonites in Canada, 1786–1920* (Toronto: Macmillan, 1974); and SAMUEL FLOYD PANNABECKER, *Open Doors: The History of the General Conference of the Mennonite Church* (Newton, Kans.: Faith and Life Press, 1975). On Hutterites, see VICTOR PETERS, *All Things Common: The Hutterian Way of Life* (New York: Harper Torchbooks, 1965/61);* JOHN A. HOSTETLER, *Hutterite Society* (Baltimore: Johns Hopkins Press, 1974); and JOHN A. HOSTETLER and GERTRUDE ENDERS HUNTINGTON, *The Hutterites in North America* (New York: Holt, Rinehart & Winston, 1967).* An excellent film on the Hutterites has been produced by the National Film Board of Canada.

75. For the Doukhobors, see GEORGE WOODCOCK and IVAN AVAKUMOVIC, *The Doukhobors* (Toronto and New York: Oxford University Press, 1968); and

HARRY B. HAWTHORN, ed., *The Doukhobors of British Columbia* (Vancouver: University of British Columbia Press, 1955).

76. The standard work on Mormonism is THOMAS F. O'DEA, *The Mormons* (Chicago: University of Chicago Press, 1957).* See also BRYAN WILSON, *Religious Sects* ("The Many-Sided Sect—Mormonism"); and MARVIN S. HILL and JAMES B. ALLEN, eds., *Mormonism and American Culture* (New York: Harper & Row, 1972).*
77. HOSTETLER, *Amish Society*, p. 28 ff.
78. Ibid., pp. 34–35 and p. 43. For some interesting parallels in early Christian development pertaining to the evolution of liturgical garb, see DOM GREGORY DIX, *The Shape of the Liturgy* (London: Dacre Press, 1945), pp. 404–405.
79. For sources on the Doukhobors, see note 75. The following discussion is derived primarily from WOODCOCK and AVAKUMOVIC.
80. On the Mormons, see note 76. On JOSEPH SMITH, see FAWN M. BRODIE, *No Man Knows My History: The Life of Joseph Smith* (New York: Knopf, 1945/71). See also Chapter 3.
81. MARK TWAIN, *Roughing It* (New York: New American Library/Signet Classics, 1962),* Chap. XIII.
82. For Mormon folklore, see AUSTIN and ALTA FIFE, *Saints of Sage and Saddle* (Bloomington, Ind.: Indiana University Press, 1956). For a briefer account, see RICHARD M. DORSON, *American Folklore* (Chicago: University of Chicago Press, 1959),* pp. 112–21.
83. DORSON, *American Folklore*, p. 118.
84. See THEODORE ROSZAK, *The Making of a Counter Culture* (Garden City, N.Y.: Doubleday Anchor, 1969), for a critique of the scientific worldview and an advocacy of a return to a traditionalistic cosmos.

3

Popular Religion and the Modern World

PROTESTANTISM AND MODERNIZATION

The religious revolution of the sixteenth century which engendered Protestantism was inextricably bound up with the strands of a broader transformation of the Western world. Martin Luther's insight and impact did not take place in a vacuum; without the supportive context of wide-scale social, intellectual, economic, and political change, Luther would most likely have lived out his life as a gifted, eccentric Augustinian monk. Religious change correlates with more general cultural movement, and the Reformation was no exception. In order to understand the origins and the phenomenal success of Protestantism, we have to be aware of the cultural and social matrix in which it was incubated and nurtured.

One approach to the complex of factors that converged to result in the age of the Renaissance and Reformation is to regard them as the coming together of technological innovation and a state of mind congenial to the implications of such innovation.[1] Again, the simple presence of genius is not sufficient to result in a technological revolution; da Vinci and Edison may well have remained in obscurity had not the culture around them been receptive to their work, and provided them with problems for solution and an eagerness to accept their answers. Long-term trends of interest in the expansion of geographical and technological horizons and mastery of the physical environment reached a "critical mass" at this time. The state of receptivity among those with the power to support and implement innovation was the *sine qua non* for the outburst of creative energies that was looked upon even at the time as a "Renaissance," a rebirth of human creative potential.

The first major impact of a new interest in both technological innovation and the broadening of horizons took place in the realm of navigation. The opening of Africa to European trade and colonization by the Portuguese during the fifteenth century, followed by the more dramatic Spanish "discovery" of the New World by Columbus and the circumnavigation of the globe by Magellan, made possible and perhaps inevitable an irreversible transformation of the economy and the world picture of the West. It also provided the physical arena in which the logic of the emergent religion and culture of Protestantism could unfold itself most fully in the centuries to come.

The other major technological development that provided the material basis for the spread of Protestantism was printing with movable metal type. Among the first works to emerge from Gutenberg's press were the Bibles and Psalter of 1457.[2] When Luther and others began during the following century to make vernacular translations of Scripture available, one of the major material preconditions for the rapid spread of Protestantism was ready. A steadily increasing rate of literacy encouraged by both ideological and social factors paved the way for Protestantism to emerge as a genuinely popular religion in the sense that all who could read could now set about the task of interpreting Scripture for themselves. The seventeenth century especially saw the burgeoning of whole new genres of religious literature (or subliterature) ranging from Bibles and tracts to the enormously popular *Acts and Monuments of the English Martyrs* of John Foxe and the Baptist John Bunyan's *Pilgrim's Progress.*[3] Together with the King James translation of the Bible, these latter two works would constitute the core of a common Protestant culture that would inform the American as well as the English popular sensibility.

Technology, particularly in the realms of transportation and communication, was only one of a number of components to converge in that process of development which sociologists now refer to as "modernization." The nascent urban life of the later Middle Ages now began to manifest itself more fully in the emergence of cities that were genuinely cosmopolitan centers rather than simply overgrown villages. Rationalized and centralized bureaucratic structures were slowly displacing local custom as the basis of governance in the newly consolidated nation-states. The execution of Charles II by Parliament marked the end of the notion that kingship was a sacramental function legitimated entirely by tradition and supposed divine authority.[4] Capitalism on a national and international scale was shifting the attention of an increasingly powerful bourgeoisie away from military honor toward the systematic acquistion of a self-increasing wealth as the primary desideratum of human life. In England especially, the consequences of these simultaneous and interrelated developments proved crucial in creating a population willing to pull up stakes and colonize the new lands across the Atlantic, as well as providing a climate propitious for the new ideology that would give shape to the new society which these pioneers were beginning to mold.

The relationship of Protestantism to modernization is anything but simple. Max Weber, in *The Protestant Ethic and the Spirit of Capitalism,* provided a classic if highly controversial interpretation of this relationship in his contention that these novel religious and economic tendencies continually reinforced each other's development, although neither could be convincingly posited as the direct cause of the other.[5] Less disputed, perhaps, is the linkage between Protestantism and the emergence of modern science. The impetus to investigate, analyze, and ultimately to control the forces of nature through human effort and intelligence found much greater encouragement from a religious attitude which called for a radical separation of the divine and natural realms. For Protestants, the question of the compatibility of Biblical and empirical interpretations of the natural realm and its workings would not become problematical until the upheavals in geology and life sciences of the nineteenth century. In the meantime, such an eminent Puritan spokesman as Cotton Mather saw no contradiction between his role as theologian and preacher on the one hand and his status as Fellow of the Royal Society on the other. Nature, in short, had been desacralized.[6]

Just as the general process of modernization was erratic and subject to periodic arrests and reversals, however, so was the relationship of Protestantism (hardly a uniform or unified movement in itself) to that process. Luther was certainly more medieval than modern in his outlook on the political and social spheres, as were the American Puritan followers of John Calvin. The Boston merchant Robert Keayne's "Apologia," in which he defended himself against accusations of violation of the Puritan doctrine of the "just price," can hardly be interpreted as a defense of an emergent capitalistic ethic.[7] Rather, Keayne was in fundamental agreement with the Puritan acceptance of the traditionalistic (and Thomistic) medieval prohibition of usury, and was in fact defending himself against charges of delinquency rather than rebellion.[8] Similarly, John Winthrop's exposition of the authority of the magistrate in 1645 was based on essentially medieval notions of the ordering of society along traditionalistic lines of hierarchical arrangement.[9] In the phrase of the political scientist Michael Walzer, Puritanism (and, more generally, Protestantism as a whole) might best be characterized as an "ideology of transition," at times legitimating such radical acts as the execution of an anointed monarch, at other times departing scarcely at all from the centuries-old precepts and practices of medieval Europe.[10]

If the ideas and deeds of the avant-garde of Protestantism were often so out of harmony with the spirit of modernization, it should hardly come as a surprise to find that the beliefs and the way of life of ordinary Protestants should be something less than fully rationalized.[11] From the sixteenth century onward the progress of literacy was reasonably steady, especially in areas under Protestant influence, but the ability to read and write is by no means universal even in the United States of the late twentieth century. Traditional patterns of life generally persisted longer and more obstinately in rural areas than in urban centers, and an outlook on the world in harmony with the agricultural cycle and face-to-face overlapping interpersonal relationships often prevailed through preference or simple inertia. In addition, Protestantism often failed to provide symbolic mediation in times of life crises and social disorder and that was adequate or appealing to those who were not yet ready to renounce the sacrality of all except Scripture and the direct encounter of the individual with the divine. The inherently fissiparous tendencies of Protestantism, which in the United States especially was prone to multiple and repeated division, provided institutional structures through which popular interpretations of Christianity, which often spilled over into heterodoxy and even magic, could flourish.

Another tendency with Protestantism which is probably inherent in most religions was the confusion of religious with political ends. Emile Durkheim interpreted religion as the symbolic representation of a social collectivity to itself.[12] The incipient universalism of Christianity has never triumphed entirely over the powerful retrogressive pull toward tribalism which every social group experiences, especially in times of stress, crisis, and sudden change. The role of religion in general and Protestant Christianity in particular in helping to create, legitimate, expand, and defend political communities has often been a major source of extra-ecclesiastical symbolic and religious activity in both England and the United States. Conversely, the rejection of social structures and distinctions has also been a powerful motif in American symbolic life, and has often stood in dialectical tension with the creation or legitimation of those very structures. The interaction of these two tendencies, together with the periodic eruption of symbolic behavior more characteristic of traditional than modernized societies, will form the substance of the following discussion of popular Protestantism in the United States.

POPULAR MOVEMENTS IN BRITAIN AND ON THE CONTINENT

The flurry of popular expressions of religiosity that would characterize much of the American experience was in many ways a continuation and intensification of developments originating in Europe during the later medieval and Reformation periods. The reorganization of European (and British) society and culture that took place during these centuries was extremely disruptive for vast numbers of people, and that disruption was frequently expressed in religious rather than explicitly political terms. "Mainstream" Protestantism, particularly Calvinism and its offshoots, may be interpreted as a systematic program for coming to terms with and channeling the forces of modernity, an effort to turn a potentially destructive social chaos into an ideologically informed order dedicated to the glory of God.[13] For others, however, chaos had its uses. During this period many groups began to emerge throughout Europe which could not find satisfaction in the new religious and secular establishments then in the process of formation, and instead created symbolic systems which elevated disorder of one sort or another to a normative status. This motif of "anti-structure," which we shall discuss more fully in the context of American phenomena, characterized many of these movements that adumbrated and occasionally were directly translated into the American context.

The social and economic changes that began to accelerate during the later Middle Ages led periodically to revivals of millennial expectations, usually forming around a charismatic prophet who had arisen from the ranks of marginal intellectuals or lower clergy.[14] The clientele for these movements were often, though not always, displaced urban workers who were caught between the vanishing stability of an old rural order which they had left and the precarious opportunities of the rising commercial and industrial cities, especially those of the Rhine Valley. Such movements were usually anticlerical and, in general, directed against the structures of a society that had shut out many from the opportunities which it was opening up for others. The idea of a purely political protest movement was not yet a live possibility for medieval people. What was in large measure an expression of social, political, and economic malaise could only take religious expression. That expression usually came, appropriately, in the form of a vision of a new kingdom in which the first would be last and the last first; in which status distinctions would either be eliminated or reversed; and in which the burden of seeking an existence by the sweat of one's brow would be forever eliminated.

Protestantism, anticipated by the protests of the Lollards in England and the Hussites in Bohemia, also brought with it movements for radical change. The Radical Reformation, which arose more or less spontaneously in myriad forms throughout parts of Germany and the Low Countries especially, was a congeries of small sectarian movements, most of them of the pietist sort, which rejected the claims of worldly governments in favor of a strict adherence to such perfectionist counsels of the Gospel as pacifism and communitarianism.[15] From these movements came the contemporary Amish, Hutterite, and Mennonite groups we discussed in a previous chapter. Others, such as the movement by Thomas Müntzer and the millennial community erected at Münster by John of Leyden, Matthys, and Bockelson, were infused with chiliastic expectation. They practiced nakedness, polygamy, and violence against all opponents until they were ruthlessly put down by the surrounding political powers. At a time when social change was rampant and religious uniformity had suddenly vanished, almost anything could happen and seemingly, for a brief period, did.

Of more direct historical relevance to the American scene is the proliferation of sectarian groups which arose during the extreme confusion of the years of the Civil War and the interregnum in England. Again, the symbolic importance of the execution of King Charles I can hardly be overemphasized. As Christopher Hill has implied in the very title of one of his works, this was a time when the world was indeed turned upside down, when appeals to the future began to displace legitimation based on history and precedent.[16] It was also a time when the sweeping social changes that had begun with the dissolution of the monasteries in the time of Henry VIII had created widespread social disruptions and confusion, when millions of Englishmen and women no longer experienced the order and security which the traditional feudal agrarian system had provided for them for centuries. The conflict between Anglican and Puritan parties had already brought about severe religious discord at the highest levels, and the lower orders were by no means backward in contributing to this profusion of religious expression among the people.

Among the groups that arose or flourished during the period between 1640 and 1660 were the Ranters, the Diggers, and the Fifth Monarchy Men. The Ranters were in a way the most radical, but also the least political.[17] Their symbolic behavior was chiefly that of boundary destruction and inversion, as in their blasphemous songs and acts, prolific cursing, and suspension of normal rules of sexual conduct. They considered themselves free spirits, liberated from ordinary norms of behavior by their state of perfection. Needless to say, they almost completely lacked organization and the movement (if it can be called that) was rapidly dissipated with the return of normal civil authority and social expectations. Although they were to exert little direct influence on subsequent movements, their anticlericalism, antinomianism, and a rather curious sort of perfectionism were indicative of the sorts of behavior and beliefs which, in different combinations, would characterize later forms of religious expression in America as well as England.

The Diggers, a small offshoot of the more political Leveller movement of civil war times, were led by Gerrard Winstanley.[18] For Winstanley, the decline of the cultivation of unused common land was a grievous indication of the disappearance of communal spirit in rural England. Its restoration thus became the main symbolic and, to a degree, practical issue in his program for recalling the world to a properly Christian state of affairs. He considered Jesus Christ the Head Leveller, standing in opposition to the forces of evil represented by royalty, aristocracy, the clergy, and the legal profession—in short, the offices constituting the hierarchical structures of society. Winstanley's vision was that of a return to the primordial purity that had existed before the Fall. This was a variety of the primitivistic thought that has been a leitmotiv in Western thought from antiquity till the present. In order to realize this vision, Winstanley actually set about establishing small "Digger" colonies upon unoccupied land, in defiance of the principles of private property. Needless to say, these experiments were rapidly nipped in the bud by the forces of duly constituted authority and outraged landholders. His universalistic vision of a humanity freed from the consequences of the Fall not of Adam, but of what was wrought in each individual through the bondage of individual property, was an interesting anticipation of later, more secularized socialist and communist theories of property owning and its alienating effects on humanity.

The most properly millenarian of the Civil War sects were known as the Fifth Monarchy Men.[19] Their name was derived from the Book of Daniel, which prophesied that the four great earthly monarchies would be superseded by a fifth, millennial kingdom which would endure forever. The notion of the imminent coming of the millennium had been common currency for some time, and became part of the mythology of the Puritan movement in its fight against the forces of popery and monarchy together. The Civil War naturally heightened expectations of the end of the world as it was known, and the execution of the king was taken by many as a sign that the end was indeed at hand. For the Fifth Monarchists, this generalized expectation became specific, and they called vigorously for a new regime of the elect which would preside over the earth when the new order would be inaugurated. (They disagreed among themselves, however, as to the exact way in which this would happen.) Rather unfortunately, they fell to making specific predictions about the date of the millennial event, and, as is inevitable in such cases, experienced some rather extreme disappointments.

The Fifth Monarchy Men exhibited a number of characteristics common to many such movements of their own and later times. Although people from across the social spectrum participated in the movement, members of the "mechanic classes," especially those in the cloth trades from London, were heavily represented. There was a strong note of social protest in their opposition to lawyers, great merchants, and trade monopolies, and in the adoption by some of the Quakers' refusal to acknowledge social or civil rank. However, the movement was anything but antinomian. It enunciated a Puritan call to morality and revival of the Mosaic code, and called for a reign of the elect to impose discipline upon others until the Fifth Monarchy was inaugurated. The combination of the Restoration and the failure of millennial expectation, however, proved to be too much, and the movement rapidly collapsed after the 1660s.

The movement arising out of this time with the most direct historical import for American religion was that of the Quakers.[20] The early English movement led by George Fox and represented in its most eccentric guise in the antics of James Nayler (who made a triumphant entrance into Bristol on a donkey) was far removed from the later introversionist sect which would evolve in Pennsylvania during the following century. Their behavior in these early stages exhibited many of the extremes of "enthusiasm": prophesying, miraculous healings, disruption of worship services, and even nakedness. Although they shared some of the behavioral extremes of the Ranters, they were in fact far closer to orthodox Christianity doctrinally, and, perhaps surprisingly, were virtually alone among the Civil War–engendered sects in surviving far beyond the few decades of their origins.

Early Quakerism was more of a movement, a climate of opinion, than an organized religious group, and eventually, when it found itself durable, acquired a more distinctively sectarian character. It drew its members from a broad spectrum of society—just as did the early American "Awakenings" before they became routinized into organized revivalism—but seems to have appealed especially to those involved in commercial and geographically mobile occupations, rather than to the more tradition-minded peasantry and aristocracy. (Fox himself was the son of a weaver, an occupation especially given in England and on the Continent to participation in "radical" movements.) Its flourishing was a sign that society was still very much in transition, and that many Britons still had not settled into an organized ideological expression that adequately interpreted their perception of their place in a volatile society.

The most notable feature of early Quaker symbolic expression was its opposition to boundaries of any sort. The notion of the "Inner Light" blurred the distinction between man and God in its mystical affinities, and eliminated the need of any intermediary organization or structures between the two. The Quaker undercutting of the normative and final authority of scriptural revelation in favor of the ongoing illumination of individuals through the Inner Light similarly eliminated another form of structural mediation, and emphasized instead the continuous rather than the disjunctive relationship between the human and the divine. Quaker worship lacked any formality or sacramental apparatus, and meetings were simply a physical and social setting in which testimonies of the Spirit within individuals could be expressed and correlated. The spiritual boundary that separated the elect and the damned irrevocably one from the other within Calvinistic Puritanism also disappeared in Quaker thought, to be replaced by a proto-universalistic notion of salvation as a condition of illumination through Inner Light.

Quakers became especially controversial in both England and America at least as much through their insistence on social as on theological boundary repudiation. Neither sex nor social class were conditions for full participation in the movement, and all believers were of equal quality. Their refusal to take oaths, to remove their hats in the presence of a magistrate, or to use the formal "you" in their speech were all self-conscious symbolic expressions of their unwillingness to acknowledge differences either among persons or in the quality of response demanded in different social situations. Finally, their pacifism was a dramatic gesture of refusal to comply with the demands of the state, and an additional expression of their nonrecognition of political or social boundaries or structures as a basis for human relationships.

PROTESTANTISM AND COMMUNITY BUILDING: STRUCTURE AND ANTI-STRUCTURE

One of the principal functions which Mircea Eliade ascribes to religion is the symbolic transformation of chaos into order.[21] Order and chaos, of course, can exist at a number of levels, whether external or internal, geographical or psychological, political or spiritual. For the settlers of the new American continent, chaos characterized all these realms of existence, and their religion—that brand of English Calvinism known as "Puritanism"—was the informing structure through which they attempted to create order at all levels. To this day, the churches on the town greens of New England symbolize the centrality of religion in the communal sense of order and value, and that symbolism later was to spread west across much of the continent.

The religion of the Puritans can hardly be called "popular" in any meaningful sense, even though in England it stood in opposition to the beliefs, symbols, and structures of the "Establishment" of King, Court, and *Ecclesia Anglicana.* This highly literate and tightly organized opposition regarded by Michael Walzer as the prototype of the revolutionary elites of later centuries was soon to become the "Establishment" once it had acquired physical space and consolidated its power in the New World.[22] Its members were neither delinquents nor anarchists. They believed firmly in the necessity of a tightly structured society, and just as firmly that they and not the Stuart monarchy possessed the divinely ordained master plan for such a structure. The commonwealths of New England (Rhode Island to some degree excepted) were the result. Although their polity, both civil and ecclesiastical, was considerably more representative of public sentiment than was that of their English counterparts, the Puritan leadership constituted at best a "speaking aristocracy" responsible for the governance of a "silent democracy."

From the beginning, however, the Puritans had to face challenges to their authority from both within and without. Incursions into Massachusetts territory by Quaker missionaries were a constant nuisance, and evoked such a fear on the part of the Puritans that several Quakers were, after repeated lesser chastisement, executed. From within, Roger Williams and Anne Hutchinson demurred from the teachings and structures of orthodoxy and were finally exiled to that repository of dissent and opprobrium, Rhode Island.[23]

The episode of the heresiarch Anne Hutchinson is especially interesting for our purposes.[24] Her teaching that the Puritan saints were deluded in their belief that all or most of them were among the elect, and that only she and a small number of her followers (who alone had the power to recognize one another) were in fact the real chosen, was hardly conducive to her achievement of widespread popularity among the leaders of the Massachusetts Bay faithful. Moreover, her belief that she and her fellow saints were free from all law through the fact of their election—the doctrine of antinomianism—added fuel to the already menacing flames. That she was female in a society in which women were not entitled to any direct voice in theological or political affairs was in keeping with the general tenor of her teachings, and exacerbated the degree of her offense. Both her doctrine and her person provided a potent symbolic rallying point for many Puritans.[25] This was especially true of women who were experiencing malaise brought about by the tightly structured society and rigorous regimen entailed by the Puritan experiment, but who were unable to express their discontent in a focused political idiom. Her expulsion into the wilderness of Rhode Island was a temporary victory for the overly structured Puritan establishment, but this triumph was destined by the laws of sociology (if not those of God) to prove evanescent.

The repudiation of the constraints of political, social, and doctrinal structures expressed in Hutchinson's antinomian teachings is a good illustration of the mode of symbolic expression which the anthropologist Victor Turner calls "anti-structure."[26] At the basis of this concept is the idea that social systems necessarily incorporate two antithetical principles within themselves in a dialectical relationship, and cannot continue to function successfully for very long unless allowance is made for the expression of both of these principles. "Structure," on the one hand, is the principle of organization and stability that must necessarily prevail as the dominant mode of operation if everyday life is going to take place in normal, undisturbed fashion, and all the elements of the social order are to perform their functions in some degree of harmonious interaction and cooperation. However, any organization has a natural tendency to run down, to rigidify, to become subject to over-routinization and simply concern itself with its own perpetuation. (Anyone who has had some experience with university or governmental bureaucracies should immediately recognize what I am talking about here.)

To some degree, the inevitable succession of generations works against this trend through the periodic infusion of "new blood" into the system. However, this process is not usually enough to stave off the hardening of institutional arteries. If stultification on the one hand and revolution on the other are to be avoided, a principle of "anti-structure," some mechanism through which the principle of structure itself is periodically criticized, repudiated, or suspended, must be built into the system. In normal, secular situations, reform movements or perhaps an institutionally supported "ombudsman" is sufficient to keep the system working. However, in situations of extreme social tension, such expedients may be insufficient; where such mechanisms are totally lacking, moreover, drastic outbursts of anti-structural sentiment and activity may even be anticipated.

Religious movements and organizations are particularly subject to this dialectical tension, since the destruction of boundaries and structures is one of the most enduring and potent forms of religious expression. In any religious population of sufficient size, there will be some members who feel the call to heroic piety, to emulate (in a Christian framework) the evangelical counsels of perfection which deny the necessity of compromise with earthly weakness and limitation. When society becomes complex and diverse enough, this impulse may become prophetic, and aim not so much at individualistic perfection as at the overturning and abolition of the structures of the broader society itself when they are perceived as oppressive. When the process of secularization has proceeded far enough and religious legitimations for such expression no longer seem compelling, the anti-structural impulse may express itself in revolutionary movements such as Marxism, which, at least in its earlier stages, had a strong millenarian dimension guised in a metaphysical rather than religious vocabulary.

The medieval Catholic Church recognized this principle of social maintenance implicitly in its institutionalization of monasticism. Here the principle of anti-structure became routinized into what Turner calls "normative communitas"—that is, a stable, institutional context in which religious *virtuosi* could live a life of heroic piety in a communal situation; in which all status distinctions are eliminated (except the necessary one between the ritual elder, or abbot, and the other monks); and in which all manifest their common spiritual status in simple, egalitarian costume and general way of life (e.g., communal dining).[27] Monasticism had originated within Christianity in the ascetic, often bizarre and excessive practices of individual virtuosi as Simeon Stylites (the prototype, perhaps, of the marathon flagpole-sitters of the 1920s).[28] It was the organizational genius of the Roman Church which transformed and channeled these energies into a more routinized form, so that, instead of being suppressed as socially disruptive, the monks could play a positive (if closely supervised) role within the economy of salvation.

With the advent of Protestantism, however, tolerance of and provision for such diversified forms of religious inclination diminished considerably. The Calvinistic way was straight and narrow, and made little provision for pluralism of expression or conduct. Thus, in the American context, anti-structural modes of expression were usually extra-ecclesiastical in character. The facility with which new organizations could be formed after Independence made it likely that these movements would either rapidly burn out or become routinized into new sectarian, and, eventually, denominational structures before very long. Such "established" groups as the Congregationalists and Presbyterians were reluctant to make accommodations with the irrepressible forces of anti-structure, and thereby lost their hold on large numbers of the population once religious liberty became a widespread option on an intra- as well as intercolonial (or state) basis.

The suppression of the antinomians in Massachusetts Bay contained a profoundly ironic dimension. In England, Puritans had themselves played the role of dissenters, and had been attacked by the establishment as heretics, subversives, and anarchists. With the achievement of hegemony in New England, however, this role was dramatically reversed. Puritanism rapidly changed, in Perry Miller's phrase, "from a revolution into an administration," which almost from the beginning found itself in the role of defender of right belief and good order. ("Orthodoxy is my doxy; heterodoxy is your doxy.") During the remainder of the Colonial period (and beyond), the major theme of popular religion was to be its role as contrapuntal advocate of "anti-structure" against the increasingly inflexible structures of established Calvinistic orthodoxy.

By the early decades of the eighteenth century, increasing social and economic diversification combined with routinized forms of orthodox religious practice to produce, in the eyes of such concerned observers as Jonathan Edwards, a conspicuous decline in vital piety.

During the 1730s Edwards, the Congregational minister in Northampton, Massachusetts, capitalized on the general sense of malaise and disorientation that seemed to be prevalent in his congregation to launch what amounted to a revitalization movement within Puritanism. By raising anxieties to a fever pitch and giving them ideological focus through his dramatically effective preaching, Edwards managed to channel hitherto diffuse energies into a program for restoring Calvinism, purged of many of its Puritan theological accretions, to what he regarded as its earliest purity. This movement of repristination was not dramatically successful in institutional terms, but it did help pave the way for the more dramatic religious upheaval known as the "Great Awakening" which would be stimulated by George Whitefield during the following decade.[29]

The vital element of personal conversion which became a *sine qua non* for full religious and political status in the Puritan community had been carefully counterbalanced by mechanisms of social control and a theological emphasis on the individual as part of a covenanted community; therefore, even dramatic instances of personal religious experience seldom burst their bonds to become the occasions of social disruption. By the eighteenth century, however, covenantal theology and control mechanisms had fall into such desuetude that they could no longer hold in and channel the energies which the preaching of such an enormously charismatic preacher as the English Calvinist Whitefield was able to release on an intercolonial scale.

American Calvinism, whether of the Congregational or Presbyterian variety, had heretofore been firmly rooted in the medieval tradition of parochiality. The church one attended was determined by one's place of residence, and the New England "church on the green" in fact served as a symbolic center, a sort of *axis mundi,* for each community. Whitefield, in his role as "the Grand Itinerant," seriously challenged this principle of the coincidence of religious and vicinal allegiance through his tactic of itinerant preaching. He thus became the instrument of what was perhaps the first common experience residents of all of the Atlantic colonies had ever shared—the witnessing, or hearing of a first-hand account, of his preaching. It is hardly surprising that this challenge to local allegiances should have been viewed with profound alarm by those settled clergy who would soon take on the name of "Old Side" or "Old Light."

Edwards, the chief theoretician and apologist for the "New Lights," encouraged to some degree this disruption of traditional boundaries. He had a vision of a nascent resurgence of revived Christianity that would transcend all the old structures, to bring about a gradual but in fact millennial reconstitution of the world under the leadership and example of the brotherhood of those whose consciousnesses or, in fact, whole beings, had been transformed through the revitalizing experience of conversion. For Edwards, however, this would necessarily take place within an institutional framework, and would provide a principle of reconstruction for the whole of society.[30]

Other elements of leadership within the Awakening were less committed to order and structures than was Edwards. The increasing number of opponents of the movement grew steadily more alarmed by a number of phenomena which the original impetus of Whitefield's example had stimulated: widespread itinerancy, and corresponding neglect of the principles of parochial autonomy; spontaneous preaching, in defiance of the Puritan tradition of homiletics based on carefully prepared notes and sermons laid out in rational argument with precise scriptural quotation; exhortation by laypeople, lacking regular ordination, seminary training, or even formal education of any sort; and finally, of most concern especially in New England, emotional preaching designed not to expound the word of God systematically and with care to draw out its applications, but rather to stir the affections of the congregation, to bring about the dramatic and sudden change of heart that was now said to be the essence of salvation.[31]

This "enthusiasm," as it was called by its detractors, occasionally took the form of some rather bizarre excesses of puritan zeal, reminiscent of the great vanity-burnings of Savonarola.[32] Dr. Alexander Hamilton, a visiting Edinburgh physician, noted one of these outbursts with some amusement:

> Sunday, August 26 [1743, New London, Conn.] I went home at 6 o'clock, and Deacon Green's son came to see me. He entertained me with the history of the behaviour of one [James] Davenport, a fanatick preacher there who told his flock in one of his enthusiastic rhapsodies that in order to be saved they ought to burn all their idols. They began this conflagration with a pile of books in the public street, among which were Tillotson's Sermons, Drillincourt on Death, Sherlock and many other excellent authors, and sung psalms and hymns over the pile while it was a burning. They did not stop here, but the women made up a lofty pile of hoop petticoats, silk gowns, short cloaks, cambrick caps, red heeled shoes, fans, necklaces, gloves and other such apparell, and what was merry enough, Davenport's own idol with which he topped the pile, was a pair of old, wore out, plush breaches. But this bone fire was happily prevented by one more moderate than the rest, who found means to perswade them that making such a sacrifice was not necessary for their salvation, and so every one carried of[f]their idols again, which was lucky for Davenport who, had fire been put to the pile, would have been obliged to strutt about barearsed, for the devil another pair of breeches had he but these same old plush one which were going to be offered up as an expiatory sacrifice.[33]

Extravagant and unrepresentative as this particular episode may have been, it is significant in its illustration of symbolic behavior of the anti-structural variety. The primitivistic theme of a periodic cleansing and return to origins—what Mircea Eliade called "the eternal return"—is a significant countercurrent in Western religious behavior contrasting with the emphasis on historical progress and development that became dominant with the rise of mainstream Protestantism. Puritanism itself, in fact, contained an element of this symbolic modality in its election rituals, at which the preaching of "jeremiads" recalled the faithful from their deviant paths to a return to original purity. (The name "Puritanism," for that matter, denotes an emphasis on purification, as does "Reformation" imply re-forming and a return to primitive Christian origins.) The motif later became significant in the early nineteenth century in the "restorationist" movement of Alexander Campbell and Barton W. Stone, who regarded their following (later to become the Disciples of Christ) as an antidenominationalist return to the unstructured purity of New Testament Christianity.[34]

The Atlantic colonists and their religion were never to be the same after the Great Awakening. As Perry Miller and Alan Heimert have pointed out, the traditionalistic principle of religious affiliation on the basis of territoriality was definitively superseded by the modernistic notion of voluntarism.[35] Both religious groups (later to be called "denominations") and individual churches were rent asunder by the uncontainable ferment of enthusiastic religion, and communities that had previously been bound together in ecclesiastical unity were now confronted with an irreversible diversity of religious options. (The continuing presense of two Congregational churches side by side on the New Haven Green is a tangible reminder of this fission.) The resulting "reshuffle and new deal," which resulted in, among other things, a revitalization of the rather moribund Baptist community, takes us into a realm of historical sociology that is beyond our proper scope.[36] However, despite the resultant and inevitable routinization of the enthusiastic impulse into denominational form, the hold of traditionalistic structures on American religious life had now received a standing challenge. Popular religion had come into its own as a major force of anti-structure, and would play an even more important role in the ferment of the nineteenth century.

The Great Awakening of the 1730s and 40s established a pattern that would be emulated again and again during the nineteenth century (and, according to some interpretations, the twentieth as well). What is generally known as the Second Great Awakening occurred in two principal phases.[37] The first, which began in Connecticut during the 1790s, was not really a popular movement in that it was carefully guided and nurtured by such stalwarts of the Congregational establishment as Timothy Dwight, the learned president of Yale College. It was for the most part an effort on the part of the "Establishment" to direct the social berlin College he dabbled in perfectionist theology and social reform ovements, his composition of a bulky systematic theology of his own s indicative of his basic love for form and order. His message was ndamentally neither popular nor radical; rather, it was based on a ofound desire to tame the human wilderness, to subdue social and oral chaos, and to transplant to the West, in an idiom acceptable to its tlers, the traditional New England patterns and values in which he nself had been reared.

A number of more genuinely radical and popular forms of symic expression, all in one way or another providing an anti-structural nterpoint to the dominant society, emerged during the antebellum iod. The Shakers, for example, were one of the most radical and cessful of the utopian communities whose number and variety made h an impression on the endless stream of European observers who ted America in quest of exotic novelties which they might report to r countrymen.[42] The Shakers had their origins in a combination radical Quakerism and enthusiastic French influence in midnteenth-century industrial England. Out of this milieu emerged one he most original and controversial religious leaders in the Angloerican ambit, "Mother" Ann Lee.

Ann Lee, who in many ways resembled her female successor in gious leadership, Mary Baker Eddy, was a poorly educated and oughly unhappy woman who had the gift of formulating a symbolic social antidote to her particular ailments and griefs. She responded er extremely problematic marital situation and difficulties in lbirth through an ideological repudiation of sexuality. This eventureceived institutional expression in the Shaker practice of celibacy segregation of the sexes. After considerable persecution in England, nd a handful of followers emigrated to New York State, where they n to found communitites and to evangelize widely. The recently ed lands of the Western Reserve and Kentucky were propitious for endeavors, and a number of colonies were founded both in New and and the newer areas.

The Shakers were in many ways a Protestant (or at least nonolic) exemplar of the institutionalized *communitas* which sticism had represented in Roman Catholicism. Shaker celibacy, nunal ownership of goods, subordination of the individual to the rity of ritual elders, simplicity of lifestyle, and vicinal segregation all direct parallels to the more traditional Christian expressions of rawal from the world for the collective cultivation of godliness. nonks and nuns of the Roman Church, however, had been not only dox in their beliefs but the most fervent upholders of orthodoxy the Christian community. The Shakers, on the other hand, were

malaise generated by the aftermath of the Revolution into constructive channels—that is, the revitalization of what again was perceived by many as a decline in vital piety. This aspect of the Second Awakening is analogous in both temporal sequence and general function to the Edwardsean revivals in Northampton of the 1730s.

The second phase, which had little direct connection with the first, consisted in the extraordinary enthusiasm generated in the camp meetings in Kentucky and the adjacent frontier area during the first decade of the following century.[38] During these excitements, preachers from a variety of denominations would hold forth simultaneously and in apparent harmony before great throngs assembled over a considerable expanse of territory for the event. Participants frequently experienced dramatic physical seizures, and such "exercises" as "barking," "jerking," and the like were commonplace. Blacks as well as whites participated, emphasizing the nearly complete, if rather transitory, anti-structural character of the proceedings.

In a sense, the frontier awakening resembled the sort of religious experience described (with perhaps questionable accuracy) by Emile Durkheim in his *Elementary Forms of the Religious Life* (1917). As with Durkheim's aboriginal Australians, the frontier people were scattered over a large territory where they lived in isolation and hardship. The camp meetings, however, provided an occasion for coming together into a community, and the quality of emotion generated by this coming together can easily be described by Durkheim's term "effervescence." Their existence as a group took on a character transcending their impoverished life as individuals, and the resultant outburst of energy and enthusiasm expressed itself in religious form. The ecstatic experience of participation in an event in which collective involvement and excitement made it possible for individuals to submerge themselves in the collectivity, moreover, may have served the latent function of providing the rudimentary experience of participating in a community. Thus was laid the groundwork for the subsequent religious and social organization of the frontier people into more settled and stable patterns. However, the chaotic character of the initial experiences was an apt symbolic reflection of the unsettled social experience of early frontier life.

The continued influx of settlers into the frontier area, together with the desire of many of the frontier people to escape from the isolation and hardship of their scattered and remote little farms and cabins, insured that the camp meetings in their earliest and most spontaneous forms would not be possible for very long. Throughout the South (and it should be remembered that much of the South remained frontier country till nearly the time of the Civil War), the camp meeting became a regular feature of religious life during the next few decades of the nineteenth century. In his study of what he refers to as "plain-folk camp-meeting religion," Dickson D. Bruce, Jr., points out how the routinized camp meeting came to provide the elements of institutionalized anti-structure which made possible for many a collective "rite of passage" from frontier chaos into the order of settled community life.[39] The meeting included in its course (which stretched over several days) a point at which all present, including preacher and congregation, male and female, black and white, entered into a common physical area and partook of a common religious experience. This experience of *communitas* provided an important counterpoint to the social distinctions that characterized the structure of the settled parts of the region as a whole. On the one hand, the social and moral chaos of frontier life was forever repudiated and left behind. On the other, a new life in a rigidly structured community, in terms of both moral self-discipline and acceptance of rigid social, sexual, and racial roles, was made more palatable through the release experienced in the "communitas" process. Spiritual equality compensated for the supposed necessity of inequality, and heaven loomed ahead as a realm where the ecstatic communitas experienced only momentarily in the camp meetings would be restored on an eternal basis.

In the northern part of the frontier region, where role distinctions were real but less rigid, a similar vehicle for socialization was developed through the revivalistic work of Charles G. Finney and his imitators and successors.[40] Finney was a lawyer from the "Burned-Over District" of upstate New York who, after experiencing a dramatic conversion himself, fell to work to apply the principles of Yankee know-how to turning revivalism into an ongoing process. Where Edwards and other supporters of the First Great Awakening had interpreted the wave of conversions and enthusiasm as a divinely sent blessing, Finney maintained that revivals were events that could be initiated, organized, and carried through by human effort. Finney was a sort of spiritual engineer, and his impact on the routinization of the revival in subsequent American experience was enormous.

Finney's task was in many ways much easier than that of his Southern counterparts. His clientele were much closer socially and psychologically to the "civilization" that had nurtured them than were the Scotch-Irish pioneers who had left rural Virginia and Carolina behind. Calvinist social values and religious ideals were only lightly concealed in the consciousness of the new settlers of Ohio and western New York, and it did not take too great an effort to restore them, in somewhat transformed fashion, to the surface.[41] Finney's tactics were more oriented toward the individual than were those of the camp-meeting preachers. After arousing a group to a state of high excitement through intense preaching, he

would invite those on the brink of a breakthrough
bench," where direct efforts of the revivalist might be co
them. Such "new measures" as the anxious bench an
meeting drew fire from the more traditional evangelica
they seemed to work. Before long the towns and cities
were filled with Finney's converts, and what had forn
aggregations of settlers were now transformed i
grounded and united communities.

With Finney and his work, we have really left be
"anti-structure." However, we might pause for a mo
Finney's career in the context of "popular"religion.
revivals were anything but popular in their calculati
genuine spontaneity. Compared with the "effervescer
earlier meetings in Kentucky, they resemble nothin
blooded feats of social engineering and manipulation
parison with contemporary events in New Engla
character becomes much more apparent. Finney
trained not as a clergyman but rather as a lawyer. Al
ordination of a sort, he clearly lacked the usual cred
cal status, and himself admitted that he neither kn
about the finer points of Presbyterian doctrine. H
outside the structures and supervision of the est
tions, and were clearly examples of "extra-ecclesias
did, however, serve as a recruiting agency for loc
much of the success of the revivals depended o
personal charismatic power. Although the techniq
devised were of great utility in promoting the wo
doubtful whether their success would have been
not been for the commanding presence of the gr
(The success of Finney's predecessor George W
measure dependent on the same personal force. It
Itinerant that he could reduce a crowd to tears s
the word "Mesopotamia.")

From the perspective of New England, Fin
primary representative of the challenge of Weste
ern tradition. In broader context, however, Finn
a force of conservatism. Orthodox Congreg
byterianism may have been moderately effective
among the better educated in-migrants from
Middle States, but many even of these were n
purely traditional message once they had move
lay in instilling the ideological groundwork for
settled community among these very people. A

certainly eccentric from the standpoint of tradition. Mother Ann came to be viewed as a new incarnation of the godhead, the female counterpart of Jesus Christ who had now appeared to complete the revelation which her male predecessor had only begun.

The notion of a female divinity was perhaps the most extreme expression of the anti-structural quality of the Shaker experiment. Whatever indirect influence women may have exercised in antebellum culture, they were almost uniformly barred from positions of religious and other sort of leadership. Ann Lee's semi-divine status did not result in the limitation of female leadership within the movement to herself, either. Women held coordinate positions of authority within the Shaker communities even after the passing of Mother Ann, and their situation was one of genuine, if celibate, equality. The other features of communitas which the Shakers shared with Catholic monks were also in direct contradiction to the norms of the dominant culture. Although their influence upon that culture was more aesthetic than religious (and that primarily during the twentieth century), the Shakers did persist in maintaining themselves as a successful community far longer than most of their utopian contemporaries, and a handful were still maintaining their traditional life in one or two New England locales far into the twentieth century.

The symbol of the outsider as the bearer of redemption also entered the American symbolic vocabulary, this time on a massive scale, through the phenomenally popular *Uncle Tom's Cabin* (1851/52) of Harriet Beecher Stowe.[43] Stowe was the daughter of the powerful evangelist and conservative reformer Lyman Beecher, and the wife of the theologian Calvin Stowe. Although she eventually abandoned her ancestral (if somewhat softened) Calvinism in favor of the Episcopal church, she never showed the slightest inclination toward involving herself in the nascent women's movement. Nevertheless, much of the success of her indictment of slavery was the result of her depiction of the weak and dispossessed—women, children, and blacks—as the real bearers of the message of the Gospel. Her character Uncle Tom, who during the 1960s came under undeserved fire as the symbol of toadyism toward whites, in fact served as a scarcely disguised Christ-figure whose greatest triumph came through his unmerited suffering and death.

Stowe's work can in fact be taken not only as a thoroughgoing indictment of the entire nation for collaboration in maintaining the dismal institution of slavery but also as a covert (and perhaps even unconscious) attempt to subvert the masculine hegemony on worldly affairs—including theology—which characterized the official social structure on the United States. In any case, *Uncle Tom's Cabin* took its place with the *Book of Martyrs* and the *Pilgrim's Progress* as one of the evangelical classics available on a mass scale first through serialization in popular journals and shortly afterward in book form at an easily affordable price.

Another enemy of slavery, William Lloyd Garrison, was much more open about his criticism of American society on all counts, and utilized some of the most dramatic symbols of anti-structure ever heard in general public discourse in his abolitionist rhetoric.[44] Garrison, the product of a Baptist heritage, an unstable family, and later Quaker influence, launched an unmitigated frontal attack on the institution of slavery and all those individuals and institutions implicated in its perpetuation in his periodical *The Liberator* (1831–1865). He rapidly assumed the role of one of the most controversial and hated figures of his time, and was placed under a virtual death sentence by several Southern state legislatures.

Much controversy has arisen over the question of Garrison's actual influence and the wisdom of his tactics, but these are not questions we can here resolve. What is important for us to note is the role which the symbolism of *communitas* and anti-structure played in his rhetoric. Garrison would have been satisfied fully with nothing less than the realization of the Kingdom of God on earth, and that kingdom was to be characterized primarily by the obliteration of all earthly social distinctions. Garrison was not simply opposed to slavery and other iniquities based on race. He was also incensed over what he perceived to be the injustices inflicted on women in American society, and precipitated a major schism within the ranks of the abolitionists through his insistence that women be accorded full membership and rights of leadership within that movement. In like fashion, he espoused virtually every contemporary cause (and there were many in the air) which he saw as conducive to the achievement of a society in which all the arbitrary barriers to full equality had been removed forever.

One of the most interesting features of Garrison's rhetoric was his recognition and critique of what would later be called the "Civil Religion." Garrison saw both Church (i.e., evangelical Protestantism) and State as implicated in a blasphemous conspiracy to maintain the iniquitous institution of slavery through their acceptance of the *status quo* ordained by the Constitution. Where many contemporaries viewed that document as virtually sacred in its authority as the constitutive charter of a nation in an at least informal covenant with God, Garrison denounced it instead as "a covenant with death and an agreement with Hell." Americans, charged Garrison, worshipped not Jesus but George Washington; more outrageously, he asserted that

> [i]n this country, Jesus has become obsolete. A profession in Him is no longer a test. Jesus is the most respectable person in the United States. Jesus sits in the President's chair of the United States. Zachary Taylor sits

> there, which is the same thing, for he believes in Jesus. He believes in war, and the Jesus that "gave Mexicans hell."[45]

Garrison was not, of course, asserting that Jesus would have approved of the American government's position on war and slavery. (We might note here that Garrison was a pacifist as well.) What he was really doing was attacking the ready use many Americans were prone to make of the symbols of Christianity as a legitimation for their rather dubious social and political stances and activities. The churches were as bad as the politicians in this regard, and Garrison was not loath to exempt even the Bible from his attacks when that document was utilized in justification of iniquity. Many of Garrison's words, in fact, point to the conclusion that he recognized instead a higher law that was finally superior to any human writings and that was knowable through conscience and inspiration alone. (The Declaration of Independence, however, came fairly close to embodying the principles on which this law rested.) Garrison came close, in short, to a position of transcendental anarchism. Both his widespread notoriety and his contempt for structures give him a prominent place in our chronicle of the varieties of popular anti-structuralism in the American experience.

RELIGION, TIME, AND HISTORY: PROVIDENCE AND PROPHECY

One theme that runs through all of American religious history, and through popular religion in particular, is a concern with the nature of time and the process of history.[46] Attitudes toward time and history, in fact, comprise one of the most distinctive features of what has been described as a specifically Western consciousness. In most of the primitive and peasant cultures we discussed earlier, the perception of time is geared to the annual round of the seasons and the cycles of the agricultural year.[47] Life tends to be patterned on supposedly eternal archetypes, and deviation from these behavioral norms is regarded not as progress but as regression into chaos. Nor is this attitude restricted to "primitive" cultures. The liturgical calendar of the Roman Catholic Church is very much based on a cyclical model, and the events that took place in the "strong time" of the life of Jesus become the paradigms that are endlessly repeated every year in the prescribed sequence of masses and holy days.[48] Many of these festivals, such as Christmas, Easter, and All Saints' Day, are in fact superimposed upon an older, pre-Christian cycle of observances, and their correspondence with actual historical events in the life of Christ is minimal indeed.[49]

The religion of the ancient Hebrews, however, broke with this traditionalistic pattern of temporal observance, and began to move in the direction of interpreting time as a linear sequence from specific historical origins to an ultimate consummation.[50] The paradigmatic event for the Hebrews was their deliverance out of Egyptian bondage into the Promised Land by Moses, but this was by no means the beginning and end of their meaningful history. Yahweh remained active throughout their collective life, and continually intervened to reward or punish them according to their faithfulness in observing the conditions of his covenant.

Early Christianity was caught up in a frenzy of apocalyptic expectation, and consequently placed little emphasis on the significance of events in the temporal sphere.[51] After this eschatological expectation had faded, the medieval church, which was geared to the life of a feudally organized agricultural society, demonstrated little interest in long-term divine plans as they were worked out in the historical arena. It was not until the Renaissance and Reformation that a new conception of and interest in history and its corollary, progress, began to emerge as a major intellectual and theological motif.

The general tendency of the Reformers was to emphasize the remoteness of God from the immediate realm of historical affairs, and to stress the importance of divine Will and Law as revealed in Scripture as the norms for human activity. God did take an interest in the course of history, but was not prone to intervene very frequently in the direct guidance of that course. Rather, especially for the Calvinists, his predestined band of the elect was charged with the execution of his Will, and their ultimate success was insured by the omnipotence of the source of their election.

On the other hand, it was not so easy to purge the world of all traces of the supernatural. Luther, for example, possessed a vivid sense of the immediate presence of the Devil, and at one time is supposed to have hurled an inkpot at his satanic tormentor. The Reformers may have striven mightily to rid the world of popish superstition, saints, sacraments, and other forms, but they and their Roman antagonists were equally susceptible to belief in the insidious activities of witches.[52] The general alliance of Protestantism with the process of modernization, which expressed itself in increasingly rational and abstract interpretation of the natural and social orders, was by no means complete, even at the "elite" level. Only with the Enlightenment of the eighteenth century would this process of rationalization and desacralization be realized, and the Enlightenment can hardly be regarded as a popular movement.

The relationship of Protestantism to the process of modernization can be interpreted fruitfully in terms of the notion of "providence."

Providence is a general term for the intervention of God in the affairs of the world. As opposed to magic, it emphasizes the free will of God, whose intervention cannot be coerced but must come freely (although petitionary prayer may prove efficacious if God is favorably disposed toward the petitioner). Providence oscillates between two poles: "general" and "special." At its most general, as in the theistic Enlightenment, God is seen as a "watchmaker" who sets the universe in motion, equipped with a program that will ultimately redound to the good of all. At an intermediate level, as in the case of ancient Israel, God superintends the welfare of a nation, rewarding and punishing its people collectively rather than individually. Special providence, which at times comes close to the magical, involves the direct intervention of the deity in the most specific circumstances. In this schema, extremely particular occurrences are attributed to the pleasure or displeasure of God. A corollary of the notion of divine providence is the attribution of earthly events, usually those of an unfortunate sort, to the active involvement of the Devil in the earthly realm. This sort of intervention may occasionally reach up to the level of intermediate providence, as, for example, in the Protestant attribution of demonic power to the papacy (or the more recent linkage of International Communism with the powers of darkness.)

At an intermediate level between the most general and specific of providences lay the Puritan interpretation of first English and then American history. Adapting the self-conception of the Israelites of old, the Puritans saw themselves and then, by extension, their land and nation, as constituting a New Israel, now perfected through the fulfillment brought about by the Incarnation.[53] God had once again entered into covenant with his chosen people, and collectively nurtured or chastened them according to their deserts. The "jeremiad" sermon form, manifested also in such verse as Michael Wigglesworth's "God's Controversy with New England" of 1662, evolved in the context of this interpretation of providence. It related various good or, more usually, bad fortunes to their causes in the moral merits and demerits of the New Englanders.[54] John Foxe's *Acts and Monuments* (the "Book of Martyrs") also helped to provide at a popular level a providential interpretation of British history.[55] Foxe argued on rather tenuous grounds that the true faith had been brought to Britain in New Testament times by Joseph of Arimathea, had managed to survive there during the intervening centuries of popish darkness, and had emerged again in its pristine splendor during the period of the Reformation. This myth of origins, and an eventual return thereunto, was easily adapted by the American Puritans, and with Puritan notions of providence helped lay the foundations for the mythical legitimation of American expansionism and imperialism during the nineteenth century.

God, moreover, regularly condescended to intervene not only in the collective affairs of humanity but also into the lives of individuals, for similar purposes of reward, edification, or chastisement. William Bradford, in his chronicle of the Pilgrim migration from the Netherlands to Plymouth, tells the story of

> a proud and very profane young man, one of the seamen, of a lusty, able body, which made him the more haughty; he would always be condemning the poor people in their sickness and cursing them daily with grievous execrations, and did not let to tell them that he hoped to help cast half of them overboard before they came to their journey's end, and to make merry with what they had; and if he were by any gently reproved, he would curse them and swear most bitterly. But it pleased God before they came half seas over to smite this young man with a grievous disease, of which he died in a desperate manner, and so was himself the first that was thrown overboard. Thus his curses light on his own head, and it was an astonishment to all his fellows for they noted it to be the just hand of God upon them.[56]

The appropriateness of the punishment fitting the crime is typical of this sort of narrative of "remarkable providences," and is considerably closer to the punitive scheme of Dante's *Inferno* than to modern notions of the economy of justice.

This concern with the exemplary providential lessons continued in "elite" thought well beyond the seventeenth century, and perhaps reached its fullest expression at that level in several works by the extraordinary Mather family (e.g., Increase's *Remarkable Providences Illustrative of the Earlier Days of American Colonization* [1684] and his son Cotton's *Magnalia Christi Americana* of 1702).[57] The Mathers and their contemporaries recorded story after story in the genre. A servant girl becomes pregnant and kills her child; when she touches the corpse later, blood returns to its face. (The idea that blood pours from a corpse when touched by its murderer had a hoary history, and was a variant of the medieval practice of ascertaining guilt through ordeal.) The daughter of a buggerer dreams of his execution before his foul deeds become known and he is in fact executed for crimes against nature. Anne Hutchinson, exiled from the Massachusetts Bay Colony for her espousal of antinomianism, gives birth to a grotesquely deformed baby. A young man is converted by the Quakers, and is later found with his head mutilated. A man loses his sight after saying that the Devil might put out his eyes if he were guilty of an offence of which he had been accused. An ecumenical touch is provided in an account by a Jesuit missionary of another man who ground up a set of rosary beads and smoked the resultant powder in his pipe. Later, he was killed when a fish bit a large chunk out of him, just as he himself had "eaten up his Ave Marias."[58]

malaise generated by the aftermath of the Revolution into constructive channels—that is, the revitalization of what again was perceived by many as a decline in vital piety. This aspect of the Second Awakening is analogous in both temporal sequence and general function to the Edwardsean revivals in Northampton of the 1730s.

The second phase, which had little direct connection with the first, consisted in the extraordinary enthusiasm generated in the camp meetings in Kentucky and the adjacent frontier area during the first decade of the following century.[38] During these excitements, preachers from a variety of denominations would hold forth simultaneously and in apparent harmony before great throngs assembled over a considerable expanse of territory for the event. Participants frequently experienced dramatic physical seizures, and such "exercises" as "barking," "jerking," and the like were commonplace. Blacks as well as whites participated, emphasizing the nearly complete, if rather transitory, anti-structural character of the proceedings.

In a sense, the frontier awakening resembled the sort of religious experience described (with perhaps questionable accuracy) by Emile Durkheim in his *Elementary Forms of the Religious Life* (1917). As with Durkheim's aboriginal Australians, the frontier people were scattered over a large territory where they lived in isolation and hardship. The camp meetings, however, provided an occasion for coming together into a community, and the quality of emotion generated by this coming together can easily be described by Durkheim's term "effervescence." Their existence as a group took on a character transcending their impoverished life as individuals, and the resultant outburst of energy and enthusiasm expressed itself in religious form. The ecstatic experience of participation in an event in which collective involvement and excitement made it possible for individuals to submerge themselves in the collectivity, moreover, may have served the latent function of providing the rudimentary experience of participating in a community. Thus was laid the groundwork for the subsequent religious and social organization of the frontier people into more settled and stable patterns. However, the chaotic character of the initial experiences was an apt symbolic reflection of the unsettled social experience of early frontier life.

The continued influx of settlers into the frontier area, together with the desire of many of the frontier people to escape from the isolation and hardship of their scattered and remote little farms and cabins, insured that the camp meetings in their earliest and most spontaneous forms would not be possible for very long. Throughout the South (and it should be remembered that much of the South remained frontier country till nearly the time of the Civil War), the camp meeting became a regular feature of religious life during the next few decades of the nineteenth century. In his study of what he refers to as "plain-folk camp-meeting religion," Dickson D. Bruce, Jr., points out how the routinized camp meeting came to provide the elements of institutionalized anti-structure which made possible for many a collective "rite of passage" from frontier chaos into the order of settled community life.[39] The meeting included in its course (which stretched over several days) a point at which all present, including preacher and congregation, male and female, black and white, entered into a common physical area and partook of a common religious experience. This experience of *communitas* provided an important counterpoint to the social distinctions that characterized the structure of the settled parts of the region as a whole. On the one hand, the social and moral chaos of frontier life was forever repudiated and left behind. On the other, a new life in a rigidly structured community, in terms of both moral self-discipline and acceptance of rigid social, sexual, and racial roles, was made more palatable through the release experienced in the "communitas" process. Spiritual equality compensated for the supposed necessity of inequality, and heaven loomed ahead as a realm where the ecstatic communitas experienced only momentarily in the camp meetings would be restored on an eternal basis.

In the northern part of the frontier region, where role distinctions were real but less rigid, a similar vehicle for socialization was developed through the revivalistic work of Charles G. Finney and his imitators and successors.[40] Finney was a lawyer from the "Burned-Over District" of upstate New York who, after experiencing a dramatic conversion himself, fell to work to apply the principles of Yankee know-how to turning revivalism into an ongoing process. Where Edwards and other supporters of the First Great Awakening had interpreted the wave of conversions and enthusiasm as a divinely sent blessing, Finney maintained that revivals were events that could be initiated, organized, and carried through by human effort. Finney was a sort of spiritual engineer, and his impact on the routinization of the revival in subsequent American experience was enormous.

Finney's task was in many ways much easier than that of his Southern counterparts. His clientele were much closer socially and psychologically to the "civilization" that had nurtured them than were the Scotch-Irish pioneers who had left rural Virginia and Carolina behind. Calvinist social values and religious ideals were only lightly concealed in the consciousness of the new settlers of Ohio and western New York, and it did not take too great an effort to restore them, in somewhat transformed fashion, to the surface.[41] Finney's tactics were more oriented toward the individual than were those of the camp-meeting preachers. After arousing a group to a state of high excitement through intense preaching, he would invite those on the brink of a breakthrough to the "anxious bench," where direct efforts of the revivalist might be concentrated upon them. Such "new measures" as the anxious bench and the protracted meeting drew fire from the more traditional evangelicals of the East, but they seemed to work. Before long the towns and cities of the Northwest were filled with Finney's converts, and what had formerly been simply aggregations of settlers were now transformed into ideologically grounded and united communities.

With Finney and his work, we have really left behind the realm of "anti-structure." However, we might pause for a moment to consider Finney's career in the context of "popular"religion. In one sense, his revivals were anything but popular in their calculation and absence of genuine spontaneity. Compared with the "effervescent" character of the earlier meetings in Kentucky, they resemble nothing so much as cold-blooded feats of social engineering and manipulation. However, in comparison with contemporary events in New England, their popular character becomes much more apparent. Finney himself had been trained not as a clergyman but rather as a lawyer. Although he received ordination of a sort, he clearly lacked the usual credentials for full clerical status, and himself admitted that he neither knew nor cared much about the finer points of Presbyterian doctrine. His revivals operated outside the structures and supervision of the established denominations, and were clearly examples of "extra-ecclesiastical" religion. (They did, however, serve as a recruiting agency for local churches.) Finally, much of the success of the revivals depended on Finney's enormous personal charismatic power. Although the techniques and methods he devised were of great utility in promoting the work of the revivals, it is doubtful whether their success would have been nearly as great had it not been for the commanding presence of the great evangelist himself. (The success of Finney's predecessor George Whitefield was in large measure dependent on the same personal force. It was said of the Grand Itinerant that he could reduce a crowd to tears simply by pronouncing the word "Mesopotamia.")

From the perspective of New England, Finney was the agent and primary representative of the challenge of Western pragmatism to Eastern tradition. In broader context, however, Finney appears primarily as a force of conservatism. Orthodox Congregationalism and Presbyterianism may have been moderately effective in gaining a following among the better educated in-migrants from New England and the Middle States, but many even of these were no longer receptive to a purely traditional message once they had moved west. Finney's genius lay in instilling the ideological groundwork for the establishment of a settled community among these very people. Although as president of

Oberlin College he dabbled in perfectionist theology and social reform movements, his composition of a bulky systematic theology of his own was indicative of his basic love for form and order. His message was fundamentally neither popular nor radical; rather, it was based on a profound desire to tame the human wilderness, to subdue social and moral chaos, and to transplant to the West, in an idiom acceptable to its settlers, the traditional New England patterns and values in which he himself had been reared.

A number of more genuinely radical and popular forms of symbolic expression, all in one way or another providing an anti-structural counterpoint to the dominant society, emerged during the antebellum period. The Shakers, for example, were one of the most radical and successful of the utopian communities whose number and variety made such an impression on the endless stream of European observers who visited America in quest of exotic novelties which they might report to their countrymen.[42] The Shakers had their origins in a combination of radical Quakerism and enthusiastic French influence in mid-eighteenth-century industrial England. Out of this milieu emerged one of the most original and controversial religious leaders in the Anglo-American ambit, "Mother" Ann Lee.

Ann Lee, who in many ways resembled her female successor in religious leadership, Mary Baker Eddy, was a poorly educated and thoroughly unhappy woman who had the gift of formulating a symbolic and social antidote to her particular ailments and griefs. She responded to her extremely problematic marital situation and difficulties in childbirth through an ideological repudiation of sexuality. This eventually received institutional expression in the Shaker practice of celibacy and segregation of the sexes. After considerable persecution in England, she and a handful of followers emigrated to New York State, where they began to found communitites and to evangelize widely. The recently opened lands of the Western Reserve and Kentucky were propitious for their endeavors, and a number of colonies were founded both in New England and the newer areas.

The Shakers were in many ways a Protestant (or at least non-Catholic) exemplar of the institutionalized *communitas* which monasticism had represented in Roman Catholicism. Shaker celibacy, communal ownership of goods, subordination of the individual to the authority of ritual elders, simplicity of lifestyle, and vicinal segregation were all direct parallels to the more traditional Christian expressions of withdrawal from the world for the collective cultivation of godliness. The monks and nuns of the Roman Church, however, had been not only orthodox in their beliefs but the most fervent upholders of orthodoxy within the Christian community. The Shakers, on the other hand, were

Donald E. Byrne, Jr., in his study of the folklore of Methodist itinerant preachers during the earlier part of the nineteenth century, has demonstrated that the notion of special providences, both positive and negative, continued well beyond the Puritan epoch.[59] The American Wesleyans experienced or encountered a whole range of phenomena which illustrated the workings of divine power in the midst of the mundane world. Circuit riders visited heaven and hell in dreams, and in such fashion were present at their own judgments. They had visions of departed relatives and colleagues, and dreamed frequently of future events, including their own demises. The impious were punished in a variety of ways, including their own deaths and those of their children. On the other hand, the virtuous (i.e., Methodists) were miraculously delivered from various perils of the wilderness in which they served, including incipient attacks by panthers, wolves, bears, rattlesnakes, bulls, and runaway horses. Financial relief was also unexpectedly provided through fortuitous gifts when resources ran dangerously low, and prayers brought about all sorts of material and spiritual blessings, including rain. As Byrne remarks, the God of these preachers was an avenging clan god, determined to protect his own and to lay low their detractors.[60] "God protects the Methodist."

As the examples show (and many more could easily be adduced), belief in special providences as divine reward or, more usually, punishment, was not the exclusive property of any religious group, but rather common to all of Christendom. God was not content to wait until the sheep and goats were sorted out at the Last Judgment; rather, he was continually occupied in righting the balance of things at every moment, and caused an immediate as well as a long-term justice to prevail in the world as a deterrent to would-be malefactors. As Keith Thomas has pointed out, it was not until a scientific world picture became more or less universal that such beliefs began to lose their hold, and even today special providences and their like have by no means been eradicated from the outlook of many.[61]

Perhaps the best theoretical key for understanding the phenomenon of special providences is Max Weber's concept of rationalization.[62] In a world in which many important relationships are still conducted on a personal basis, with direct contact between the parties involved, it is likely that such a personalistic conception of relationships will be applied to the divinity as well. Even though Calvin went a good way toward removing the divine from the everyday realm and pictured God as infinitely remote and inscrutable, his Puritan followers had not attained to such a state of impersonality in their own affairs that they could sustain this vision in all its unmitigated corollaries. Their God remained in many ways more of a feudal lord than an impersonal chief bureaucrat or remote oriental despot, and was by no means above intruding himself into the everyday run of human relationships. As a matter of fact, the neo-Calvinist God of the Barthians has not yet achieved anything like universal popularity, and is unlikely to do so in the foreseeable future.

Providence is one major concept or symbol through which the temporal process may be interpreted. At the extremes of special and general providence, history comes to a standstill, and loses its soteriological potency. In the intermediate version that became dominant in America, however, history became an extremely important category for interpreting the meaning of earthly existence.

Throughout American religious life, however, there is a pessimistic (or, depending on one's point of view, optimistic) note that runs throughout, often in a subterranean vein, and occasionally surfaces in times of distress and confusion. Millennialism—the belief that a dramatic transformation will overtake and transform the whole of the earth—is a religious modality of venerable lineage. Its origins in the Western world lie in the Jewish apocalyptic literature of the Second Commonwealth, and the Book of Daniel especially survived to become a major text for those inclined to speculate on matters eschatological. John G. Gager, in another volume in this series, has discussed the early Christian movement as a millenarian community, as well as the emergence within it of a strong missionary thrust as a means of dealing with the disappointment over the non-event of the imminently expected Second Advent.[63] By the time of Saint Augustine, the notion of a new Kingdom expressed most dramatically in the Book of Revelation had been rationalized by that great theoretician's concept that the Church itself was the Kingdom, and that it was futile to expect any dramatic and visible transformation of the whole earth by supernatural agency. The Christian Church never abandoned the doctrine of an apocalyptic end to the world, but relegated it to a remote and unknowable time in the distant future so that it no longer served as a focus for immediate expectation.

During the later Middle Ages and the English Civil War period, millennial expectations enjoyed a resurgence of popularity.[64] The belief was current among many American Puritan leaders, although it never became the basis for action of any specific or concerted sort. It was not until the time of the Great Awakening, when religious ferment provided an atmosphere susceptible to the entertainment of anti-structural activity and speculations of all sorts, that the idea gained real credence in the American colonies. However, the millenarian speculation that characterized the thought of Jonathan Edwards and his successors was of an entirely different sort from that which had informed the popular movements of earlier times.[65]

The idea of a millennial kingdom, in which all status distinctions are erased and all the world will live in peace and harmony free from want, is certainly a vision of anti-structure and *communitas* in the full sense of those terms. However, beginning with Edwards, a radical transformation in the implications of the idea began to arise. The crucial point that was to distinguish the mainstream of American millenarian thought from its usual apocalyptic expression involved the theological question of exactly in what relation the second coming of Jesus stood to the Kingdom itself. In most Christian millenarian movements, it was the expectation that Jesus would first return, then the Kingdom would come. This interpretation, which has come to be known as "pre-millennialism" (that is, Jesus would come before the Millennium, or thousand years of peace and plenty), implies a highly pessimistic attitude toward the state of the world. In such a scheme, the world is usually regarded as so hopelessly lost and corrupt that dramatic supernatural intervention is the prerequisite for any significant change.

The emergent American temperament, however, was considerably less pessimistic about the prospects for earthly life in general and for the course of American destiny in particular. Edwards was thus one of the first theoreticians of that position which has subsequently come to be called "post-millennial"—that is, the belief that the Second Coming would be the climax, rather than the commencement, of the millennial realm.[66] Where pre-millennialism is pessimistic and antihistorical, post-millennialism of this sort is optimistic about human possibilities and legitimates the historical realm as the arena in which the divine will is to be acted out and realized. America, in short, was the Chosen Land in which the culmination of God's benevolent purposes for humanity would be fulfilled in all their grandeur.

Post-millennialism in both its explicitly religious and more secularized forms—i.e., the notions of "progress" and "destiny"—was an enormously influential motif in American thought and life throughout the nineteenth century. However, its unfolding is really beyond our scope here, because its investigation would take us out of the realm of popular belief and practice into the field of intellectual and cultural history. Also, the symbolism of post-millennialism is really of a very different sort from that which we have been discussing. The gradual nature of the transformation of the social realm into an ever more perfect community does not involve the eruption of divine power into the mundane sphere until the very end, where in practice it serves more as an afterthought than as an active principle. Post-millennialism easily blurs into reformism or secular utopianism, and its religious force is readily blunted as it becomes an operative idea.

Pre-millennialism, however, fits our definition of popular religion very well, both in its actual constituency and in the nature of the symbolic process involved. The term, in fact (in the form of "millennialism" or "millenarianism"), had been adopted by anthropologists to describe "cargo cults" and other popular movements in which a dramatic transformation of the social world, often with an accompanying influx of material goods in superabundance, is immediately expected.[67] In such movements there is often no explicit or even implicit reference to the Second Coming or any other aspect of Christianity, but the basic form is similar. Such movements almost always take place in the context of rapid and distressing social change, where the supernatural powers heretofore manipulated by the old order are overshadowed in their efficacy by the technological "magic" of the white society, and a new ideology arises which promises a "buying-in" on that magic on a dramatic scale.

America, however, has not generally proved to be a very propitious arena for pre-millennial movements. Such an appeal has generally been pre-empted by various orthodoxies, post-millennial hope, secular appeals to reform and progress, or other religious or ideological options that call for an active mastery of the social environment. "Freedom's Ferment," whether expressed in utopian or evangelical form, was essentially optimistic and activist, and genuine pre-millennial pessimism has always been a distinctly minor note.[68]

One dramatic episode in antebellum history, however, has achieved lasting prominence as an example of pre-millennial fervor, and has probably received so much attention because of its exceptional nature. During the late 1830s, a Calvinistic Baptist named William Miller began to devote his attention to the interpretation of Biblical prophecy.[69] Miller was an unlikely leader for the sort of movement which in European and non-Western cultures had generally been led by inspired, charismatic prophetic figures. Miller was instead a literal-minded, rather orthodox resident of New York's "Burned-Over District" of Massachusetts lineage who through painstaking numerological speculation became convinced not only of the validity of the pre-millennial position but also that the Second Advent was imminent. At first his message was confined to a local constituency in New York, but the work of skillful publicists such as Joshua Himes, who had become a Millerite believer, gave his ideas widespread circulation throughout New England and the whole of the Northeast.

Miller was hardly an aggressive prophet, and was at first reluctant either to break with established denominational religion or to predict a specific date for the Great Event. However, as the movement gathered momentum, he was forced to give way to the increasing hostility of many orthodox ministers and to the demands of his followers and managers for a precise date. Finally, Miller settled on the year that ran from 21 March 1843 to the same date of the following year. When the appointed year had run its course with no dramatic developments, he revised the date to 22 October 1844. Expectation reached a climax that October but, as before, nothing much happened. As is necessarily the fate of all millennial movements, a great disappointment ensued, and Millerism proper came to an end.

So did Miller, who died a few years later. Some of his followers, however, were not so easily deterred. Many drifted off and were received back into the evangelical churches out of which most of them had come. Others, however, were not content to let the matter drop. As often happens in the wake of disappointed millenarian expectations, various rationalizations were made. Many believed that the problem lay in Miller's having made an error in his calculations, and returned to their numerological drawing boards to speculate on the matter further. Others were convinced that the problem lay not in the accuracy of the prediction but in the perception of what had actually happened. In this version, Christ had in fact come, but invisibly and spiritually. Those who were among the chosen were living in the millennium; for the others who lacked eyes with which to see and ears with which to hear, it was all over.

Firm evidence is lacking as to the actual nature of Miller's constituency, but two facts seem to emerge as secure: many followers were rural, and the time in which the movement flourished was one of economic depression.[70] Moreover, Millerism had arisen toward the end of a period in which religious expectations had been continually stirred through the succession of movements—revivalistic, spiritualistic, Shaker, Noyesian Utopian, Mormon—that had swept the "Burned-Over District" and large parts of rural New England as well. This territory was filled with poorer Yankees, of Puritan descent and still imbued with Puritan religious attitudes, but only partly educated and cut off from the prosperity that characterized the seaboard, urban, and commercial areas. It was, in short, a marginal area, no longer frontier but not yet fully settled, populated with poorer, less successful people nurtured in a religious culture but no longer fully under its grasp. Where the more successful of these people might well find Finney's evangelism or Noyes' perfectionism attractive, their less fortunate cousins, especially in times of a depressed economy, might well be drawn instead to a message promising immediate deliverance from earthly troubles and membership in a community of the chosen. Such redemption was contingent only on their belief and not on any secular effort of their own. Where, moreover, they saw themselves as the victims of the wealthier, more successful lawyers, businessmen, and Masons who were forming a regional middle-class aristocracy, they now had the promise of a Kingdom where such status and economic distinctions would vanish forever.

The more extreme of the Adventist groups which survived the Great Disappointment eventually found a new rallying point in the leadership of a woman from Maine.[71] Ellen Gould Harmon White had been nurtured in the provincial evangelical culture of northern New England. She had also been the victim of a childhood accident that had left her permanently impaired and precluded her further education. After participating in the Millerite excitement, she began to have a series of visions which took her on tours of the other world and provided inspiration as to how to cope with the Disappointment.

The movement that grew up around her visions and the leadership of Mrs. White and her husband—Seventh-Day Adventism—expressed itself through a shifting combination of symbolic modes. At first the anti-structural, millenarian component manifested itself vigorously in the rejection of both Catholicism and Protestantism through exegesis of the book of Revelation, as well as a refusal to participate in any civic or military activities. The name of the movement itself points to a rejection of traditional observance of Sunday as the Lord's Day, and a literalistic substitution of the Old Testament Sabbath in its place. Also, Mrs. White and her followers became increasingly concerned with matters of health and bodily purity. Diet reform was very much in the air throughout the early nineteenth century, and with good practical reason: much of the food consumed by Americans, especially in frontier areas, was unwholesome and poorly prepared.

However, the more pragmatic or ideological innovations advocated by such reformers as Sylvester Graham (inventor of the Graham cracker) were given a religious twist when adopted by the Adventists. Where millennialism had been a broad movement in the days of William Miller, welcoming believers from all groups, it was now in the process of hardening into a sect. Since the belief was no longer widely fashionable, the remnant that still clung to it were forced to draw in upon themselves through the leadership of a woman psychologically predisposed to propound symbols of inner purity and external corruption. Her major vision of 5 June 1863 instructed her that meat, alcohol, tobacco, and drug-dispensing doctors were anathema, and that she and her disciples were to rely instead on air, sunshine, rest, exercise, proper diet, and water. The common belief of the mid- and later nineteenth century that masturbation and excessive sexual intercourse (more than once a month among married couples!) were both debilitating in their excessive drawing-off of a limited supply of "our precious bodily fluids" was also given religious legitimation in this vision.

Seventh-Day Adventism went on to become a small but vigorous denomination during the twentieth century. Though its modern adherents retain many of their taboos, emphasis has been given increasingly to medical work. (Adventists today maintain several fine medical institutions.) The original "come-outer" attitudes toward political organization gradually weakened, and symbolic depictions of the United States as the two-horned beast of the Book of Revelation changed slowly into pictures of the American bison. The earlier phase of the movement, however, is significant in its combination of several important symbolic motifs: millennial expectations, an almost gnostic preoccupation with the seventh-day Sabbath as divinely ordained, and an obsession with bodily purity. Together these constitute an apt expression for a group of people united in alienation from the broader structures of society, who place little hope in earthly things and band together in fear of the contaminating effects of sexual and comestible pollution. Salvation, conversely, lay within the boundaries of the group (through avoidance of external contaminants and adherence to the symbolic shibboleth of the seventh-day Sabbath) and across the boundary of history into the millennium. As the group grew more secure and prosperous after Mrs. White's death in 1915, the emphasis on boundary maintenance relaxed somewhat, but group identity continued to be preserved through allegiance to its particular symbols.

We will return to discuss some contemporary manifestations of prophecy and millennialism in a later section.[72] We might conclude this section with a brief discussion of the role of prophecy in one of the less orthodox movements of the nineteenth century, which was nevertheless highly American in its combination of an almost exaggerated rendering of themes common in the culture of the time with a highly particularistic version of prophecy that had a distinctively post-millennial element within it.

Joseph Smith, the founder of the Church of Jesus Christ of Latter-Day Saints, or Mormonism, was almost as incautious as had been William Miller in making claims linked to highly specific circumstances.[73] Where Miller was exclusively concerned with the future, however, Smith focused primarily upon the past and present (although his message held extremely important implications for the future as well). Smith's imagination was of the highly concrete, literalistic sort that has also manifested itself in a fascination with the esoteric implications of the dimensions of the Great Pyramid, "lost tribes and sunken continents," and the literal fulfillment of the prophecies of the books of Daniel and Revelation.[74] Smith in fact seems to have adapted locally circulating stories about the American Indians being the Ten Lost Tribes of Israel into his supernaturally authenticated Book of Mormon, which consists of a rather repetitious saga of those tribes during their pre-Columbian days. What is most interesting about Smith's revelation is the close attention to detail manifested in its highly specific circumstances, with a whole panoply of angelic informants, gold tablets, and a sort of looking-glass through which the revelations written on the tablets could be translated. What was involved primarily in this prophecy was not some general, timeless ethical, spiritual, or metaphysical truth, but rather an intensely concrete story about supernatural appearances and allegedly historical events.

Smith's revelations continued as the movement which he founded began, perhaps surprisingly, to thrive, and to come into need of specific direction at various junctures. We have already seen that special providence played a major role in the self-interpretation of the Mormon experience, as in the miraculous appearance of seagulls after the first crops in Utah were threatened by insects. The significance of all these revelations and prophecies lies in their highly specific nature and reflects the social experience and perceptions of Smith, Young, and their followers. Both leaders and recruits were, in a sense, rural versions of Christian Scientists to whom we shall return in the following section. They were physically and psychologically displaced persons, cut loose from traditional patterns of communal life, and scattered throughout the small farms and towns of the only recently settled "Burned Over District" of upstate New York.[75] Success and, metaphorically, salvation, were highly concrete, and lay in the acquisition of wealth, family, and prestige. The revelation given unto Joseph Smith provided these rootless people with a highly specific spiritual history; a vision of wealth and splendor, exhibited in angels and gold tablets; and, most important, a communal organization which enabled hitherto scattered and individually powerless people to unite and thereby achieve a specific, collective, and material salvation.

THE SYMBOLIC ADJUSTMENT TO URBAN LIFE

During the fifty or so years between the Civil War and the First World War, the expansive tendencies of American society began to reverse their direction; centrifugal force gradually became centripetal. The Department of the Census announced that the frontier had come to an official end in 1890—there was no longer any significant amount of arable land left to be claimed for settlement. By 1920, the census would show that the majority of Americans were city dwellers. These decades were also characterized by a massive influx of immigrants, primarily from the less developed areas of Eastern and Southern Europe, but there was little vacant land left on which they could resume their peasant life patterns. These immigrants for the most part joined the increasingly larger number of country people, especially the younger ones, who were leaving the farms to seek their fortunes in the city. (After the First World War, blacks would take up this quest as well.) This reversal of demographic patterns had profound consequences for all Americans, and the resulting responses were symbolic as well as political and economic in character.[76]

The principal movements we shall consider in this section all adopted an implicit strategy of a basic acceptance of the new urban world, but this acceptance was modified by the maintenance of a certain tension with or distancing from that world. Some, like Christian Science, went beyond the theological boundaries of traditional Protestantism; others, like middle-class Holiness and Moodyite revivalism, remained within the fold of orthodoxy. However, they created a network of taboos and prohibitions relating to personal conduct in order to provide believers with a realm of symbolic safety through which they might operate within the world while remaining insulated from its potentially corrupting influences. Finally, as a brief look at one of the most popular novels of the period, *In His Steps,* should make clear, the major problem all of these movements confronted was that of creating symbolic identity for a nascent urban middle class.

Mary Baker Eddy, the founder of the Christian Science movement, was an emotional casualty of the changes that had been transforming New England society.[77] The Civil War had decimated the younger male population, and the newer cities of the West had begun to usurp the region's economic and cultural leadership. But Eddy was a woman who capitalized upon her own misfortunes, provided for them a symbolic resolution, and launched a phenomenally potent new religious force that appealed to the thousands of other emotionally and cognitively displaced persons who shared her predicament.

Mary Morse Baker, the precocious but inadequately educated daughter of a New Hampshire family, left her rural home to embark on a series of generally unsatisfactory marriages. These left her primarily with one son from whom she eventually became almost totally estranged. She was an ambitious and capable woman in an age when such energies lacked many suitable outlets. She was the victim of serious psychosomatic afflictions at a time when psychotherapy was virtually unknown and a subculture of "mindhealers" such as Phineas P. Quimby provided such relief (often surprisingly effective) as was then available.[78] She had little success as a wife and mother when such roles were still the most highly regarded for her sex. She had grown up imbued with Calvinist theology at a time when orthodoxy was rapidly yielding to more liberal religious forces in her native New England, and a preoccupation with sin and predestination persisted chiefly in rural backwaters and villages far from

Boston and New Haven. Finally, she found herself uprooted from the isolated but secure and picturesque New Hampshire countryside to find herself in the squalid and, in Sydney Ahlstrom's phrase, now irrecoverable sub-ethos of boarding houses in the milltowns north of Boston, adrift with other "spinsters" and marginal people who had been bypassed by the benefits of the process of modernization.[79]

This new culture was very different from that which had characterized the traditional rural life of New England, the older *gemeinschaftlich* world of face-to-face relationships, of a secure sense of continuity with the past and communal identity in the present. "Group," in the sense in which the anthropologist Mary Douglas employs the term, had become minimal, while "grid," or sense of place in a social hierarchy, was still strong but rapidly changing in character.[80] Until roughly the time of the Civil War, commercial success had combined with birth and education to create a social hierarchy in which status was partially ascribed and partially achieved. Now, however, birth and breeding counted for little, and the way was clear for the ambitious to claw their way to the top. As Howells' Silas Lapham discovered, such status could vanish as rapidly as it was attained. Many who never even began to attain it not surprisingly experienced a severe sense of displacement and alienation.

It is probably not very surprising, at least in retrospect, that the "walking wounded," those who did not fit into this new order which required skills and values unanticipated by previous generations, should manifest their *anomie* in the form of psychosomatic ailments. Mrs. Eddy herself was dramatically cured of what she was convinced was a fatal back injury through Quimby's "mind cure," and proceeded to apply her enormous skills at organization, along with her rather more limited abilities in the literary and metaphysical lines, to systematizing and spreading far and wide her gospel of "Christian Science." Symbolically, her strategy was that of denial. If both the microcosmic physical body and the macrocosmic social bodies were problematical and the sources of aches and anxieties, she would deny their very existence, not merely tinker with trying to improve them piecemeal. Mind would be all, and matter nothing. Death and sickness were simply illusions, which could be overcome neither through prayer nor medicine but through a new source of *gnosis,* a new method of interpreting Christian Scripture which produced hitherto unrealized insights about the true nature of the metaphysical realm and its application to immediate human problems.

Sydney Ahlstrom has aptly described the message of Christian Science as a "this-worldly otherworldliness."[81] This characterization emphasizes the irony that her denial of the physical and social bodies was paradoxically at the same time an affirmation of those very bodies. The emphasis of the movement was never, at least until very recently, particularly concerned with either piety or ethics. Rather, it was thaumaturgical: it was concerned with making whole the physical and psychic unity of the person which the new social forces had rent asunder. In addition, the movement's adherents only temporarily found themselves among the dispossessed or "relatively deprived." Rather, in true sectarian fashion, they soon came to constitute the most middle-class and the wealthiest (as well as the most urban and female) of American denominations, hardly an "other-worldly" situation in the context of Christian tradition.[82] In order to find health and success they had first to "lose," paradoxically, their inhibiting belief in the reality of that over which they eventually triumphed, namely sickness and failure. The organization of Christian Science adherents, characterized until recently at least by impersonal, functional relationships rather than surrogate kinship or community groups, was also significantly imitative of the emergent structure of the broader society within which they developed.[83]

The development of Christian Science as a denomination is beyond our scope here since, according to our working definition, a movement ceases to be "popular" in the full sense after it achieves organizational success and stability and its clientele enters increasingly into the ranks of the middle classes. We might note in passing, however, that the early Christian Science organization, which was at all times presided over dictatorially by Mrs. Eddy herself, for a time took on the characteristics of a witchcraft society. Mrs. Eddy was continually obsessed with challenges to her leadership, since much of her clientele was still amorphous and spinoff schismatic movements were frequent. Living in the midst of a rather tight group of disciples whose deference to her undivided authority was constantly coming into question, she came to express her fears of rivalry in her doctrine of "Malicious Animal Magnetism" (M.A.M.) or mental assassination, and was convinced that her last (and most satisfactory) husband had met his demise in this fashion. Witchcraft beliefs, under whatever name, had not in fact perished with Goody Nurse and her unfortunate companions at Salem.

Another, more "mainstream" response to the problems created by urbanization was provided by some developments within a religious tradition which had its very roots in the modernization of English society during the eighteenth century. After its transplantation to an American setting, Methodism adapted itself rapidly and successfully to the new environment.[84] Its beginnings in America were simultaneously rural and urban but, given the predominantly agricultural economy of the new nation, it flourished primarily in rural areas during the earlier part of the nineteenth century. It found its greatest opportunities especially on the frontier, both southern and western, and provided the discipline and organization for those areas which the Puritans had earlier brought to the wilds of New England. In these earlier days, it served much of the same role of turning chaos into community as had its Calvinistic predecessors.[85]

Despite its tight and effective system of organization, Methodism from its beginnings was in many senses a popular religion. Formal theological education received little emphasis in the early days, and even came in for a good deal of scorn from such "self-made" circuit riders as the legendary Peter Cartwright.[86] These circuit riders, who often wore themselves out through their strenuous efforts and died at an early age, were distinguished from the laity more by function and zeal than by training or the mystique of a priestly caste. Personal observation has convinced this writer that it is still difficult to distinguish clergy from laity at Methodist Annual Conferences.

From its beginnings, American Methodism has been given both to revivalism and to a form of perfectionism known as "Holiness."[87] The notion of perfectionism—of the individual's attaining a state of complete freedom from sin in this life—attained great popularity in many quarters during the early nineteenth century, and was espoused both by such eccentric communitarians as John Humphrey Noyes and by the more representative Charles G. Finney, who developed a theological elaboration of the doctrine while president of Oberlin College. It was this doctrine of Holiness which characterized, in its earlier stages, the transition of Methodism from a predominantly rural to an increasingly urban and middle-class denomination.

Holiness has been an emphasis within Methodism from its origins in the teaching of John Wesley. Wesley's unique doctrinal contribution was his doctrine of Sanctification, the "Second Blessing." Conversion, as with all evangelicals, was the first indispensable step in the process of salvation. However, the Christian could and should then move onward to a state of purity and sanctity in which all temptation to sin would be not only conquered but removed. This was a radical innovation in the context of Puritan-inspired evangelicalism, since earthly perfection had traditionally been denied even to the saints. Wesley's doctrinal combination of Arminianism, which allowed a measure of free cooperation on the part of the individual in the process of salvation, with Entire Sanctification, provided an irresistibly optimistic package to many inhabitants of the new nation who were temperamentally inclined to think not only well but rather extravagantly about their own possibilities as individuals and of those of the nation as a whole.

As the nineteenth century progressed, the moderates among the Methodists became inclined toward the "churchly" position that sanctification was a gradual rather than a sudden process, a notion somewhat akin to the Hartford Congregationalist Horace Bushnell's concept of "Christian Nurture."[88] Others, however, were strongly attracted to the more extreme position that sanctification, like traditional evangelical conversion, was a sudden and dramatic process which left the individual purified and transformed in no uncertain fashion.

This emphasis on sanctification, nurtured by such lay advocates as Phoebe Palmer in New York City, led to the emergence of a considerable movement within Methodism which was to have dramatic consequences for that denomination's subsequent development.[89] Shortly before the Civil War Mrs. Palmer and her husband began staging Holiness revivals and camp meetings, and her *Guide to Holiness* achieved enormous interdenominational popularity. In 1867 the first national Holiness camp meeting was held in Vineland, New Jersey, with the unofficial approval of the national church, and was followed by a long series of similar meetings throughout the remainder of the century. Permanent campgrounds were established in attractive locations throughout the Northeast and grew into a string of religiously oriented summer resorts for middle-class Holiness adherents.[90]

As the Holiness movement grew in popularity, however, it tended to weaken rather than to revitalize the parent Methodist Church. Extra-ecclesiastical apparatus such as journals and organizations for various specific purposes began to proliferate, and independent urban missions arose to reach the poorer clientele which an increasingly middle-class church was allegedly no longer serving. By the end of the century a number of schismatic groups, mostly in the Midwest and Far West, began to take form, and went their separate ways to become the extraordinarily complicated network of Holiness and Nazarene churches that continuously merged with and split off from one another during the earlier twentieth century. Doctrinal innovations such as the "Third Blessing" or "Fire Baptism" (sometimes followed by a whole string of further spiritual explosions) were characteristic of the more radical of these groups.[91]

What was in many ways a parallel development was also taking place in the later nineteenth century in the revivals of Dwight L. Moody and his accompanist Ira D. Sankey.[92] Moody was a shoe salesman from Massachusetts who moved to Chicago and began a career as the most influential revivalist since Charles G. Finney. He had little formal education, and showed even less respect than had the younger Finney for the niceties of Christian doctrine. Instead, he had an extraordinary talent for organization, promotion, and simple, heartfelt preaching, and soon attained international recognition through his revivalistic tours of America's increasingly populous cities and those of the British Isles as well.

Moody's message was simple. All that was necessary for salvation was a change of heart, a free acceptance of Jesus, which was open to all who wanted it. His appeal was primarily to the great numbers of displaced country people who were abandoning their farms and small towns for the lure of urban opportunity, but who understandably felt lost and ill at ease in an alien and forbidding impersonal world. Moody's promise of salvation based on a simple change of heart and the adoption of a virtuous lifestyle grounded in the traditional evangelical moralistic virtues and taboos was a source of reassurance and comfort for many, although its lasting effects in recruiting new members for urban churches was questionable. (It has been suggested that a sizable number of the members of his audiences already belonged to churches.)

The piety that emerged in the contexts of the Holiness movement and Moody's revivalism was best expressed not in doctrine and theology but in the new hymnody of this period, which was made accessible to all through a series of collections of Gospel songs that gained rapid popularity and tremendous sales. These songs received an enormous boost from the work of Moody's assistant Sankey, who served as song leader, composer, and popularizer.[93] Another major force was both the personality and the hymn writing of Fanny J. Crosby, the blind composer of over six thousand of these songs.[94] Her simple verses all stressed a piety free from theological complications, the tenderness of Jesus, and the ease with which the consolations he offered could be accepted.

A closer look at some of these hymns will illustrate their symbolic dynamics more explicitly. They stress first the helplessness of the individual, beset by sin, infirmity, and tribulation, unable to find solace in the world: "Just as I am, without one plea."[95] The individual is not only weak but also plagued by the temptations of the urban world, which offer fleeting pleasures and illusory consolation: drink, tobacco, sex, sharp business practices, and the easy negative pleasures of forgetting God and his worship. However, the sinner is not alone in suffering and misery. Jesus himself had been tempted, suffered terribly, and died an ignominious death on "an old rugged cross, the emblem of suffering and shame."

This very suffering of Jesus is the answer to the individual sinner's predicament. Particularly potent is the salvific and purifying power of his blood. Blood itself is an ancient and potent symbol, representative both of the primal life force and of the loss of that force through suffering and death. What now seems a rather grotesque emphasis on sanguinary imagery in such songs as "Fountain Filled With Blood," "Nothing But the Blood of Jesus," and "Are You Washed in the Blood of the Lamb?" makes considerable symbolic sense in the economy of salvation which these songs depict. The blood that is menacing and repulsive as a symbol of the suffering occasioned by the world's cruelty is symbolically reversed when transferred to a sacred context, and thus becomes redemptive and life-giving instead.

All that is necessary for salvation is the acceptance of the blood which the "Lamb," the archetypal symbol of innocence, has shed. This is not a harsh and demanding, but rather a simple and appealing process—"Softly and tenderly, Jesus is calling." The process, moreover, is intensely personal. What is called for is not intellectual acceptance of a set of abstract theological propositions, but rather acceptance of the entrance into a personal relationship with the tender, suffering person of Jesus. The process is so personal, in fact, that it often takes on strong erotic overtones in such songs as "In the Garden," where Jesus "walks with me and . . . talks with me and . . . tells me I am his own." (I leave it to the reader to discover other instances.)

After accepting Jesus, the converted sinner is called upon to "yield not to temptation[s]," to live a life of righteousness conceived in terms of personal purity and evangelical outreach to other individual sufferers. Maintenance of this state of purity calls for vigilance, to make sure that the newly purified body is not penetrated by the agencies of temptation and defilement. (We may note here some structural parallels with the social situation described in the case of the origins of Christian Science.) However, especially in the Holiness-oriented songs, the rewards are immediate and vivid. The convert dwells in a land of "corn and wine," a realization of the heavenly kingdom in the here and now.[96]

Although the hymns in most of these collections were written from the eighteenth century onward (with a concentration in the last decades of the nineteenth century), and arose out of a number of somewhat different theological settings, their publication together in various songbooks served to give them a sort of canonical quality among Evangelicals of many persuasions. The scenario one can derive from them as a collectivity runs roughly as follows. Rural people come to the city, attracted by opportunity and the bright lights, but uncomfortable and threatened by the impersonality and the contradiction to their sense of traditional values. They as yet lack the economic and personal skills with which to conquer the city on its own terms. Once they yield to urban temptations, however, they drastically weaken their ability to cultivate the discipline necessary for self-preservation, autonomy, and success. Their choice must be the easy consolations of intoxicants and sex, or the more enduring comforts of Jesus. The pain they experience through uprooting, psychological displacement, and lack of immediate success is assuaged by their identification with and affirmation of the sufferings of Jesus. Their renunciation of worldly pleasures is compensated through indulgence in the excitement of the revivals and by an emotional, sensual, almost erotic relationship with the suffering but tender Savior. The blood shed by Jesus represents at once the threat to life from the hostile external environment and the simultaneous preservation of life through the vicarious shedding of sacred blood. The fear of loss of self through penetration by external hostile forces is symbolized in the rejection of worldly pollutants such as stimulants and intoxicants. If Jesus' blood and tenderness are accepted, and if a straight-and-narrow path of life is subsequently followed, they will ultimately triumph spiritually and, quite possibly, succeed materially and socially as well.

This is not to say that the only audience for these songs and the accompanying set of symbols and mode of piety consisted of newly arrived and displaced urbanites. Many rural people adopted them enthusiastically as well. One reason for this common appeal may lie in the emergent urban culture considered not simply as a sociological reality but as a symbol too. Even if one lived far from New York or Chicago, one was increasingly aware of the city as the locus of pollution that was threatening the predominance of rural mores as the national norm. The Scopes trial brought this cultural clash into national prominence, and symbolized the very real shift in economic and cultural power that was gradually transforming the whole nation from an agricultural to an industrial base. The tenuous balance between *gemeinschaftlich* and *gesellschaftlich* values and styles which had characterized the Protestant era in America was now tipping rapidly toward the latter, and the image of the sinner beleaguered by hostile forces and dependent on Jesus alone for strength and consolation took on a potent general meaning.[97]

In addition to the institutional development of the Holiness movement and the revivalistic apparatus of Moody, the emergent urban middle classes also found a source of symbolic reorientation and self-interpretation in popular religious literature of a nondenominational character. During the antebellum period, *Uncle Tom's Cabin* had established the precedent for this kind of indigenous fiction, and had achieved an extraordinary success in providing Americans with a set of symbols through which they could organize their conflicting emotions about such troublesome and disorienting issues as slavery and the role of women in a rapidly changing society. In 1897, Charles M. Sheldon, a Congregationalist minister from Topeka, published another novel which would surpass even the saga of Uncle Tom and Little Eva as a basic text of popular Protestantism. By 1965 *In His Steps* had sold over eight million copies, a record for a work of fiction surpassed only by *Peyton Place*.[98]

In His Steps is generally categorized as one of the primary exemplars of a subliterary genre known as the "Social Gospel novel," but this designation is in a way more misleading than illuminating. The "Social

Gospel" movement of the late nineteenth and early twentieth centuries is best remembered today in terms of its leading spokesmen, especially Walter Rauschenbusch and Washington Gladden.[99] These men led a call for a reorientation of middle-class Protestantism away from a preoccupation with the conversion of the individual toward a concern with the redemption of the whole of society through the application of Christian ethical principles to the social and political realm. Their vision of the Kingdom of God conceived in terms of social redemption, however, lacked broad appeal in its liberal (in both the theological and social senses of that term) orientation. While what we might call the "High Social Gospel" of Rauschenbusch may have had a considerable impact on seminary education and the higher echelons of emergent denominational and ecumenical bureaucracies, it fell far short of becoming the "stuff" of popular Protestantism for most middle-class congregations.

In another sense, however, the term is a fitting description of Sheldon's orientation if it is qualified as a "Low" or "Evangelical" Social Gospel. *In His Steps,* at least at the most obvious level, deals with nothing if not social concerns. The basic theme and plot of the book revolve around a conscience-awakened urban minister's attempts to rouse his rather placid and comfortable middle-class congregation by asking them to consider what Jesus would do if he were confronted with any of the moral decisions they had to make. The general scheme of social betterment that informed such decisions, however, would have been familiar and satisfactory to Lyman Beecher. Moral betterment was to be achieved through a publisher's refusal to accept advertisements for liquor or to print a Sunday edition; through a college president's willingness to seek political office on a platform of prohibition; and through a society girl's forsaking a promising career in music in favor of gospel singing at evangelical services for the poor. Sheldon's vision of reform reflected a merger of evangelical morality and conservative Progressivism, and nowhere approached what now seem to be the rather tame but then quite radical calls for social legislation—for example, reforms in wages-and-hours laws and child labor—which other Social Gospel spokesmen were advocating.

Another peculiar characteristic of the book, as Wayne Elzey has pointed out, is that very little finally seems to come of asking the question "What would Jesus do?" in terms of immediate external results.[100] By the end of the book a fair number of the formerly idle rich (or at least prosperous) have taken to asking themselves the crucial question on a regular basis, and are living lives very much in keeping with prevailing standards of evangelical morality. However, many of them suffer serious reversals in their temporal fortunes as a consequence (the newspaper editor, for example, comes to woe at the hands of the liquor interests).

More pertinently, little if any changes occur in the lives of the vast numbers of urban poor for whose sake these sacrifices have ostensibly been undertaken. Following in the steps of Jesus apparently leads nowhere but to failure. This denouement stood in marked contrast to the more pragmatic and goal-oriented platform of the disciples of Rauschenbush and, at a later period, those of Reinhold Niebuhr.

One way of interpreting this rather surprising outcome is to view it as a continuation of the same logic we saw to be at work in *Uncle Tom's Cabin.* At one level, *In His Steps* can be read as a reaffirmation of the timeless Christian message of the Cross, the way of suffering which leads to earthly failure but ultimately to redemption in another realm. At another level, it can be seen as the attempt of a class of people which perceived itself as increasingly impotent—in this case, the middle-class Protestant clergy—to redefine success in terms that conform to its own perception of its situation in the world. Ann Douglas, in *The Feminization of American Culture,* argues persuasively that this is precisely the tactic initiated by Harriet Beecher Stowe in her earlier fiction and taken up by a covert coalition of liberal ministers and women writers and editors in the sentimental religious fiction and journalism of the later nineteenth century.[101] Although relegated by the dominant masculine culture to positions of impotence, these groups tried to turn the tables symbolically on their oppressors by depriving them of moral justification for their hegemony on worldly power.

Wayne Elzey has also advanced a compelling interpretation of *In His Steps* which presents a very different picture of Sheldon's real (i.e., his covert) message. According to Elzey, the real problem the book addresses is not so much ethical or spiritual as conceptual. The urban middle-class audience Sheldon was addressing found itself increasingly squeezed from two directions. On the one hand, the "robber barons" of the newly powerful industrial economy flaunted their contempt for traditional virtues and morals through their patterns of conspicuous consumption and their neglect of the welfare of their employees. (In fact, it is not clear whether Sheldon was attacking these *nouveaux riches* as much as he was attacking an Americanized version of the stereotypically decadent European aristocrat.) On the other hand, the cities were rapidly filling up with the untamed, the unwashed, and the unchurched of the lower orders, many of them foreign-born and incapable of conforming to middle-class standards of decent behavior. This threat from both above and below was naturally alarming to a new middle class that was not yet secure in its social and economic status in a society in which all was still flux.

According to Elzey, who uses a typology derived from the anthropologist Claude Levi-Strauss, Sheldon provided these beleaguered members of the middle class with a set of opposed images which they could utilize in order to think clearly about their situation and find comfort in it, even though they might often seem to be fighting against hopeless odds. Both upper and lower classes were exemplars of menacing vices, but each also possessed redeeming and corresponding virtues as well. The upper classes were decadent, but they were also rational and efficient. The poor were subject to excesses of animal passions, but they were also warm and spontaneous. One suffered from an excess of culture and a deficiency of nature; with the other, the reverse prevailed. What was necessary was a class that combined the virtues of both while eliminating the vices of each.

Needless to say, the middle class filled this prescription precisely. They represented what for Levi-Strauss was the golden mean which human beings have always sought after: the proper balance of nature and culture. Jesus, the mediator between the divine and human who incorporated both these realms of being into his own nature, was the natural symbol for this balance—hence, one only needed to follow "in His steps." Whatever misfortunes might befall the middle class thereafter, they could rest secure in the knowledge that their way of life alone represented the true course prescribed by God for humanity to follow, a mixture of intelligence and self-control with human warmth and kindness. Their triumph might prove more intellectual than political, but at least the universe made sense.

A final aspect of the emergence of popular Protestantism among the American middle class which deserves at least a passing mention is the emergence during the early twentieth century of a distinctive genre of devotional iconography and artifacts. Nineteenth-century Evangelicalism had inherited the iconoclasm of its Puritan forebears, and American Protestantism consequently had developed little in the way of an indigenous artistic expression. The increasing interest in church architecture which began with the Episcopal Church and spread to other denominations during the nineteenth century, together with a general rediscovery of European and especially Catholic culture, helped prepare the groundwork for a revival of religious art at a variety of levels. (The phenomenon of Baptist Norman and Methodist Gothic churches was a sign of this general trend.) Another source of inspiration at the popular level was the Pennsylvania Dutch tradition of folk art, including samplers with pious mottoes for hanging on the wall. (Laminated plaques reading "God Bless Our Mobile Home" may well be direct descendants of this earlier pietism.)

The major influence of popular Protestant religious art, however, was probably the sentimental didactic painting of the Victorian period which was made widely available through such means of mass distribution as the chromolithograph. Such now-familiar scenes as "The Good Shepherd," with Jesus minding a flock of real sheep, or "Heart's Door," with Jesus aglow in light, holding a lantern, and knocking at a rather medieval-looking entranceway, are squarely in the popular tradition of which pre-Raphaelitism was the "high" expression. Although most of this work was presumably the product of commercial artists, it stands in the folk tradition in its anonymity.

Only a later work, Warner Sallman's "Head of Christ" (1924), is generally associated with a specific artist, although little seems to be known about him beyond his name. Despite its late date, however, the Sallman work is very much in the style of the earlier popular tradition. It depicts a Jesus whose idealized, non-Semitic features are highlighted against a dark background in a probably conscious echo of the style of the later Renaissance. The long hair and gentle features evoke a sense of androgyny, if not femininity, and Jesus seems more liminal than distinctively sexual. (Jesus' period costume of a long robe further accentuates his indeterminate sexuality.) The long popularity of this style, which now seems to be complemented but not displaced by a more contemporary idiom, testifies to the conservatism of popular art. Sallman takes his place with N. C. Wyeth and Norman Rockwell as a major contributor to the development of a popular American style, and it is likely that his mass-produced and -distributed artifacts will continue in their popularity for many years to come.[102]

ALTERNATIVES TO URBANIZATION: PENTECOSTALISM AND THAUMATURGY

Christian Science, Methodist Holiness, Moodyite revivalism, and the Evangelical Social Gospel novel were all attempts of the newly forming middle strata of America's cities to create a symbolic interpretation of their experience. Although each movement expressed a tension between its adherents and the society into which they were gradually becoming integrated (a process in many cases abetted by their religious practices), their fundamental orientation, at least at a covert level, was toward acceptance of that society. None of these movements seriously attempted to withdraw from society or to predict its imminent end as part of the divine scheme. Rather, that society could be made habitable for Christians once its structures were modified or, more usually, once the individual believer was sufficiently modified in thought, deed, and feeling to be able to resist the temptations and trials that surrounded him. These movements were, in short, geared to the needs and expectations of an emergent urban middle class.

For many who were neither urban nor of the middle class, however, these strategies had little to offer in their original forms. Many Americans still lived in rural areas or small towns, and had neither the desire nor the opportunity to move to the cities. Many of these, together with some of their urban counterparts, had no realistic hope of ever attaining the comforts of middle-class life. The benefits of modern science, medicine, and technology were denied them, and the idea that progress and reform could combine with these forces to create a pleasant, orderly, and optimistic world in which they might thrive till it came time for them to return happily to their Maker seemed irrelevant and foolish. Although Pentecostalism and its offshoot, the faith-healing movement which followed the Second World War, were not entirely confined to the urban and, especially, the rural poor,these were in fact the people who formed its natural constituency.

Pentecostalism was the true successor in many ways to the enthusiastic movements that had characterized the religion of the frontier during the first two Great Awakenings.[103] Although the geographical frontier had come to an end in 1890, America was by no means lacking thereafter in areas characterized by a marginal civilization, midway between order and chaos. Black in-migrants to urban areas following the First World War left behind them the emotional comforts of family and familiar surroundings to begin anew, in the socially disorganized ghettos of Harlem, Chicago, and Los Angeles, and found apt expression of that disorientation in the store-front churches and cultic groups that proliferated there. Appalachia remained at the margins of American life, and its white residents forged an interpretation of their experience in the tiny sects that proliferated in rural Tennessee and West Virginia. Still other whites, better off materially and at least minimally educated, sensed that the life of farming and decent evangelical values in which they had been nurtured was rapidly yielding to the new civilization of the cities that lured away their sons and daughters in increasing numbers.

It was in these interstices of society that the new movement took root and then flourished and spread. Pentecostalism had forerunners in England during the nineteenth century and on a small scale among the American Shakers, but it did not reach "critical mass" in this country until around 1900. It originated in the wake of the Holiness movement first in the Midwest, then in the South and on the Pacific Coast. From the small towns and farming country of Kansas and North Carolina to the Los Angeles ghetto, the movement grew spontaneously, manifesting itself in scattered sites and small churches and sectarian groups until it reached national and eventually international proportions. Many middle-class people became attracted to the movement and provided leadership, theology, and institutional structures, but it always flourished most intensely among the socially dispossessed. (For example, it has attained widespread popularity in our own time among the Puerto Rican immigrants of New York City.) It continues to increase at a prodigious rate in Latin America, and may well be called *the* popular religious movement of the twentieth century, not only in the United States but throughout the entire Western world.

Pentecostalism emerged in the context of the Holiness movement which had grown out of Methodism during the second half of the nineteenth century. Where Holiness had been something of a doctrinal innovation, Pentecostalism was instead a sort of restorationist movement, a primitivistic return to the practices of the earliest Christian community. In its advocacy of the active practice of such gifts of the Spirit as glossolalia (tongue-speaking), the movement demonstrated its hunger for unmediated religious experience, for direct evidence that God was making his presence felt in each individual just as had been the case at the earliest, "strong" time of the founding of the community.

Tongue-speaking, though not the only practice of Pentecostals, is perhaps the movement's most distinctive feature. In many ways it resembles the ecstatic seizures which the more frenzied participants in the First and Second Great Awakening underwent. Individuals abandon themselves totally to the work of the Spirit, and lose all individuality in the process of participation in a greater, transcendent reality. (The trance states entered into by the shamans of the American Indians and other primitive peoples are another analogous form of ecstatic behavior.)[104] Glossolalia, moreover, is primarily an anti-structural form of symbolic expression. In the repudiation of rational discourse for the ecstatic utterance of a rapid flow of syllables with no discursive content, the forms of structured, everyday modes of communication are left behind in favor of pure, unmediated flow. Whatever communication thus achieved is at the prerational level; what is valued above all is "pure experience," uncontaminated by any attempt at interpretation or structuring.

Another aspect of the anti-structural character of the Pentecostal experience is in its organization, at least in the early phases before the movement became routinized into standard denominational forms. As in the Cane Ridge and other Kentucky camp meetings, participants of both sexes and all races were able to take an active part, even to the point of assuming leadership roles. When the Spirit was moving, no earthly structures were allowed to get in the way. What Turner calls "spontaneous communitas" was the result in its purest form.[105] The unstructured character of the meetings themselves, where ritual, liturgy, and preaching were superseded by spontaneous expressions of the Spirit, was also in keeping with the general symbolic mode of the movement.

Pentecostalism, however, was not wholly focused on glossolalia. The faith-healing movements that arose after World War II and the "gift" of being able to heal illnesses and even to raise the dead was also alleged to come from the Spirit, and to be a revival of the charismatic practices of the Apostolic Age.[106] After it had achieved some measure of organization, the movement also adopted many of the behavioral taboos characteristic of a variety of sectarian groups which we will discuss in the next section.

Perhaps the most controversial offshoots of the Holiness and Pentecostal movements are the snake-handling cults that have arisen in isolated rural communities in Kentucky, West Virginia, and other parts of Appalachia and the upper South. These meetings, which have been vividly documented in the film *Holy Ghost People,* are characterized by many of the same practices that take place in the mainstream of Pentecostal worship: tongue-speaking, gospel-singing, dancing, occasional ecstatic seizures, informal testimonials and homilies.[107] However, a difference becomes very apparent when a basket of rattlesnakes is brought out and the serpents are thrown about among the participants while they are caught up in music and dance. The same groups occasionally add variations, such as the drinking of a thimble-full of strychnine (the "salvation cocktail") or the passing of a lighted blowtorch over the face and hands.

On one level, these practices can be seen simply as an extremely literal interpretation of Mark 16:17–18, which promises that the followers of Jesus shall cast out demons, speak in new tongues, and not be harmed by taking up serpents or drinking deadly things.[108] This does not resolve the question as to why this, as opposed to numerous other passages in Scripture which raise rather serious problems when taken at face value, should have been chosen for literal adherence. One suggestion is offered by Wayne Elzey, who argues that such practices involve a symbolism of inversion.[109] Where such practices as drinking, gambling, and nonmarital sexuality fall under a taboo in daily life, structurally similar practices become positively sacred when performed in a sacred context. Thus intoxication and sexual ecstacy, though forbidden in secular life, are signs of possession by the Spirit when they seize the participant at a Pentecostal worship service. Similarly, gambling—in this case with one's life, by playing with rattlesnakes, poison, or fire—takes on a similar "positive charge" when performed in a sacred manner. The sacred, in short, carries a "plus-or-minus sign" in front of it: what is most feared in some contexts is most prized in others.

Another clue to the symbolism of the charismatic movement can be found in its social character. A striking feature of the service depicted in *Holy Ghost People* is that the people in attendance at the service were from widely scattered localities. Many had come, obviously at great inconvenience, from up to a hundred miles' distance to participate. The community, in short, had no immediate and restricted vicinal base. The snake-handlers were rejecting the principle of geographical organization, and assembling voluntarily from localities scattered over a broad district (although most, if not all, were presumably members of a common cultural group). Their attraction by a perfectionistic ideology rather than common residence thus emphasizes, along with their particular and extreme practices, their rejection of the structures of the world as sources of meaning, and their choice instead of participation in a select community constituted and bound together by adherence to self-created danger and risk. Both speaking in tongues and snake handling can thus be seen as similar rejections of the ordinary forms and cautions of the mundane world in favor of a sacred disorder and danger.

Mainstream Pentecostalism, like most such movements, has shown a tendency to lose some of its original spontaneity in its creation of national or international denominational structures. (The international and interracial character of the movement, however, are important signs of a rejection of social conventions and structures ordinarily observed rigorously by such non-Pentecostal fundamentalist groups as the Southern Baptists.) A recent interesting phenomenon has been the emergence of "Neo-Pentecostalism" among such traditionalistic, liturgical groups as Roman Catholics and Episcopalians.[110] The popularity of charismatic practices among a generally well-educated, middle- to upper-middle-class clientele makes it clear that a simple "deprivationist" hypothesis is insufficient to account for ecstatic behavior as "compensatory." A more satisfactory theory would try to take into account common structural elements in the social experience of both poor Appalachians and sophisticated suburbanites who turn to tongue-speaking and other "gifts of the Spirit" as an appropriate and gratifying form of religious expression. We might suggest that both groups find their social experience inadequate and constricting, although in different ways. Both feel trapped within rigid structures from which there is no easy escape, while only one group actually experiences economic deprivation. Ecstatic behavior, then, with its rejection of the ordinary structured worship of the established churches and its substitution of unstructured experience in place of liturgy, provides the kind of symbolic expression that corresponds to this mutual longing to escape from the realm of the mundane into the spontaneous communitas of the sacred realm. (Another way of putting the matter is in the paradox that those who find structures chaotic sometimes find chaos structuring. In other words, those who fail to find meaning in the ordinary structures of life, including worship, may find it instead in an escape into ecstatic behavior.)

The Pentecostal revival that began to sweep first the South and then enclaves of displaced Southerners in the cities of the North and the West following the Second World War was characterized not only by the hitherto primary phenomenon of tongue-speaking, but by a new emphasis on thaumaturgy or "faith healing."[111] This preoccupation was by no means novel in the history of religion. During medieval times, various prayers and sacramentals were regarded as possessing miraculous curative properties, and pilgrimages to the sites of saints' relics were a primary devotional form with explicitly thaumaturgical ends. (Such pilgrimages are still popular forms of Catholic piety.) In England, in addition, the touch of the king was said to be efficacious in dealing with scrofula and kindred ailments, and the cult of royal healing was naturally welcomed by the Stuarts as an additional legitimation of their political and dynastic claims.[112]

With the increasing confidence generated in a scientific medicine beginning around the seventeenth century, reliance on folk remedies and various forms of faith healing became increasingly relegated to the remotest and most poorly educated of the English, and it seems unlikely that genuinely magical folk healing was ever very popular among most American colonial rural folk. (Many poor white Southerners, however, became clients of the indigenous black equivalents of conjure-men and witch doctors in their dispensation of voodoo cures.)[113] Although organized medicine remained generally inefficacious and even dangerous until late in the nineteenth century, the *belief* that medicine was superior to folk practices seems to have prevailed considerably earlier.[114] Herbal remedies doubtless were part of common lore, but for the most part, they fall into the category of empirical rather than symbolic cures.

"Faith healing," which is probably the best-known sort of modern-day thaumaturgy through the enormous publicity modern mass media have made possible, began to emerge in the work of such evangelists as Aimee Semple McPherson during the 1920s, but did not come into its own as a major religious force until after the Second World War.[115] The clientele of such healers as William M. Branham, A. A. Allen, and the younger Oral Roberts was largely recruited from the dispossessed poor whites, both urban and rural, of the postwar South, although some attracted a sizable black constituency as well. For such people, basic physical health was (and often still is) a matter of pressing concern, since sophisticated medical (not to mention psychotherapeutic) resources remained beyond their financial ability or even their knowledge. Also, we should stress that the interconnection between mental, physical, and, more broadly, spiritual "wholeness" is still only dimly understood by the medical profession, and we have already seen how Mexican-American *curanderos* possess an efficacy in dealing with borderline disorders which eludes their more sophisticated medical contemporaries (or rivals). Although some of the claims and procedures of the more extreme healers may arouse a just skepticism in the "scientific" onlooker, it would be well to remember that genuine healing usually presupposes a receptivity on the part of the afflicted based on a firm will to live, which no medical technology can ever wholly supersede or provide by itself.[116]

The more temperate of the healing preachers, such as Oral Roberts (who abandoned his Pentecostal Holiness background to affiliate with the Methodists in 1968), refrained from making excessive claims either for the unfailing efficacy of their work or about the role they themselves played in the mediation of divine, healing grace.[117] They acknowledged the limitations and occasional failures their approach involved, and urged their clients to consult physicians as well. They saw their role, in short, as both ecclesiastically and scientifically ancillary; their work was intended to supplement rather than displace that of the ministers and doctors available through ordinary institutional channels.

Others, however, were not so circumspect, and reveled in claims to work outright miracles. Their implicit message was that mainstream society and "approved" patterns of thought and scientific procedure had bypassed or disappointed them; in reaction, they would take their stand outside both the natural and social orders, and therby achieve the wholeness denied to them by a hostile and alienating outside world. The Pentecostal appeal for the revival of New Testament "gifts of the Spirit" was a perfect symbolic vehicle for this stance. Jesus had clearly repudiated both the established orders of nature and society in his preaching and thaumaturgy, and dramatically held out for his followers the possibility of an alternate and infinitely better Kingdom.

The gamut of wonders worked by these latter-day thaumaturges ran from the bizarre to the brazenly exploitative. Healing miracles were, of course, the principal stock in trade. Cancer, which has taken on in recent decades an aura of almost diabolical mystery and has become a metaphor for uncontrollable and insidious corruption of any sort, was one of the most popular matters for curing. Many other diseases were cured as well, and the extraordinary A. A. Allen claimed to have healed, among other things, a case of hermaphroditism.[118] Many of the more extreme evangelists stressed their role as exorcists, and performed their cures through the casting out of the demons allegedly responsible for both mental and physical illness (presumably in imitation of the archetypal Christian thaumaturge of the Lukan Gospel). Even more spectacularly, these healers resurrected occasional clients from the dead, and William M. Branham once added an extra touch by bringing a deceased fish back to life.[119]

As with some of the black cultic leaders such as Sweet Daddy Grace and Father Divine, the radical healers made explicit or implicit claims to divine powers dependent on their own persons, and often used their status to exempt themselves, at least covertly, from the usual niceties of ethical behavior. Some were clearly alcoholics, while others lost credibility when they themselves succumbed to sickness or death.[120] Branham represented an eccentric but slightly less extreme departure from orthodoxy in his espousal of the "Jesus Only" position, thereby denying the Trinity, and not too subtly hinted that he himself occupied a special place in the dispensation of divine prophecy.[121] After his death he became the object of a cult among some of his disciples, and was believed by some either to be God and/or to be about to rise from the dead. A curious technological variant on the medieval cult of relics has manifested itself in the circulation of tapes of his sermons among his followers, presumably in the belief that they could perpetuate or recreate the charismatic powers of the living master himself.[122]

At the other end of the social spectrum, a very different application of religion to therapeutic practice characterizes the lay ministry of Ruth Carter Stapleton, sister of President Jimmy Carter. Stapleton's "gift of inner healing," as she calls it, involves the invocation of mental images of Jesus as a parent-surrogate during individual or small-group sessions of psychotherapy. She has run into considerable opposition from other Southern Evangelicals mainly on two grounds: first, that she is female, and, second, that her healing is not biblically grounded. What seems to underlie both of these objections is a question of boundary maintenance and erosion. On the one hand, a woman's assuming an active ministerial function can be seen as a violation of various New Testament injunctions to the contrary. (Southern Evangelicals have been far more resistant than Northern groups to the ordination of women.) On the other, Stapleton's technique is suspect because it borrows heavily from mainstream, though not heavily Freudian, therapeutic practice, and thus violates a cultural taboo against assimilation of "scientific" orientations into religious practice. Although her vocabulary is in considerable measure that of her Evangelical background, the content of her practice owes considerably more to Carl Rogers than to Billy Sunday.[123]

One important point about such activities as witchcraft and thaumaturgy raised by Keith Thomas might be repeated here. Since these malevolent or benevolent uses of "magic" can never be fully confirmed or disconfirmed empirically, confidence in them can last as long as they serve a purpose, whether explanatory or therapeutic, that is not provided elsewhere.[124] The frequent failures of faith-healers can always be written off to lack of sufficient faith on the part of the sufferer, to God's inscrutable purposes, or to other ultimately unverifiable causes. Witchcraft has a similar dynamic, and belief in it is buttressed by its self-fulfilling character. If people geniunely believe that they have been bewitched, they may suffer or even die as a result. It is only when a scientific worldview becomes plausible on a sufficiently broad and immediate level that resort to providential explanations, witchcraft, and thaumaturgy begins to wane.

WITCHCRAFT AND COUNTERSUBVERSION

Pentecostalism and its offshoot, faith healing, were two symbolic modes whereby the disinherited attempted to express their exclusion from the historical process and to come to terms with their situation in acceptable fashion. Pentecostalism was essentially a new version of the theme of anti-structure. It reflected in its repudiation of logical discourse a disenchantment with all socially imposed structures and conventions, and a hunger to return to a more basic reality in which those forms counted for nothing. Faith healing, similarly, was simply the latest of a venerable line of thaumaturgical systems in which the desire for immediate and highly particularistic results obscured more comprehensive theological concerns. The two intimately related movements, though expressing themselves through very different symbolic modes, nevertheless shared a sense of immediacy, a desire to break through the barriers that had cut their adherents off from what they perceived to be the material and emotional satisfactions of the "haves." If society rejected them, they would seek acceptance from God and a sense of his immediate presence in the form of the Spirit. If doctors failed to heal them and hospitals turned them away, they would seek healing from the source of all health and life instead.

As we have observed with regard to the phenomenon of Neo-Pentecostalism, however, it is dangerous to attribute religious expression simply to material deprivation, or even relative deprivation, as the major causal factor. As scholars such as Wayne Elzey (following Claude Levi-Strauss) have argued, an even more fundamental category of malaise which often expresses itself in religious and other symbolic forms is cognitive distress. Comparative cultural studies demonstrate that the level of material abundance necessary to sustain life and induce a sense of well-being is indeed minimal. This latter sense is in fact relative to actual possibilities and, perhaps more important, levels of expectation. What most people cannot tolerate for extended periods is the lack of a satisfying framework through which they can make sense out of what they perceive to be inequity or other misfortunes. Much can be endured if it can be interpreted and experienced as part of a larger whole, in which all is fundamentally well despite occasional, or even frequent, breaches of order and justice. What renders even minor ill fortune intolerable is the lack of such a cognitive framework, where no order is apparent, and existence is reduced to a series of random acts of meaningless violence.

One symbolic modality for dealing with incongruity and misfortune in the face of the breakdown or absence of more comprehensive and abstract systems of explanation is the belief in witchcraft.[125] Witchcraft seems to be nearly as old as human society itself. Although some peoples, such as the African, seem especially prone to a preoccupation with witchcraft beliefs, virtually all primitive and peasant groups have their version of the practice.[126] An increase in witchcraft preoccupation seems to correlate also with rapid and disturbing social change of particular sorts, and the relevance of this aspect should become clear as we examine the proceedings at Salem more carefully.

The Salem "witch hunt" was actually the last gasp of a veritable mania of witch hunting that swept over both Protestant and Catholic Europe during the sixteenth and seventeenth centuries.[127] Witchcraft and allied magical practices had lived a sort of half-life throughout Christian Europe during the Middle Ages without ever attracting a great deal of attention, despite occasional clerical attempts to suppress or punish particular cases through whose malevolent exercise serious harm was thought to have been done. However, on the Continent, agents of the Inquisition during the late fifteenth century constructed an elaborate mythology of witches' Sabbaths and pacts with the Devil out of confessions extracted under torture, and their bizarre fantasies attained enormous popularity during the ensuing centuries. England, where judicial torture was never permitted, was virtually alone in escaping the mania, which resulted in the torment and death of thousands upon thousands, mostly of old, outcast women, during this period of frenetic religious and social dislocation. (Scotland succumbed to the witch craze; England did so only briefly during the interregnum, when traditional legal restraints were suspended and Matthew Hopkins, the notorious Witch-Finder, worked his baleful work.) What happened at Salem, in short, was a Colonial addendum to a much more general social fever and was very limited in its effects, duration, and direct consequences.

There seems to be little doubt that some forms of witchcraft were actually practiced in both Old and New England during the sixteenth and seventeenth centuries. This has been both substantiated by historical research and rendered plausible by a consideration of the persistence of the folk heritage even among peoples well started along the road toward modernization. The increase in witchcraft trials in England during this period is illuminative of the general process of social transformation that was taking place in contemporary English rural life.[128] Most of the accused were poor, socially marginal, often widowed old women who were forced by necessity to beg and borrow frequently from their neighbors. The medieval social code had made such neighborliness mandatory as a Christian duty. However, the displacement of this code of indiscriminate charity was gradually yielding to the Puritan notion of individualistic self-help and good works oriented toward the edification of the ambitious and godly poor. The clash between these two ethics, together with the absence of a comprehensive program of public poor relief, generated a sense of ethical confusion among many of the villagers who managed to scratch out a living but had little surplus to bestow. These people were inclined in any case to favor the sanctions of the new order as a pretext for abandoning the traditional constraints and obligations of village neighborliness. Their residual guilt feelings, however, often seized upon any minor (or major) misfortune that occurred to them after they had turned such a crone away from their door, empty-handed, grumbling, and possibly muttering dire imprecations, as evidence of witchcraft. This judgment would often be sustained by their peers, and the unfortunate woman might well be punished as a witch.

In New England, witchcraft sustained itself through the combined heritage of English folk belief and some new elements introduced by West Indian slaves. The actual occasion of the witch craze of 1692 lay in the accusations by several young girls temporarily rendered hysterical through some dubious adventures with the prediction of the future, itself a common form of traditional folk magic. Chadwick Hansen has written a persuasive account of the actual psychological mechanism of hysteria in his *Witchcraft at Salem* (1969); he leaves the reader with little doubt that a genuine fear of witchcraft based on its actual practices existed, and that the hysterical symptoms were in fact authentic.[129]

The problem, however, is why the most learned ministers and judges of the Bay Colony should have been temporarily caught up in the hysteria themselves, and why the whole community should have proceeded to such drastic action on the basis of what seems to us today the flimsiest of evidence.[130] The first question may be answered in two ways. First, as we have seen, belief in the Devil and in his traffickings with ordinary folk had by no means been banished even from the world picture of intellectuals by this time, though it was decidedly on the wane in many quarters. Secondly, and more relevantly, the whole colony was in a crisis, since its charter had been suspended and its very status as a sociopolitical unit based on a distinctive and exclusivist ideology was in serious doubt owing to political changes in England. The Mathers and their contemporaries easily lapsed into the ready-made symbolic answer to their specific fears and diffuse anxieties over collective survival, and were willing, at least briefly, to entertain the possibility that they were the victims of a supernatural and diabolic conspiracy. They came to their senses soon after the events had taken their course, but too late to rectify the damage that had already been done through the execution of the accused.

A preoccupation with witchcraft in the Anglo-Saxon world, however, had traditionally been much more common among the folk than with their leaders. The Salem outbreak was a genuinely grass-roots outbreak of symbolic behavior rather than an elite's attempt at some sort of social control. The key to what really happened at Salem has been provided recently in the collaborative scholarship of Paul Boyer and Stephen Nissenbaum in their *Salem Possessed: The Social Origins of Witchcraft* (1974).[131] Through a careful analysis of the concrete social setting of the accusations made at the time, these two historians have in fact unraveled in very convincing detail the sociogenesis of a seemingly irrational or inexplicable wave of behavior.

The Salem of the 1690s was not, in fact, a unified political or social entity. Salem Town, which we now know as Salem proper, was rapidly becoming a prosperous and sophisticated *entrepot* of foreign trade, and was far removed in many ways from the traditionalist village mentality in which witchcraft and accusations were likely to flourish. The residents of Salem Village (now Danvers), however, were not nearly as fortunate as their more cosmopolitan neighbors. Their village was a rather anomalous affair. It had in 1672 become a separate community from the Town, but it still lacked at the time a government or church of its own. Its layout was random, and it lacked the center which traditionally provided New England towns with their spatial, sociopolitical, and ontological orientation. Moreover, it lacked mechanisms for settling intravillage squabbles efficiently at a time when social tensions were very much on the rise.[132]

Social problems in the district were at the time becoming acute through the increasingly obvious contrast between the prosperity and autonomy of Salem Town and the disorganized, going-to-seed quality of life in the Village. The Village, moreover, was hemmed in on all sides by other municipalities and had no room to expand. It became divided into factions—namely, the more prosperous Villagers who relied on the Town for their livelihood, and those who had been left behind to a more meager existence within the confines of the Village itself. The tension manifested itself specifically in quarrels over the shaky local church, which was served by a rather unsteady failed merchant named Samuel Parris.[133]

The witchcraft accusations, after they began to emerge in the specific context of the hysterical girls, were not surprisingly seized upon most avidly by the supporters of Parris. These were themselves the victims of a rapidly developing social change from a traditionalist to a capitalistic economic order that was leaving them stranded in the wake of Salem Town's progress. Their victims, however, were not those Villagers who were themselves the most wealthy and successful. Such a course presumably seemed too obvious even at the subconscious level to be sustained for very long. Rather, the accused tended to be marginal people, such as the tavern-keepers along the Ipswich Road, who made their livelihood not from the Village but depended rather on the increasing commerce and travel which the new order in the Town was generating. Others of the accused included those who had fallen on the hardest of times, the analogues of the dispossessed old widows in English villages who often were said to be witches, as well as other, more prosperous folk whose increase in fortune was implicitly perceived as the result of their allegiance to the life and values of the Town rather than the Village.[134]

What thus seems to have taken place at Salem is a veritable textbook illustration of the witchcraft typology developed by Mary Douglas in the first edition of her *Natural Symbols* (1970). According to Douglas, symbolic behavior of various sorts tends to correlate with specific types of social structure (or lack thereof). The kind of society in which witchcraft accusations flourish is characterized by Douglas as possessed of "low grid" and "high group."[135] By grid is meant a coherent sense of order and hierarchy among a society's members, the kind of explicit structure based on ascribed status usually found in feudal communities. The social disorganization represented by the emergent proto-capitalistic order of Salem Town, where status was based on achievement rather than ascription and traditional roles were no longer either stable or normative, was clearly wreaking havoc among the Villagers. These latter were becoming increasingly the victims of the new order, and lacked the security of an established traditional society into which to retreat. (We should remember here that Salem Town was a sort of "liminal" entity, neither formally organized community nor frontier wilderness, in which mutual relationships, obligations, and lines of authority were never clearly drawn or recognized.)

"Group," on the other hand, involves a sense of belonging to a clearly defined social unit, at least in terms of ethnic and/or geographical boundaries. Thus, just as "grid" in Salem Village was clearly minimal, a strong sense of "group" was inescapable because of the hemmed-in character of the Village's physical location. Its situation was clearly claustrophobic. Urban people had opportunities for new livelihoods provided by the sea, and an increasing anonymity which removed their private concerns from the public domain. Genuinely rural people, if discontented with their lot, still had the opporunity to illustrate the Turner "frontier thesis" by pulling up stakes and heading out toward Northampton and Stockbridge. The Villagers, however, were caught in the middle. They had nowhere to go, either geographically or economically, and became increasingly turned in upon themselves, unconsciously looking for a scapegoat through which their misfortunes could be explained and their claustrophobia relieved. At least in retrospect, witchcraft accusations were an obvious answer.

Except perhaps in some isolated zones of extreme cultural lag, the belief in witchcraft receded to the point of disappearance in the centuries following the Salem trials. However, the basic symbolic activity of witchcraft is simply the most explicit and obvious exemplar of a form of symbolic activity that has by no means vanished from American life. In situations of cultural confusion and social stress similar to that of Salem during the 1690s, misfortune has continually been attributed to sources which for all intents and purposes are identical with witchcraft, and it is by no means accidental that certain rather odious forms of political activity are still referred to as "witch hunting." The perennial desire to impose order upon chaos by blaming the latter on internal agents in league with powerful, insidious, and perhaps superhuman external agencies did not die at Salem, and the determination to rid the social body of these agents continues to the present day.

David Brion Davis has provided a term by which these latter-day campaigns to rid the land of "witches" may be conveniently designated: "countersubversion."[136] The movements to which Davis explicitly gives this name—the campaigns against Masons, Mormons, Catholics, and Southern slave-holders which took place during the middle span of the nineteenth century—are essentially identical in their basic structure to witchcraft and witch hunting. All involve the perception of a conspiracy to undermine the structures and values that underlie American society through the allegiance of a particular group with insidious external agents bent on the subversion of that society. Whether those agents are material—e.g., the papacy— or supernatural, as in the case of witches in league with the Devil, is not really very important. What matters is that internal problems, usually the result of role confusion and the perceived lack of clear lines of authority, are attributed to the conspiratorial alliance of disloyal "insiders" with malevolent "outsiders." The solution advanced to this problem is usually a call for the destruction or banishment of the guilty insiders, who are thus transformed into "scapegoats."

As Davis has pointed out, the basic structure of "countersubversion" has remained unchanged through centuries of American experience, while the objects of accusations of conspiracy have varied enormously.[137] During the Colonial period, Puritan fears of the Roman Catholic Church, which it identified with the Anti-Christ, provided the main focus for such fears. Since Catholics were virtually nonexistent in New England, the symbol of the Pope as the agent of Satan led to little if any actual countersubversive activity, although it did provide a convenient means of instilling and maintaining group loyalty through the creation of a common negative identity.[138] During the Revolutionary period, anti-Catholic sentiment faded in the face of the new political alignment with Catholic France, and King George instead assumed the dubious role of chief satanic conspirator. Americans thus severed themselves from their traditional identification with Britain as the home of liberty and the new Chosen People, but this did not seem to cause great anxiety to the formulators of the new symbolic system through which providential destiny was utilized to legitimate political action.[139]

After Independence, new sources of conspiracy had to be sought out in order to provide potential countersubversives with an enemy on whom the responsibility for the anxieties created by a not as yet fully formed and ordered society could fall. Lyman Beecher, for example, was wont to accuse both French Jacobins and Roman Catholic Jesuits as fomentors of conspiracy, unlikely bedfellows indeed. For a time the Bavarian Illuminati were viewed with alarm, but a more likely (and real) bearer of the Enlightenment tradition was found in the Masons. Freemasonry, whose members had included such improbable conspirators as Washington and Franklin, was subject to suspicion on two grounds: it made a great deal of the secrecy of its ritual, and, perhaps more important, its membership was drawn almost exclusively from what many perceived to be the more privileged orders of society. Aristocracy had been the enemy during the Revolution, and the Masons now seemed to be aspiring to play the same role, an intolerable one in a militantly egalitarian society. Anti-Masonry actually coalesced into a serious political party for a brief period, but in the long run the movement dissipated itself, and the Masons gradually evolved into simply another middle-class fraternal organization.[140]

More serious, perhaps, was the increasing anti-Catholic sentiment which found political expression in the Know-Nothing Party (which briefly controlled several state legislatures and other political offices).[141] The underlying social causes of the nativism (or fear of the foreign-born) which this party and its successors represented were in many ways economic, since the influx of Irish and later Southern and Eastern European immigrants represented a threat to the jobs of many native-born American workers. (The same process would later take place on the West Coast in the opposition to and subsequent restriction of immigration from the Orient.) Protestant leaders such as Lyman Beecher were also uneasy about the potential threat to American political and religious institutions which they saw in these hordes of poorly educated and unacculturated men and women who seemed ripe for direction from Rome.

Some of the more extravagant expressions of this fear took as their focus the mystery that seemed to surround the celibate clergy and nuns and the cloistered precincts in which they resided. Works with such lurid titles as *Jesuit Juggling, Secrets of Nunneries Disclosed,* and *Rosamund; or, a Narrative of the Captivity and Sufferings of an American Female under the Popish Priests in the Island of Cuba* achieved a wide circulation, and regaled the reader with such stories as that of "a clerical plot to capture negro boys, kill them, and grind them up into sausage meat."[142] Davis has aptly pointed out that the authors of these books delighted in detailed descriptions of sex and sadism, enjoying the satisfaction of attributing their practice solely to the enemies of the Republic.[143]

Perhaps the best known of these works was Maria Monk's *Awful Disclosures of the Hotel Dieu Nunnery of Montreal* of 1836.[144] Maria Monk, who subsequently came to an ignominious end, claimed that she had escaped from a Montreal convent at which she and her sisters had been compelled to enter into sexual relationships with depraved priests. After the nuns had borne their children, the priests, she said, would administer baptism, then strangle the unfortunate infants and bury their remains in the convent cellar. The fact that her allegations were demonstrated to be baseless did little to dampen the popularity of her work and that of her many successors. Although her adventures were pure fabrication, they contributed to an increase in the tensions that had already led to the burning of the Ursuline convent in Charlestown, Massachusetts in 1834 and would erupt in anti-Catholic rioting in Philadelphia during the following decade.

Mormonism provoked a similar response that was also to culminate in violence.[145] The esoteric character of Mormon revelation and the group's propensity for withdrawing into separatistic communities combined with the unorthodox (and, to "Gentiles," rather titillating) practice of polygamy to provoke hostile responses, first by the armed mobs who assassinated Smith, and later by the federal government itself. The Mormons were eventually pressured into abandoning polygamy, and ironically have come to embrace the norms and mores of "mainstream" American culture in an exaggerated form.

Countersubversive activity received new impetus after the Civil War from the "new immigration" which flooded the cities of the East Coast with Europeans unaccustomed to American ways.[146] Their attitudes toward alcohol and ready allegiance to political bosses who looked after their immediate material needs in a way Yankees were unable or unwilling to do aroused considerable anxiety among many of the native-born. The crusade for Prohibition, which eventually culminated in the Eighteenth Amendment and the Volstead Act at the end of the First World War, was brought about by an alliance of liberal and conservative Protestants (with the help of some of the more assimilation-minded members of the Catholic hierarcy.)[147] Although these people as a group can hardly be characterized as exemplars of the "paranoid style in American politics," their attitude toward the consumption of alcohol—and their implicit condemnation of traditional European Catholic folkways—displayed some of the characteristics of "countersubversion." The extravagant propaganda prepared by such groups as the Women's Christian Temperance Union, which recounted rather doubtful anecdotes about whiskey-sodden men bursting into flames after lighting a match, implicitly attributed to alcohol a virtually demonic power that was irresistible to mere mortals. This notion of a fascinating, insidious alien force which could corrupt even the virtuous bore a striking resemblance to that attributed to the Catholics, Mormons, and other enemies of an earlier time, as well as to the characteristics that would later be attributed to Communism in the 1950s and marijuana in the following decade.

During the twentieth century, countersubversives have formed an odd fellowship indeed. The Ku Klux Klan, one of the durable of such organizations, was originally organized during the years following the Civil War, and then emerged again in more virulent form during the 1920s.[148] Its program of opposition to blacks, Catholics, and Jews attracted many who were sympathetic as well to the Fundamentalist movement, and it spread far beyond its native South to attain major political power in Indiana and other midwestern states. The Klan's tactics of secret activity and its love of elaborate ritual illustrate one of the points Davis has made about earlier countersubversive movements—viz., that their tactics ironically ape those of the subversive movements which they are supposedly counteracting. Only conspiracy, it would seem, is capable of combating conspiracy.

The rhetoric of the Klan is also illustrative of another major feature of the symbolic preoccupations of countersubversives. Their stress on ethnic and racial purity is an example of the microcosm-macrocosm parallel discussed earlier in the context of "Ghetto Catholicism" (which was, ironically, one of the Klan's principal enemies and targets). Following Mary Douglas, one might well argue that the classic "strong group–weak grid" typology characteristic of witchcraft societies is the dominant symbolic theme at work here. The preoccupation with fears of penetration from without is also readily susceptible to Freudian analysis, which a group of psychiatrists have provocatively applied to the similar symbolic behavior of contemporary groups opposed to the fluoridation of public drinking-water supplies.[149] Perhaps the best treatment of the whole syndrome has been done by the film director Stanley Kubrick, whose psychotic General Jack D. Ripper in the film *Doctor Strangelove* is preoccupied with the contamination of his "precious bodily fluids."[150]

Dr. Strangelove is basically a satire on the excesses of the right-wing obsession with Communism which cast a baleful shadow over much of the political activity of the 1950s. (It has been observed that science-fiction films of the period, such as *The Invasion of the Body-Snatchers,* [1956] also dealt with the theme of invasion by enemy aliens.)[151] Ironically, the most conspicuous exemplar of the anti-Communist crusade was Senator Joseph McCarthy of Wisconsin, a Roman Catholic who received at least tacit support from several prominent members of his Church's hierarchy.[152] One of the major motifs of McCarthy's campaign was that of internal subversion, the allegation that the Army and the State Department were being infiltrated by Communists or their sympathizers who were passing on military and diplomatic secrets to the enemy. It is ironic that many of McCarthy's allies and successors were right-wing Fundamentalist ministers such as Carl McIntire and Billy James Hargis, who can scarcely be described as sympathetic toward Roman Catholicism.[153]

Another ironic twist in the convoluted development of twentieth-century countersubversive movements has been the association of anti-Communism with anti-Semitism. Again, one of the most prominent advocates of the conspiracy theory as an explanation for the Depression of the 1930s was Father Charles Coughlin, the "radio priest" who broadcast to a national (and ecumenical) audience from his Shrine of the Little Flower in Royal Oak, Michigan.[154] Coughlin began his public career as a supporter of the New Deal, but later turned against Roosevelt and began to attack a rather doubtfully documented conspiracy of international bankers with at least implicit Jewish connections. Even more virulent advocates of this theory circulated the spurious "Protocols of the Elders of Zion" in an attempt to portray Jews as engaged in an international conspiracy. (Jews, of course, had been the targets of similar attacks for centuries, and were popularly believed during the Middle Ages to be in league with the Devil.)[155] Although many Jews in fact demonstrated sympathies with Communism during the 1930s, more recent developments in the Soviet Union have made it clear that Communist nations are at least as prone as capitalists to revive the age-old propensity for utilizing the Jews as scapegoats for their own internal difficulties.[156]

FUNDAMENTALISM AND EVANGELICALISM

As should be clear by now, the various modalities of symbolic behavior which we have been discussing are by no means separate and distinct when they become expressed in concrete historical circumstances. Their expression is by no means accidental, since each seems to appear with some degree, if not of predictability, at least of fittingness as certain social situations appear and reappear in the course of history. Certain symbols and forms of symbolic action, moreover, appear to exert an "elective affinity" for one another, and the story of popular religion can be told as the interactions of these mutually attractive symbols and their formations into clusters which historians designate as "movements."

The movement known as "Fundamentalism," which began to take shape around the beginning of the twentieth century, is a good illustration of this phenomenon.[157] Although individuals and groups have designated themselves as "Fundamentalists" (and, for that matter, continue to do so), there are only broad common emphases which all of these people share (e.g., allegiance to the "Five Points" of Orthodoxy enunciated in 1910). However, all who subscribe to even these tenets cannot be described as Fundamentalists, since many who prefer to call themselves "Evangelicals" take exception to the connotations the term carries with it.

Fundamentalism, in fact, might be described (in a very loose sense) as the "Little Tradition" which exists symbiotically with the "Great Tradition" of Protestant Orthodoxy in general and of Evangelicalism in particular. Although people styling themselves "Fundamentalists" might be found anywhere, the probability is that the better educated and more sophisticated adherents of the same set of theological tenets will designate themselves "Evangelicals" instead. "Fundamentalism" is usually associated with a set of cultural attitudes which look upon "sophistication" with suspicion or hostility. Its adherents tend to regard themselves as a subculture that constitutes a "saving remnant," loyal to genuine, traditional American values and scornful of those who have abandoned those values for "modernism." Its opponents, on the other hand, describe it as characterized by "anti-intellectualism, bad manners, and obscurantism."[158]

Fundamentalism is often associated with a rural setting, but it would be more accurate to associate it with a state of mind sympathetic to traditional rural values. As Ernest Sandeen has pointed out, its theological roots can be traced to the Niagara Bible Conferences which were conducted primarily by urban ministers during the later nineteenth century.[159] Another major source of Fundamentalist theology was the dispensationalist reading of Scripture formulated by the English sectarian John Nelson Darby and popularized in the United States through the annotated Scofield Reference Bible.[160] According to this scheme of interpretation, the sacred history of both Jews and Gentiles can be divided into a number of discrete periods, or "dispensations," each of which has been placed under a separate covenant handed down by God through which men would relate to him. The last of these, which is yet to come, is known as the Fullness of Time or the Kingdom, the Millennium in which Christ would restore the Davidic monarchy and rule for a thousand years.

This dispensational interpretation of Scripture was based on a rather strained arrangement of Biblical texts into a rigid order. This same method of literal and rationalized interpretation also underlay the other main doctrinal bulwark of Fundamentalism—namely, the "Five Points" mentioned earlier. These points, which are based on the application of deductive reasoning to various scriptural texts, include the Virgin Birth, the "Satisfaction Theory" of the Atonement, the bodily resurrection of Jesus, the verbal inerrancy of Scripture, and the authenticity of the Gospel miracles.[161] The main emphasis, in short, is on the preservation of the particularistic, supernatural elements of revelation, together with a legalistic interpretation of the soteriological transaction.

Fundamentalism, however, is much more a state of mind and a cultural configuration than a set of theological propositions. Although the Fundamentalist spirit dominates a number of loosely allied institutions, such as the Moody Bible Institute, the Southern Baptist Convention, and the Campus Crusade for Christ, it has no central organization and no really codified orthodoxy.[162] Episcopalians may (however improbably) be Fundamentalists, and many members of sects or denominations that are predominantly Fundamentalist may prefer to describe themselves as Evangelical. One may say, perhaps, that Fundamentalism is to the Baptists and similar denominations as the Holiness movement of the nineteenth century was to institutional Methodism. It is a loosely organized but reasonably coherent movement (rather than a set of structures) which dominates some institutions and plays a part in the life of others.

Another way of looking at Fundamentalism is to consider it as the coming together of a number of the motifs and symbolic modalities of popular religion that had earlier manifested themselves in America in other contexts into a new constellation. We have already seen that dispensationalism is one of the principal undergirdings. Millennialism, which is a corollary of dispensationalism, also plays a prominent part in the Fundamentalist worldview, and the idea of a "rapture" in which all the "saints" will be taken up to Heaven before the final battle of Armageddon has achieved a good deal of popularity recently. (Some 1970s bumper stickers read "The Rapture—What a Way to Go!") Countersubversive motifs have been linked with Fundamentalism from its beginnings, and radio preachers such as Billy James Hargis and Carl McIntire continue to denounce alleged Communist infiltration of liberal church groups and other American institutions. Most Fundamentalists adhere to the taboos of nineteenth-century Evangelicalism, such as prohibitions on smoking, drinking, and dancing, and some of the more extreme sectarian groups extend this emphasis to a ban on such unlikely matters as neckties[163] and bobbed hair. (This is clearly a manifestation of the tendency we saw earlier among the Amish to elevate the general cultural practices of an earlier period and a particular social class to normative sacred status.)

Fundamentalists, however, are given to expressions of anti-structure only in tightly restricted contexts. Many Pentecostals, for example, tend toward Fundamentalism in their general attitude toward scriptural interpretation and worldly "vanities," but many Fundamentalists regard Pentecostal practices as excessive. The most basic thrusts of the movement are toward boundary drawing and maintenance, fear of pollution from external sources, and a tendency toward rigidity in all aspects of both religious and secular life (if such a distinction can be drawn).

The historical context for this characterization is rooted in the clash between urban and rural values that began to polarize during the early twentieth century; we have already discussed this. It became increasingly clear that the campaign for an informal evangelical hegemony on American mores was failing. (Prohibition was perhaps its last major gasp.)[164] Many Protestants were abandoning Orthodoxy in an attempt to come to terms theologically with the modern world through Liberalism and the Social Gospel; native-born Protestants themselves were in danger of numerical and political eclipse by the increasing numbers of Catholic, Jewish, and unchurched immigrants arriving from Europe in increasing numbers. Moreover, the general dominance of a rural culture, with its stress on face-to-face *gemeinschaftlich* relationships and the initiation of the individual through conversion into a coherent, homogeneous community, was rapidly becoming eclipsed by the impersonal, heterogeneous, apparently corrupt and chaotic culture of the industrialized cities. Protestants of many different denominations and backgrounds, rural and tradition-oriented urban, began to coalesce into a common movement for self-defense.

Billy Sunday, the ball-player-turned-revivalist successor to Dwight L. Moody as the nation's most prominent evangelist, was one of the first major spokesmen for this nascent movement.[165] Sunday adopted and improved upon Moody's basic organizational strategy for urban revivals, and also retained aspects of Moody's emphasis on traditional small-town manners and values. In other ways, however, Sunday's style was significantly different from that of Moody's. Where Moody had been persuasive, Sunday was aggressive. Where Moody had been conciliatory, Sunday was openly hostile toward those persons and forces he regarded as his enemies. Where Moody had been mildly theatrical, Sunday was an outright showman. His tactics, which owed perhaps as much to vaudeville as to traditional homiletic technique, achieved considerable attention (and notoriety) in the media, and left both him and his audiences exhausted at the end of his more energetic services.

Sunday is interesting primarily as an exemplar of the curiously symbiotic relationship between Fundamentalism and the broader stream of American culture. On the one hand, he was the self-conscious exponent of the "old-time religion," a phrase that could become significant only in contrast with the emergence of "new-fangled" religion (i.e., "modernism.") He was a militant defender not only of evangelical mores, as in his aggressive advocacy of Prohibition, but also of such more "secular" values and concerns as laissez-faire capitalism, "rugged individualism," and the hyper-patriotism that swept the nation after its entrance into the war against the Kaiser. On the other hand, his style and tactics were redolent of anything but the tradition of mainstream Protestant orthodoxy. His extremely theatrical tactics, his love for contemporary slang which bordered on vulgarity, his mastery of crowd manipulation, his sizable financial gains from his revival tours, and his emphasis on publicity and statistics on those who had "hit the sawdust trail" to shake his hand (thereby presumably accepting Jesus) all pointed to his implicit acceptance of the values of the depersonalized, urban, commercial society which he was explicitly "giving hell." His success was paradoxically his ultimate failure, in that the disparity between his overt and covert messages soon became apparent to those who cared to think about them at any length. Moreover, as had been the case with Moody (and would also prove the case with Sunday's more dignified successor, Billy Graham), the "conversions" made at his revivals often proved superficial and ephemeral, and the churches that had sponsored them in the hopes of increasing their memberships gradually became disillusioned with his failure to "deliver" any enduring "goods."

After the Allied victory over the Hun and the advent of Prohibition, Sunday was ironically eclipsed in the popular eye by those secular entertainments whose style he had for a time so successfully imitated. Revivalism had for some decades served as a kind of popular entertainment. It provided a place where people could gather in large numbers to witness, and even participate in to a considerable degree through singing and "hitting the trail," a public display of edifying theatricality. (The more "elitist" and dignified "Princes of the Pulpit," such as Henry Ward Beecher in Brooklyn and Phillips Brooks in Boston, had also shared in this role.) With the advent of radio, motion pictures, and professional sports (especially baseball) during the 1920s, however, Sunday and his less successful imitators found this function denied to them in increasing measure as more and more people came to prefer their entertainment to be undiluted with piety.

Sunday's reaction to his dwindling appeal, and to the increasingly "secularized" culture that lay behind this decline, was one of increasing virulence and hostility.[166] His message had always been at least mildly nativistic (he had remarked during the World War that if Hell were turned upside down, one would find "Made in Germany" stamped on the bottom), and this emphasis grew increasingly pronounced as his following dwindled.[167] He no longer found very fertile grounds for his work in the great cities of the North, and began to concentrate his efforts in the smaller cities of the South which were more receptive to his message. His rhetoric increasingly partook of the vocabulary of countersubversion, and he began to denounce "wets," foreigners, liberals, and radicals as roughly interchangeable menaces to "the American way of life."[168] In his last years he abandoned what was left of his earlier optimism about the promise of America and began to make overtly millenarian predictions about the imminent end of the world. His own world came to an end with his death in 1935, by which time he was a nearly forgotten anachronism on the broader American religious scene.

The most dramatic and well-publicized clash between Fundamentalism and "modern culture" came in the Scopes trial of 1925.[169] The confrontation of the spokesman for the Old Order, William Jennings Bryan, and that of the New, Clarence Darrow, was itself a masterpiece of theatricality, and was carefully staged by both sides as a symbolic encounter between the two Americas. Its details are now a virtual part of American legend dramatized in the film *Inherit the Wind,* and do not need to be recounted in detail.[170] For many Fundamentalists and Liberals it became an almost apocalyptic, archetypal confrontation. The issue of the teaching in the public schools of the theory of evolution, an interpretation of human development in apparent contradiction with a literalistic reading of the opening chapters of Genesis, has remained as a symbolic touchstone in the unresolved struggle of Fundamentalism to retain a voice in the general culture late into the twentieth century.

After the ballyhoo of the Scopes trial (which had been acerbically reported for the *Baltimore Sun* by the sardonic H. L. Mencken) had subsided, Fundamentalism continued to survive in large measure as the ethos of the regional subculture of the South until the postwar Pentecostal revivals brought about a more general interest in many of its emphases. Billy Graham, a young North Carolinian who had studied briefly at the ultra-Fundamentalist Bob Jones University (then located in Cleveland, Tennessee), began his extensive career as a revivalist preaching a message of anti-Communism and pre-millennialism, but gradually came to identify with a more moderate evangelical stance as his popularity with the general population increased.[171] Graham's anti-Communist message (which was ironically shared by many prominent Roman

Catholic spokesmen of the time) was given an even more strident expression by the radio preachers Carl McIntire and Billy James Hargis, whom we mentioned earlier under the rubric of countersubversion. Fundamentalism generally attained a broader national audience during the 1950s and 1960s through its increasingly effective use of the mass media, including television, mass-circulation paperbacks, and even comic books. Its natural medium, however, was the radio.[172] Its intensity was best conveyed through what Marshall McLuhan has called a "hot medium" in which listeners can more actively involve themselves (as opposed to the "cool" medium of television, where the viewer is essentially passive.)[173]

During the late 1960s and continuing into the next decade, Fundamentalism and Evangelicalism (which, again, are often difficult to distinguish very effectively) received a new impetus on college campuses through the activities of the Campus Crusade for Christ and the older and more academically oriented Inter-Varsity Christian Fellowship. Campus Crusade, which has achieved an especially remarkable success at the time of this writing, was the creation of a California businessman-turned-evangelist named Bill Bright (formerly of "Bright's California Confections.")[174] Bright began the movement during the early 1950s on the UCLA campus, and his enthusiasm and genius for organization and fund-raising helped it to spread rapidly over the entire United States and beyond.

Campus Crusade and similar organizations have helped to rid Fundamentalism to some degree of its rootedness in the racism, nativism, and rejection of all manifestations of contemporary mores and styles that clung to it when it maintained itself primarily as the symbolic self-interpretation of the farms and small towns of the South and Middle West. However, the embracing of the "mod" style that characterizes Campus Crusade has generated some of the same dynamics of cultural symbiosis that came to afflict Billy Sunday.[175] The movement's rather uncritically individualistic attitude toward social questions has placed it in an implicit alliance with conservative and even right-wing politics. This conservatism has recently met with militant opposition by many members of the Inter-Varsity movement, who prefer to describe themselves as "New Evangelicals."[176] The Crusade's similarly uncritical rejection of contemporary Biblical scholarship, even of the sort acceptable to many Evangelicals, has resulted in an ahistorical and even anti-intellectual approach to theological questions which many Evangelicals find counterproductive. Finally, its preoccupation with numerical success and the propensity of its founder for labeling any sudden financial windfall as "miraculous" emphasize the movement's implicit acceptance of some of the more worldly norms of the broader culture to which Billy Sunday had earlier fallen prey.[177]

One of the major emphases that distinguish latter-day Fundamentalism from Evangelicalism is the former's pre-millennialist inclination. A remarkable illustration of this doctrine can be found in a series of pocket-sized comic books produced by Chick Publications and distributed widely by Campus Crusade and other groups. These books present, through a very able use of cartoon graphics, a condensed version of the major emphases of Fundamentalism, and a corresponding denunciation of other contemporary enthusiasm such as the drug culture and the peace movement. A strong emphasis is given to the necessity for making an immediate decision for Jesus, and the consequences of delay are dramatized in a sometimes terrifying fashion. A particularly compelling work in this series is entitled *The Beast,* a contemporary interpretation of the unfolding (in the modern world) of the apocalyptic events predicted in the Book of Revelation. (The "Beast," for example, arrives in Jerusalem in what appears to be a Buick Electra.)[178] A more prosaic version of this same scenario can be found in Hal Lindsey's *The Late Great Planet Earth,* in which Revelation is also translated (often through rather doubtful philological evidence) into a prediction of the beginnings of the end of the world in the political situation of the contemporary Middle East.[179]

The contradiction (or symbiotic tension) in Fundamentalism and the more extreme varieties of Evangelicalism is also illustrated in the (perhaps unkind) anecdote about the millennialist preacher who was observed planting shade trees in his back yard. (It is also apparent in "Jesus Is Coming Soon" signs engraved in concrete.)[180] Although the adherents of Fundamentalism preach an imminent end to the world and denounce worldly practices, the tactics they utilize and the values and style of life they espouse stand in apparent contradiction to the actual expectation of such a consummation. The actual message that is projected is one of ambivalence: the world is evil and doomed, but one is free to enjoy it and to plan for the future as long as one does not acknowledge the desirability of doing so. A possible resolution of this contradiction is provided in the argument that the world may escape disaster if it (and especially America) repents in time, but this eventuality (the possibility of which is the rationale for evangelism) seems unlikely. The essential logic of the movement is similar to that of Christian Science: by the eschewal of a few specific actions (moralistic taboos) and one great negation (the historical prediction of the apocalypse or the metaphysical denial of evil) one is thereafter enabled to live in the world in relative serenity, untroubled by moral ambiguity or the necessity of contemplating political and social evils as proximate rather than ultimate difficulties. To invoke a cliché, one may thereby have one's cake and eat it too.

If the distinctive literature of present-day Fundamentalism is apocalyptic, that of Evangelicalism is considerably more accommodative of mainstream American culture, though not unambiguously so. On the one hand, the basic strategy of such best-selling works as Marabel Morgan's *The Total Woman* (1975) and Cavanaugh and Forseth's *More of Jesus, Less of Me* (1976) is a harnessing of the self-improvement and "do-it-yourself" motifs of the 1950s to a Jesus-centered devotionalism. This strategy can best be described, in Bryan Wilson's term, as "manipulationist": supernatural means are invoked to achieve very this-worldly ends—e.g., sexual fulfillment, happy marriage, and a female figure harmonious with middle-class canons of desirability.

This affirmative literature, which preaches devotion and asceticism (i.e., dieting) for "inner-worldly" ends, is counterbalanced with another theme. One extremely popular Evangelical work is Dale Evans Rogers' *Angel Unaware* (1953), which deals with the life and death of her daughter, a child with Downe's syndrome. It is basically a work of theodicy, and explains how apparent misfortune actually brings with it a positive good greater perhaps than that which would have been possible under seemingly more favorable circumstances. Another adversity that has its uses is martyrdom. A particularly popular contemporary author in a genre that begins for Protestants with Foxe's *Acts and Monuments* is the Lutheran pastor Richard Wurmbrand, a Jewish convert who spent considerable time in Communist prisons. His newsletter, *Jesus to the Communist World, Inc.*, prints reports of Communist persecutions of Christians throughout the world. In addition to accounts of Russian persecution of Baptists, Wurmbrand's catalogue of publications includes the autobiography of the Roman Catholic Cardinal Mindszenty, who had been imprisoned by the Hungarian Communist regime for many years. (A Wurmbrand film consists of Bishop Sheen's interview with the Pastor.) It is clear that Communism has displaced Catholicism as the anti-Christ symbol, but it is equally clear that suffering has a positive aspect. Group identity is reinforced by persecution, and the Communists are rendering Christians an unwitting service by making possible heroic witness to the faith.

Where Fundamentalism continues to maintain an aggressive posture toward the dominant culture while actively adopting many of its values and practices, Evangelicalism seems to have taken a position much like that of pre-Vatican II Catholicism. Evangelicals in many ways are indistinguishable from most other people in their everyday styles, but nevertheless maintain an at least conceptual distance from others through a world picture derived in part from traditional Protestant and Catholic orthodoxy and in part from popular middle-class American culture.[181] A shared opposition to such common enemies as Communism and abortion has actually brought Evangelicals and Catholics into frequent cooperation, and Billy Graham's crusade at Notre Dame is a good indication of an increasing awareness of mutual purpose. While extreme Fundamentalists and Tridentine Catholics may despise one another as well as the more liberal wings of their own traditions, it seems that liberal as well as Evangelical Protestants are sensing that they may have more in common with their respective Catholic counterparts than with those who share their tradition but not their worldview.

THE "CIVIL RELIGION"

One of the most distinct features of the American experiment has been, from its very beginnings, an acknowledgement of the pluralistic character of the American people.[182] For a mixture of ideological and practical reasons, the Founding Fathers recognized that, since a wide variety of religions were already represented in the colonies at the time of their coming together into a union, none of those religions could be taken as normative. One of the grievances of the colonists against the British was the fear that the latter would attempt to install an Anglican bishop across the Atlantic, thus jeopardizing the *de facto* freedom (at least for themselves) the New England Calvinists and other dissenters enjoyed.[183] The federal government was from the beginning prohibited by the First Amendment from favoring any religion with its aid, and the last of the states to exercise this prerogative brought the practice to an end in 1832. Here was indeed something new under the sun: a nation in which corporate identity was not to be undergirded and preserved through the overt and particular supernatural sanction embodied in an official, established Church.[184]

Society, however, abhors a symbolic vacuum. Although the varied peoples who now constituted the United States of America might have been committed legally and to some degree intellectually to the *novus ordo seclorum* ("the new order of the ages"), few were content with a purely secular interpretation of collective life. It was inconceivable to most Americans that a polity could exist simply as a pragmatic device to provide such services as defense, highways, and garbage collection for the heterogeneous collection of individuals who for one reason or another found themselves living within common geographical boundaries. Pluralism might have been a political necessity or even an intellectual *desideratum,* but out-and-out secularism was (quite literally) unthinkable.

As has been widely noted, the people of the new nation had two strains of ideology at hand on which they might draw for an interpretation of their common endeavor.[185] On the one hand, the Puritan interpretation of historic collective purpose was by no means confined to New England. (Jefferson and Franklin, in fact, had proposed Exodus motifs for the new Great Seal.) The Puritan self-interpretation of a nation in covenant with God was a powerful one in that it provided a supernatural legitimation for what was in fact a voluntaristic undertaking, as well as a vocabulary and ritual for periodic reaffirmation of communal symbols and values and an interpretation of misfortunes. The frequent days of fast and thanksgiving declared by the Continental Congress during the Revolution stood in unbroken continuity with Puritan practice. King George and a corrupt British aristocracy, moreover, displaced the Church of Rome as the symbolic agent of the anti-Christ, and provided the struggle for independence with a demonology new in content but old in form.

The Enlightenment, a new intellectual force opposed in many ways to all traditionalistic religion, supplied its own vocabulary and imagery to the revolutionary struggle.[186] The very phrase "Civil Religion" has been traced to the writings of Jean-Jacques Rousseau, and that worthy's American counterparts—Washington, Madison, Jefferson, John Adams—shared in large measure his belief that civic virtue depended in some degree on religious commitment. Jefferson, himself perhaps the most hostile of the Founding Fathers to traditional beliefs, nevertheless invoked the name of the deity and the sense of a divinely ordained American mission as part of his vision of the new nation's nature and possibilities. The God of the Enlightenment was much more akin to the most general sort of providence than was the much more particularistic deity of the Puritans, but he nevertheless played an important role in the Enlightenment cosmology in which the new nation was to play a major part.

Catherine Albanese has described in some detail the metamorphosis this amalgam of ideological elements underwent when it merged with (and became a causal factor in) the historical experience of the Revolution. As in all modern revolutions, the leaders of opinion self-consciously set about creating a set of images, slogans, and rituals, of public acts and words, which would capture the public imagination and galvanize the less committed into action. The Liberty Tree took on a central place in this imagery from early on, and provided a symbolic center around which previously disorganized masses of people could be given ideological centering and purpose.[187]

The cult of George Washington that emerged during the Revolution and reached its heights during the nineteenth century is a good example of the issues involved in dealing with that aggregation of symbolism which has recently come to be called "Civil Religion."[188] In popular literature, most eminently in Mason ("Parson") Weems' extraordinarily successful *Life of Washington* (1800), the first president was virtually apotheosized, and presented not so much as simply a military and political leader but rather as a cross between an exemplary Protestant and a demigod.[189]

This cult of Washington—together, at a later date, with that of Lincoln as well—was to become a staple of the eclectic system of iconography and symbolism which would rapidly develop around the political life of the new nation. Its primary vehicle was the mass of schoolbooks which the American phenomenon of the "common" (public) school would engender.[190] The writers or editors of these books, of which the graded *Readers* of William Holmes McGuffey were the most successful, self-consciously set about not only to produce tools for the promotion of universal literacy but also to provide the new generation of readers with a set of values and an orientation toward the world that would equip them to deal with the as yet largely formless experience of growing up American.[191]

The basic attitudes these texts inculcated were evangelical and ethnocentric (a combination that often went together during the nineteenth century.) McGuffey's works, in fact, were rather mild in this regard. While on the one hand they strongly emphasized such Protestant attitudes as the "work ethic," temperance, and a belief in special providences, they nevertheless refrained from the excesses of racism and nationalism that were characteristic of many of the other works of this genre. The collective purpose of such works was to provide young people not simply with functional skills but with an entire world picture that was religious in essence and Protestant in its particular emphasis.

What is noteworthy about this whole enterprise, however, is the diffuse character of the symbols involved. Such "condensed symbols" (in Mary Douglas' sense[192]) as "predestination," "the Trinity," and "Jesus Christ" could scarcely be permitted in the curriculum of schools that had avowedly been created to serve a heterogeneous population which theoretically shared no common religious commitment. The informal strategy of Evangelicals to circumvent this difficulty was to propagate the "secondary" rather than the "primary" symbols of Protestantism. If they could not teach dogma, they could at least (and perhaps with greater long-run success) inculcate the values, the implications for daily living, that were derived from these "primary symbols." Collectively, these values came to constitute the "American Way of Life" which eventually transcended denominational and confessional barriers and became the common world interpretation of a significant majority of Americans of all origins. Among these values and beliefs were the sanctity of private property; the virtuousness of hard work in one's "calling"; individual judgment and responsibility; love of country and confidence in the providential character of the American experience. Allied to these, although less universally acceptable, were such specifically evangelical emphases as temperance and Sabbatarianism.

More specifically, however, the symbolic center of this diffuse system of religiosity was the national polity. Although the interpretation of this polity was eclectic and included elements of the universalistic rhetoric of the Enlightenment, its core can probably best be described as an ecumenical Protestant tribalism. Its heros, such as Lincoln and Washington, were presented in a distorted form which emphasized (or invented) their specifically evangelical virtues and piety, even though neither figure in actuality approximated that ideal very closely. Its interpretation of the national experience was shaped in large measure along the lines of providential guidance of national destiny, with an increasing emphasis on the inherent chosenness of the American people and decreasing attention to the judgmental aspects of the Puritan jeremiads.

The ecumenical character of this process is visible in the "canon" of sacred songs that began to accrue during the course of the nineteenth century. The (perhaps musically unfortunate) national anthem to which we still adhere tenaciously was composed by the Episcopalian Francis Scott Key, a member of a denomination that was only gradually escaping the stigma of "loyalist" it had perhaps justly acquired during the Revolution. The militant note of the anthem (all four verses of which should be read for full effect) was not typical of all of the patriotic hymns that succeeded and augmented it, but it is hardly aberrant. The next major contribution was "America" ("My Country 'Tis of Thee," ironically sung to the tune of "God Save the King/Queen"), the composition of the Baptist minister, Samuel Francis Smith, in 1832.[193] Its specifically New England imagery points to the continuing phenomenon of America's having a "double founding": the first by the Pilgrim and Puritan fathers during the 1620s and 30s, the second, and more universal, with the Constitution.

Some national hymns, such as "Hail! Columbia" have for the most part fallen into disuse. Two others, both by women, have survived to this day. Julia Ward Howe, a radically inclined Unitarian sympathizer, was the author of "The Battle Hymn of the Republic," a hymn both militant and redolent of the imagery of the Old Testament (although one of its later verses pays an at least nominal acknowledgement to Jesus).[194] The gentler "America the Beautiful," written by an English professor at Wellesley, omitted any call to arms in favor of a vision of "alabaster cities . . . undimmed by human tears." Its author, Katherine Lee Bates, was a Congregationalist.[195]

Again, one of the media through which this symbolism was propagated was the common (public) school. As Martin Marty points out, it is difficult to find quantitative verification of how extensively such religiosity was in fact expressed, but it seems probable that at this level at least it was extensive.[196] Incorporating exercises such as the flag salute, the pledge of allegiance, and the occasional recitation of portions of "national scripture" such as the Gettysburg Address, a loosely organized ritual did indeed evolve during the late nineteenth and early twentieth centuries which grew progressively more remote from specifically evangelical connotations as the nation and its schools grew unavoidably more pluralistic.

It is significant that educational systems have been a principal means for the propagation of this symbolic activity, since the process of socialization (of which education is a major component) is one of the most crucial ways in which a culture preserves and transmits itself. Education has traditionally been a highly sensitive topic for Americans, not only because of its role in the attainment of upward social and economic mobility but also because of its function as a repository of a sense of collective identity. Allied to education in this sense is the realm of athletics. Although sports have become increasingly professionalized during the twentieth century (but have by no means lost their ritual quality, as the singing of the national anthem before various contests indicates), their link with education still remains strong. The ritual encounter of two teams, usually representing two competing communities, is at one level a very basic manifestation of tribalism. The rhetorical identification of basic (and sometimes conflicting) American values such as individualism and teamwork is highly significant here, as is the persistence of an elaborate iconography (trophies, half-time shows, floats with patriotic motifs) in their performance.

At a more crucial level, however, the tribalism that underlies athletic competition is even more apparent in the phenomenon of war. The origins of "Civil Religion" in the rhetoric and iconography of the Revolution which we discussed earlier is an apt demonstration of this point. War at its most serious is nothing less than a struggle for collective survival, and such an elemental human undertaking necessarily engenders symbolic interpretation and legitimation. As in the educational process, the very survival of a culture is at stake, only in this case in more immediate and decisive fashion.

The nature and quality of symbolic response, however, has varied with the character of each particular war and the "national mood" during those times. The Spanish-American War and the War of 1812, for example, were never perceived by many to be vital to national survival, and rhetoric rather than genuine symbolic action was their typical accompaniment.[197] The Civil War was a more authentically popular conflict, and much of the nation on both sides seemed to regard it as a war with truly providential significance. (Both sides, in fact, sang "The Battle Hymn of the Republic."[198])

The world wars of the twentieth century evoked differing responses. The First World War provoked an almost hysterical outpouring of nationalist sentiment, and its major symbolic mode took the form of countersubversion.[199] Americans of German descent or birth were often in literal danger of their lives, and all vestiges of German culture were systematically suppressed or renamed. (The process through which sauerkraut became "liberty cabbage" and the unoffending dachshund was metamorphosed into a "liberty hound" is humorous only in retrospect.) Conscientious objectors took such an idealistic stance only at the risk of their physical safety, and the "Red Scare" which followed the end of the hostilities was very much in keeping with the wartime spirit. America was in the process of changing from a "pure" Anglo-Saxon Protestant rural nation to a polyglot urban people, and it is perhaps not surprising that the anxieties raised by this transformation were expressed in so militantly xenophobic a fashion.

By the time of the Second World War, much of the hysteria that had characterized the First had subsided.[200] Japanese-Americans, to be sure, were treated shabbily, but their case was in a sense more the exception than the rule. Much of the rhetoric and iconography of the conflict, though hardly subtle, was much less overtly tribal than had been that of the earlier international crisis. Perhaps the most typical propaganda tactic was that disseminated through motion pictures, which by now had become one of the most widespread and effective media for mass communication. Almost every war film had an obligatory roll-call, in which soldiers with Yankee, Polish, Italian, Irish, Jewish, and various other ethnic names were all summoned or cited. Another feature of such films was the "Why We Fight" lecture (e.g., that in *Destination Tokyo*), in which Cary Grant or a similar figure delineated the American Way of Life and contrasted it with that of the Germans or the "Japs." The emphasis, in short, was on values (or "diffuse symbols") rather than primary or condensed symbols. While the flag and other condensed symbols are still important, the focus has shifted to such concepts as democracy, pluralism, liberty, and other verbal abstractions. There is still a latent xenophobic tendency in the German-Japanese demonology, but this is undercut substantially by the necessary acknowledgment of the fact of American ethnic mixture.

The Korean "police action" and the Vietnam "conflict" were both characterized by a peculiar mixture of cosmopolitanism and tribalism. Each, at least in theory, was justified on the grounds of America's international responsibility to keep the peace and maintain liberty throughout the entire "free" world. Korea, however, was fought in the context of the McCarthyite "red baiting" of the fifties, and the polarization of the nation in which the American presence in Southeast Asia resulted is part of our immediate memory. The reversion to condensed symbolism in the 1960s and early 1970s, especially in the form of American flag decals and lapel pins (as well as flag patches for trousers, often placed in irreverent sites), was indicative of the primal nature of the emotions involved. The symbolic modes of countersubversion and anti-structure dominated rational thought about the validity of the conflict for a number of years until, seemingly, the massive expenditure of energies (and lives) exhausted all sides. It is worth noting that where the earlier 1960s had been characterized by the symbolic (as well as political) clash between "tribes" based on race and tradition (black versus Southern white), the later years of the decade witnessed a polarization along lines of age, education, and social class.

Another characteristic of the symbolism and iconography of the "Civil Religion" worth noting is its self-conscious character. Since America was a "new nation" in both a temporal and a sociological sense, it had no really indigenous body of traditional imagery on which to draw for its symbolic self-interpretation. American Indians had been cast aside as barbaric and inappropriate for symbolic use for many years, until they finally surfaced on one-cent pieces toward the end of the nineteenth century (after they were no longer a serious threat to anyone.) The nation's oldest traditions ran back only to seventeenth-century New England (Virginia, for a variety of reasons, never really captured the popular historical imagination), and even the Pilgrims were themselves a self-consciously and voluntarily assembled group rather than a "race" or a "nation."

One important aspect of the "Civil Religion" has thus been an oscillation between the assimilation and interpretation of genuinely common experiences, such as the Civil War, and the attempt to construct a usable past. The eclectic character of its symbols has been apparent from the beginnings, as we saw in the Revolutionary period. Often the symbols, especially condensed and diffuse symbols, have been in conflict. Liberty and pluralism, for example, have on repeated occasions run head-on against the implications of the flag which, despite its rather arbitrary and continually changing design, has often functioned as a tribal totem.

The late nineteenth and early twentieth centuries were a particularly fertile time for the self-conscious cultivation of the national symbolic canon, and also illustrative of the tensions and contradictions embodied in that formation. The Civil War had been a genuinely national crisis, and the casualties resulting from it far exceeded those undergone by Americans in any war before or since. The "martyrdom" of Lincoln produced a tragic hero for many. The celebrations of Memorial Day and of Lincoln's Birthday which were the result often evoked genuine communal solidarity, as W. Lloyd Warner's study of the former has demonstrated.[201]

On the other hand, the vast numbers of immigrants entering America during this period raised considerable anxieties in many as to whether these newcomers could be successfully acculturated into the American system of symbols and values. Some reactions, such as those of the immigration restriction movement spokespersons, were only xenophobic. Others, however, looked to the schools as assimilative mechanisms, and stressed the need for the development of a perhaps rather artificial common heritage. The numerous patriotic, veterans', and genealogically minded organizations that proliferated during this period were in part the result of this collective insecurity about roots and identity, and partly the sponsors of new measures for both assimilation and the maintenance of "racial purity."[202] Where earlier generations had reveled in their rootlessness and lack of a constricting heritage and tradition, many of their descendants turned instead to a cult of origins in an attempt to find a secure prototype for their identity in an increasingly confusing and pluralistic society. (As the art critic Alfred Frankenstein has remarked, "Genealogy is to New England what astrology is to California.")[203]

Finally, although much of the symbolic apparatus of the American people (or peoples) was contrived and even commercial in origin, some genuine patriotic folklore (as opposed, perhaps, to "fakelore"[204]) also arose in this period. As Lloyd Lewis points out in his undeservedly neglected *Myths After Lincoln,* motifs with parallels in traditional cultures began to cluster around the slain and increasingly apotheosized leader.[205] Many people, for example, were convinced that John Wilkes Booth had not in fact been killed by federal troops, and was still alive and living under a new identity.[206] (A number of claimants to the rather dubious title gradually made themselves known.[207]) Similarly, a considerable number of visitors to Lincoln's grave in Illinois were convinced either that the body was missing or that it had become petrified. (It had, in fact, received a very thorough embalming.[208]) Much was made over Lincoln's recurring dreams, and the legend arose that he had received oneiric warnings of his impending death.[209] More generally, an aura developed around Lincoln which elevated him to the status of a preternatural being, a divine agent or perhaps a *theios aner* (divine man).[210] The ready identification with the Christian *mythos* of the divine man sacrificially slain made this apotheosis all the easier. On the one hand, Lincoln was the American Christ; on the other, he was our indigenous

King Arthur or Zapata, absent but not destroyed. To add a dualistic dimension to the cultus, John Wilkes Booth displaced Benedict Arnold as the Judas-figure of treason, betrayal, and evil.[211]

Although the phenomenon of "Civil Religion" is by no means unique to the United States, the peculiar character of those States has given rise to an amalgam of symbolic behavior that is indeed unique. In some ways, American Civil Religion is analogous to the wide variety of strains and variants which make up any of the world religions that comprehend a wide and diverse population. At one level, theologians reflect, and occasionally agonize, about the compatibility of Civil Religion with Christianity, Judaism, or humanistic ethics. (Others, it might be added, debate as to whether such a thing as Civil Religion actually exists.) The religion's votaries—politicians, clergy, teachers, and other public functionaries—conduct the actual rites. The laity—the American public—participate with enthusiasm or indifference, and engage with varying degrees of self-consciousness in potentially devotional acts such as senior-class trips to Washington. Finally—and perhaps, in a way, most authentically—folk cults of American leaders spontaneously emerge from time to time, and range in their manifestations from supernaturalistic legends to commercialized souvenirs, verse, and what-not. (After the assassination of John F. Kennedy, a particularly egregious example of this latter category appeared in the form of a verse entitled "Special Delivery from Heaven.") Although "Civil Religion" is in most of its aspects an "invented" (or even "manufactured") sort of symbolic behavior, it nevertheless wells up from time to time, especially in periods of national crisis, as an expression of deep collective drives toward ritual which are otherwise accorded little opportunity for expression in an increasingly desacralized culture.

NOTES

1. On the relationships between the Renaissance and Reformation and the development of science, see E. A. BURTT, *The Metaphysical Foundations of Modern Science* (Garden City, N.Y.: Doubleday Anchor, 1954);* RICHARD S. WESTFALL, *Science and Religion in Seventeenth Century England* (Ann Arbor, Mich.: University of Michigan Press, 1958/73);* and more broadly, THOMAS S. KUHN, *The Structure of Scientific Revolutions* (Chicago: University of Chicago Press, 1962/70).*
2. MYRON GILMORE, *The World of Humanism 1453-1517* (New York: Harper Torchbooks, 1952/62),* p. 188.
3. See JAMES D. HART, *The Popular Book: A History of America's Literary Taste* (Berkeley and Los Angeles: University of California Press, 1950/61),* Chap. 1 ("The Practice of Piety"). On Foxe, see WILLIAM HALLER, *The Elect*

Nation: The Meaning and Relevance of Foxe's Book of Martyrs (New York: Harper & Row, 1963).

4. On the implications of regicide, see MICHAEL WALZER, *The Revolution of the Saints: A Study in the Origins of Radical Politics* (Cambridge, Mass.: Harvard University Press, 1965),* p. 10 and *passim.*
5. MAX WEBER, *The Protestant Ethic and the Spirit of Capitalism* (New York: Scribner's 1904–05/20/58).* For the scholarly debate that has ensued: see ROBERT W. GREEN, ed., *Protestantism, Capitalism, and Social Science; The Weber Thesis Controversy* (Lexington, Mass.: Heath, 1959/73).*
6. See note 1 above, and, for a popular discussion, HARVEY COX, *The Secular City* (New York: Macmillan, 1965),* Chap. 1 ("The Biblical Sources of Secularization").
7. BERNARD BAILYN, ed., *The Apologia of Robert Keayne* (New York: Harper Torchbooks, 1965).*
8. On usury, see BENJAMIN N. NELSON, *The Idea of Usury* (Chicago: University of Chicago Press, 1969), and JOHN T. NOONAN, *The Scholastic Analysis of Usury* (Cambridge, Mass.: Harvard University Press, 1957). On the American Puritan economic ethic, see STEPHEN FOSTER, *Their Solitary Way: The Puritan Social Ethic in the First Century of Settlement in New England* (New Haven, Conn:.: Yale University Press, 1971), and essays by PERRY MILLER, HERBERT W. SCHNEIDER, EDMUND S. MORGAN, and others in MICHAEL MCGIFFERT, ed., *Puritanism and the American Experience* (Reading, Mass.: Addison-Wesley, 1969),* especially sections II B and III A.
9. PERRY MILLER, "Jonathan Edwards and the Great Awakening," in DANIEL AARON, ed., *America in Crisis* (New York: Knopf, 1952).
10. WALZER, *The Revolution of the Saints,* p. 301.
11. KEITH THOMAS, *Religion and the Decline of Magic* (New York: Scribner's, 1971), Chap. 6 ("Religion and the People"), and pp. 663–68.
12. EMILE DURKHEIM, *The Elementary Forms of the Religious Life* (New York: Free Press, 1915/65).
13. Two major exponents of this position are MICHAEL WALZER in *The Revolution of the Saints* and CHRISTOPHER HILL in *Society and Puritanism* (New York: Schocken, 1964/67)* and other works. See also RICHARD D. BROWN, *Modernization: The Transformation of American Life 1600–1865* (New York: Hill & Wang, 1976).*
14. For the story of these movements and an analysis of their social composition and leadership, see NORMAN COHN, *The Pursuit of the Millennium: Revolutionary Messianism in Medieval and Reformation Europe and Its Bearing on Modern Totalitarian Movements* ((New York: Harper Torchbooks, 1957/61).* See also MALCOLM LAMBERT, *Medieval Heresy: Popular Movements from Bogomils to Hus* (New York: Holmes & Meier, 1977); GORDON LEFF, *Heresy in the Later Middle Ages* (New York: Barnes & Noble, 1967); ROBERT E. LERNER, *The Heresy of the Free Spirit in the Later Middle Ages* (Berkeley and Los Angeles: University of California Press, 1972); R. I. MOORE, *The Birth of Popular Heresy* (London: Edward Arnold, 1975); JEFFREY B. RUSSELL, ed., *Religious Dissent in the Middle Ages* (New York: Wiley, 1971);* and DEREK BAKER, ed., *Schism, Heresy and Religious Protest* (Cambridge, England: Cambridge at the University Press, 1972).
15. The most thorough study of such movements is in GEORGE H. WILLIAMS, *The Radical Reformation* (Philadelphia: Westminster, 1962). For a very brief

overview, see ROLAND BAINTON, *The Reformation of the Sixteenth Century* (Boston: Beacon, 1952/56),* Chap. 5 ("The Church Withdrawn: Anabaptism").

16. CHRISTOPHER HILL, *The World Turned Upside Down: Radical Ideas During the English Revolution* (Harmondsworth, Middlesex: Penguin, 1972/75).* This work provides a very good survey of the varieties of religious and political ferment of the time in England. I am indebted to Professor THOMAS COKELY for calling my attention to this work.
17. For the Ranters, see HILL, Chaps. 9 and 10; A. L. MORTON, *The World of the Ranters: Religious Radicalism in the English Revolution* (London: Lawrence and Wishart, 1970); G. F. S. ELLENS, "The Ranters Ranting: Reflections on a Ranting Counter Culture," *Church History,* 40, 1 (March 1971), 91–107; and NORMAN COHN, "The Ranters," *Encounter,* 34 (April 1970), 15–25.
18. For Winstanley and the Diggers, see HILL, *World Turned Upside Down,* Chap. 7, and CHRISTOPHER HILL, ed., *Winstanley: The Law of Freedom and Other Writings* (Baltimore: Penguin, 1973);* and A. A. MITCHELL, "Gerard Winstanley and the Diggers," *History Today,* 19 (May 1969), 338–44. For the Levellers, see JOSEPH FRANK, *The Levellers* (Cambridge, Mass.: Harvard University Press, 1955).
19. On the Fifth Monarchy Men, see HILL, *World Turned Upside Down,* (consult index for specific scattered references), and P. G. ROGERS, *The Fifth Monarchy Men* (London, New York, Toronto: Oxford University Press, 1966).
20. On the English Quakers, see HILL, *World Turned Upside Down,* Chap. 10 and *passim;* HUGH BARBOUR, *The Quakers in Puritan England* (New Haven, Conn.: Yale University Press, 1964); WILLIAM C. BRAITHWAITE, *The Beginnings of Quakerism* (Cambridge, England: Cambridge University Press, 1955) and *The Second Period of Quakerism* (Cambridge, England: Cambridge University Press, 1961); and, for a detailed study of English Quaker social origins, RICHARD T. VANN, *The Social Development of English Quakerism 1655–1755* (Cambridge, Mass.: Harvard University Press, 1969).
21. See MIRCEA ELIADE, *inter alia, The Myth of the Eternal Return or, Cosmos and History* (Princeton, N.J.: Princeton University Press, 1954/71).*
22. See WALZER, *The Revolution of the Saints.*
23. A good study of the role of dissent within New England Puritanism is KAI T. ERIKSON, *Wayward Puritans: A Study in the Sociology of Deviance* (New York: Wiley, 1966).*
24. For a brief account of the Hutchinson episode, see EDMUND S. MORGAN, *The Puritan Dilemma* (Boston: Little, Brown, 1958),* Chap. X ("Seventeenth-Century Nihilism"). More extended treatments can be found in DAVID D. HALL, ed., *The Antinomian Controversy, 1636–1638: A Documentary History* (Middletown, Conn.: Wesleyan University Press, 1968) and WILLIAM K. B. STOEVER, *"A Faire and Easie Way to Heaven": Covenant Theology and Antinomianism in Early Massachusetts* (Middletown, Conn.: Wesleyan University Press, 1978). See also the biographical sketch of Hutchinson by EMERY BATTIS in JAMES, JAMES, and BOYER, eds., *Notable American Women* (Cambridge, Mass: Harvard University Press, 1971), II 245–47.
25. On women and their relationship with religion and society in England and America during this period, see EDMUND S. MORGAN, *The Puritan Family* (New York: Harper Torchbooks, 1944/66),* especially Chap. II ("Husband and Wife"); MARY P. RYAN, "Adam's Rib: Women in Agrarian Society,"

Womanhood in America from Colonial Times to the Present (New York: Watts/New Viewpoints, 1975);* JAMES T. JOHNSON, *A Society Ordained by God: English Puritan Marriage Doctrine in the First Half of the Seventeenth Cenutry* (Nashville: Abingdon, 1970); ROLAND A. BAINTON, *Women of the Reformation,* 2 vols. (Minneapolis: Augsburg, 1974/75);* KEITH V. THOMAS, "Women and the Civil War Sects," *Past and Present,* 13 (April 1958), 42–62; and ETHYL MORHAN WILLIAMS, "Women Preachers in the Civil War," *Journal of Modern History,* I, 4 (December 1929), 561–69.

26. VICTOR TURNER, *The Ritual Process: Structure and Anti-Structure* (Chicago: Aldine, 1969),* Chaps. 3–5.
27. Ibid., p. 132.
28. A good survey of this religious style can be found in DAVID KNOWLES, *Christian Monasticism* (New York and Toronto: McGraw-Hill, 1969).*
29. On the Awakening in general, see AHLSTROM, *Religious History,* (New Haven: Yale University Press, 1972), Chaps. 18–20; EDWIN SCOTT GAUSTAD, *The Great Awakening in New England* (Chicago: Quadrangle, 1957/68);* and ALAN HEIMERT and PERRY MILLER, eds., *The Great Awakening* (Indianapolis and New York: Bobs-Merrill, 1967).* The best study of Edwards is probably PERRY MILLER's *Jonathan Edwards* (Cleveland and New York: Meridian/World, 1949/64);* for collections of his work see CLARENCE H. FAUST and THOMAS H. JOHNSON, eds., *Jonathan Edwards: Representative Selections* (New York: Hill & Wang, 1935/62)* and OLA ELIZABETH WINSLOW, ed., *Jonathan Edwards: Basic Writings* (New York: New American Library/Signet Classics, 1966).* For Whitefield, see STUART C. HENRY, *George Whitefield: Wayfaring Witness* (New York and Nashville: Abingdon, 1957). Two recent brief studies of the Awakening in particular and revivalism in general are ROBERT D. ROSSEL, "The Great Awakening: An Historical Analysis," in *American Journal of Sociology,* 75 (May 1970), 907–25, and WILLIAM G. MCLOUGHLIN, "Revivalism," in EDWIN S. GAUSTAD, ed., *The Rise of Adventism* (New York: Harper & Row, 1974). These latter two essays attempt to put these phenomena within the context of broad social dynamics.
30. HEIMERT and MILLER, "Introduction" to GAUSTAD, *The Great Awakening,* pp. i–lxi.
31. See especially GAUSTAD, *Great Awakening,* p. 70 ff.
32. An interesting survey of the term "enthusiasm" and its implications for religion is RONALD A. KNOX, *Enthusiasm: A Chapter in the History of Religion with Special Reference to the Seventeenth and Eighteenth Centuries* (New York: Oxford University Press, 1950/61).* KNOX's book provides excellent background for all the movements we have discussed thus far in this section, and is written from an urbane English Catholic viewpoint.
33. Quoted in DAVID S. LOVEJOY, *Religious Enthusiasm and the Great Awakening* (Englewood Cliffs, N.J.: Prentice-Hall, 1969),* pp. 67–68.
34. On the Disciples, see DAVID EDWIN HARRELL, JR., *Quest for a Christian America: The Disciples of Christ and American Society to 1866* (Nashville, Tenn.: Disciples of Christ Historical Society, 1966); WINIFRED E. GARRISON and ALFRED T. DEGROOT, *The Disciples of Christ: A History* (St. Louis: Bethany, 1958/64); and WILLIAM E. TUCKER and LESTER G. MCALLISTER, *Journey in Faith: A History of the Christian Church (Disciples of Christ)* (St. Louis: Bethany, 1975).
35. *The Great Awakening,* p. xlvii.

36. On the consequences of the Awakening, especially for the Baptists, see Clarence C. Goen, *Revivalism and Separatism in New England* (New Haven, Conn.; Yale University Press, 1962); William G. McLoughlin, *Isaac Backus and the American Pietistic Tradition* (Boston: Little, Brown, 1967)* and his monumental *New England Dissent, 1630–1833: The Baptists and the Separation of Church and State,* 2 vols. (Cambridge, Mass.: Harvard University Press, 1971); and Gaustad, *Great Awakening,* Chap. 7 ("Institutional Effects of the Great Awakening").
37. On the Second Great Awakening, see Ahlstrom, *Religious History,* Chap. 26; Richard D. Birdsall, "The Second Great Awakening and the New England Social Order," *Church History,* 39 (September 1970), 345–64; Richard Carwardine, "The Second Great Awakening in the Urban Centers," *Journal of American History,* 59 (September 1972), 327–40; and Charles Roy Keller, *The Second Great Awakening in Connecticut* (New Haven, Conn.: Yale University Press, 1942–68 [Archon reissue]).
38. Ahlstrom, *Religious History,* Chap. 27; Catherine C. Cleveland, *The Great Revival in the West 1797–1805* (Chicago: University of Chicago Press, 1916 [Peter Smith reissue 1959]); Bernard Weisberger, *They Gathered at the River: The Story of the Great Revivalists and Their Impact upon Religion in America* (Boston: Little, Brown, 1958),* Chap. II.
39. Dickson D. Bruce, Jr., *And They All Sang Hallelujah: Plain-Folk Camp-Meeting Religion, 1800–1845* (Knoxville, Tenn.: University of Tennessee Press, 1974).
40. For Finney, see Ahlstrom, *Religious History,* Chap. 28; Weisberger, *They Gathered at the River,* Chap. IV; Whitney R. Cross, *The Burned-Over District: The Social and Intellectual History of Enthusiastic Religion in Western New York, 1800–1850* (New York: Harper Torchbooks, 1950/65),* Chap. 9 ("The Evangelist") and *passim;* William G. McLoughlin, *Modern Revivalism: Charles Grandison Finney to Billy Graham* (New York: Ronald, 1959), *passim;* McLoughlin, ed., *Lectures on Revivals in Religion by Charles Grandison Finney* (Cambridge, Mass.: Harvard University Press, 1960).
41. For the argument that religion was a primary means of taming the frontier and subduing it according to traditional cultural patterns, see Cross, *The Burned-Over District,* which describes the social composition of that area, T. Scott Miyakawa's, *Protestants and Pioneers: Individualism and Conformity on the American Frontier* (Chicago: University of Chicago Press, 1964), argues explicitly against the "Turner thesis"—that is, the argument for the primacy of the frontier experience in shaping American character and institutions. See also Louis B. Wright, *Culture on the Moving Frontier* (New York: Harper Torchbooks, 1955/61), which is essentially conservative in its emphasis.
42. On the Shakers, see Edward Deming Andrews, *The People Called Shakers* (New York: Dover, 1953/63),* and numerous other works by Andrews; and Marguerite Fellows Melcher, *The Shaker Adventure* (Cleveland: Case Western Reserve, 1941/68).* On Mother Ann Lee, see the brief biography by Andrews in Edward T. James et al., eds., *Notable American Women,* II, 385–87. See also Ahlstrom, *Religious History,* pp. 492–94.
43. On Stowe, see *Notable American Women,* III, 393–402 (biographical essay by Barbara M. Cross). The best study of Stowe's work is Charles H. Foster, *The Rungless Ladder: Harriet Beecher Stowe and New England Puritanism*

(Durham, N.C.: Duke University Press, 1954). See also Chap. V of PETER W. WILLIAMS, *A Mirror for Unitarians: Catholicism and Culture in Nineteenth Century New England Literature* (doctoral dissertation, Yale University, 1970). Many editions of *Uncle Tom's Cabin* are readily available in paperback.

44. Two good biographies of Garrison are JOHN L. THOMAS, *The Liberator* (Boston: Little, Brown, 1963), and WALTER M. MERRILL, *Against Wind and Tide* (Cambridge, Mass.: Harvard University Press, 1963). A convenient collection of excerpts from GARRISON's publication *The Liberator* can be found in TRUMAN NELSON, ed., *Documents of Upheaval* (New York: Hill & Wang, 1966).* See also PETER W. WILLIAMS, "A Note on William Lloyd Garrison and the Civil Religion," *Ohio Journal of Religious Studies,* 4, no. 2 (October 1976), 90–94, and LEWIS PERRY, *Radical Abolitionism: Anarchy and the Government of God in Antislavery Thought* (Ithaca, N.Y.: Cornell University Press, 1973).
45. Quoted in NELSON, ed., *Documents of Upheaval,* pp. 215–16.
46. SIDNEY E. MEAD, for example, begins his classic interpretation of American religion, *The Lively Experiment* (New York: Harper & Row, 1963), with a chapter entitled "The American People: Their Space, Time, and Religion." MEAD argues that, where Europeans had interpreted their experience primarily in terms of historical time, Americans shifted their frame of reference to the vast space which confronted them. American writers of the nineteenth century were similarly concerned with America as the new land where time and history were abolished, and beginnings *de novo* in seemingly limitless space free from the burden of history were now possible. See, for example, R. W. B. LEWIS, *The American Adam* (Chicago: University of Chicago Press, 1955);* HENRY NASH SMITH, *Virgin Land: The American West as Myth and Symbol* (Cambridge, Mass.: Harvard University Press, 1950; Random/Vintage paperback reissue);* and DAVID W. NOBLE, *The Eternal Adam and the New World Garden* (New York: Grosset & Dunlap, 1968)* and *Historians Against History* (Minneapolis: University of Minnesota Press, 1965).*
47. On the phenomenology of time perception and its social implications, see GEORGES GURVITCH, *The Spectrum of Social Time* (Dordrecht, Holland: D. Reidel, 1964).
48. See the interesting if not necessarily reliable work by ALAN W. WATTS, *Myth and Ritual in Christianity* (Boston: Beacon, 1968).* Implications of changes of temporal conceptions for the Reformation can be found in HORTON DAVIES, *Worship and Theology in England,* Vol. II (*From Andrewes to Baxter and Fox, 1603–1690*), Chap. 6 ("Calendary Conflict: Holy Days or Holidays?") (Princeton, N.J.: Princeton University Press, 1973); CHRISTOPHER HILL, *Society and Puritanism* (New York: Schocken, 1964),* Chap. 5 ("The Uses of Sabbatarianism"); WINTON U. SOLBERG, *Redeem the Time: The Puritan Sabbath in Early America* (Cambridge, Mass.: Harvard University Press, 1977); and E. P. THOMPSON, "Time, Work-Discipline, and Industrial Capitalism," *Past and Present,* 38 (December 1967), 56–97. More related bibliography on the specific subject of holidays can be found in notes 33 to 41 in Chapter 4.
49. See FRANCIS X. WEISER, *Handbook of Christian Feasts and Customs: The Year of the Lord in Liturgy and Folklore* (New York: Harcourt, Brace & World, 1952).

50. See G. ERNEST WRIGHT, *God Who Acts: Biblical Theology as Recital* (London: SCM Press, 1952).*
51. See JOHN G. GAGER, *Kingdom and Community: The Social World of Early Christianity* (Englewood Cliffs, N.J.: Prentice-Hall Studies in Religion, 1975)* on early Christian apocalyptic.
52. See KEITH THOMAS, *Religion and the Decline of Magic,* Chap. 3 ("The Impact of the Reformation") and *passim.*
53. Two recent studies of this theme are ERNEST LEE TUVESON, *Redeemer Nation: The Idea of America's Millennial Role* (Chicago: University of Chicago Press, 1968), and CONRAD CHERRY, ed., *God's New Israel: Religion Interpretations of American Destiny* (Englewood Cliffs, N.J.: Prentice-Hall, 1971).* For more remote background, see WILLIAM HALLER, *The Elect Nation* (New York: Harper & Row, 1963), and GEORGE H. WILLIAMS, *Wilderness and Paradise in Christian Thought* (New York: Harper & Brothers, 1962).
54. In CHERRY, *God's New Israel,* pp. 44–54.
55. On Foxe, see HALLER, *The Elect Nation.* See also the Appendix to WINTHROP S. HUDSON, ed., *Nationalism and Religion in America* (New York: Harper Forum Books, 1970).*
56. From WILLIAM BRADFORD, *Of Plymouth Plantation,* in PERRY MILLER, ed., *The American Puritans: Their Prose and Poetry* (Garden City, N.Y.: Doubleday Anchor, 1956),* p. 14.
57. On the Mathers, see PERRY MILLER, *The New England Mind: From Colony to Province* (Cambridge, Mass.: Harvard University Press, 1953),* and ROBERT MIDDLEKAUFF, *The Mathers: Three Generations of Puritan Intellectuals 1596–1728* (New York: Oxford University Press, 1971); and DAVID LEVIN, *Cotton Mather: The Young Life of the Lord's Remembrancer, 1663–1703* (Cambridge, Mass.: Harvard University Press, 1978).
58. These anecdotes are all taken from RICHARD M. DORSON, ed., *America Begins: Early American Writing* (Bloomington, Ind.: Indiana University Press, 1950/71).* For the servant girl, pp. 118–19 (Cotton Mather); the buggerer, pp. 120–21 (Cotton Mather); ANNE HUTCHINSON, pp. 121–22 (John Winthrop); the Quaker convert, pp. 122–24 (Increase Mather); the blinded perjurer, p. 126 (Increase Mather); the Jesuit's story, pp. 128–29. On bloody corpses, see KEITH THOMAS, *Religion and the Decline of Magic,* p. 220.
59. DONALD E. BYRNE, JR., *No Foot of Land: Folklore of American Methodist Itinerants* (Metuchen, N.J.: The Scarecrow Press and the American Theological Library Association, 1975). The following examples and many others can be found throughout this rich and engaging work. BYRNE's bibliography and notes are valuable for further explorations in the folkloric aspect of American religion in general and Protestantism in particular.
60. Ibid., p. 99.
61. *Religion and the Decline of Magic,* Chap. 22 ("The Decline of Magic").
62. See WEBER, *The Protestant Ethic,* "Author's Introduction."
63. GAGER, *Kingdom and Community.*
64. On millennial thought in Judaism and early Christianity, see NORMAN COHN, *The Pursuit of the Millennium* (New York: Harper Torchbooks, 1957/61),* Chap. I. For a collection of comparative studies on the theme,

see SYLVIA L. THRUPP, ed., *Millennial Dreams in Action: Studies in Revolutionary Religious Movements* (New York: Schocken, 1970). See also BRYAN WILSON, *Magic and the Millennium* (New York: Harper & Row, 1972); YONINA TALMON, "Millenarianism," *International Encyclopedia of the Social Sciences* (New York: Macmillan/Free Press, 1968), Vol. 10, 349–62; and ERNEST TUVESON, "Millenarianism," in *Dictionary of the History of Ideas*, Vol. II, 223–25.

65. On millennialism (or "millenarianism," a variant form) during the American Colonial period, see JAMES W. DAVIDSON, "Searching for the Millennium: Problems for the 1790's and the 1970's," *New England Quarterly*, 45 (June 1972), 241–61, and his *The Logic of Millennial Thought: Eighteenth-Century New England* (New Haven, Conn.: Yale University Press, 1977); C. C. GOEN, "Jonathan Edwards: A New Departure in Eschatology," *Church History*, 28 (March 1959), 25–39; J. F. MACLEAR, "New England and the Fifth Monarchy: the Quest for the Millennium in Early American Puritanism," *William and Mary Quarterly*, 3rd series, 32 (April 1975), 223–260; NATHAN ORR HATCH, *The Sacred Cause of Liberty: Republican Thought and the Millennium in Revolutionary New England* (New Haven, Conn.: Yale University Press, 1977); and the apocalyptic writings of JONATHAN EDWARDS, ed. STEPHEN J. STEIN (New Haven, Conn.: Yale University Press, 1977). See also PETER TOON, ed., *Puritans, the Millennium, and the Future of Israel: Puritan Eschatology 1600 to 1660* (Cambridge & London: James Clarke, 1970), for English background.
66. In addition to the works cited in note 65, see also HEIMERT and MILLER'S "Introduction" to their anthology, *The Great Awakening*, for a discussion of EDWARDS' post-millennialism.
67. On these phenomena, see BRYAN WILSON, *Magic and the Millennium;* VITTORIO LANTERNARI, *The Religions of the Oppressed* (New York: New American Library/Mentor, 1963);* SYLVIA THRUPP, ed., *Millennial Dreams in Action;* KENELM O. L. BURRIDGE, *New Heaven, New Earth: A Study of Millenarian Activities* (Oxford: Blackwell, 1969), and his *Mambu: A Study of Melanesian Cargo Movements and Their Social and Ideological Background* (New York: Harper Torchbooks, 1960/70);* PETER LAWRENCE, *Road Belong Cargo* (Manchester: Manchester University Press, 1964); and PETER WORSLEY, *The Trumpet Shall Sound* (London: MacGibon & Kee, 1957).
68. ALICE FELT TYLER'S book by the quoted name (*Freedom's Ferment: Phases of American Social History from the Colonial Period to the Outbreak of the Civil War*) (New York: Harper Torchbooks, 1944/62)* is a useful survey of utopian, millenarian, and other "enthusiastic" movements during the antebellum period.
69. On Miller and the Millerites, see AHLSTROM, *Religious History*, pp. 479–80; DAVID T. ARTHUR, "Millerism," in EDWIN SCOTT GAUSTAD, ed., *The Rise of Adventism* (New York: Harper & Row, 1974), pp. 154–72; and WHITNEY R. CROSS, *The Burned-Over District*, Chap. 17 ("The End of the World"). More generally, see IRA V. BROWN, "Watchers for the Second Coming: The Millenarian Tradition in America," *Mississippi Valley Historical Review*, 39 (December 1952), 441–58, and DAVID E. SMITH, "Millenarian Scholarship in America," *American Quarterly*, 17 (Fall 1965), 535–49.
70. This discussion principally follows CROSS, *Burned-Over District*.
71. For the life and career of Ellen G. White, see RONALD L. NUMBERS,

Prophetess of Health: A Study of Ellen G. White (New York: Harper & Row, 1976), and C. C. GOEN's briefer sketch in *Notable American Women,* III, 585–88. (The following discussion principally follows NUMBERS and JONATHAN M. BUTLER, "Adventism and the American Experience," in GAUSTAD, ed., *The Rise of Adventism,* pp. 173–206. See also the bibliography and related essays in the GAUSTAD volume.)

72. Other millenarian groups such as the Jehovah's Witnesses and the Worldwide Church of God continue to arise in America, but their tightly organized sectarian character puts them beyond our scope. We might note, however, that in each case belief in the imminent end of the world (both groups experienced difficulties through their predictions of embarrassingly specific dates and subsequent rationalizations) was combined with some rather labored exegesis of the apocalyptic books of both testaments. (Herbert Armstrong, the Worldwide Church of God's founder, contended as well that the British were in fact the descendants of the Lost Tribes of Israel, an especially creative twist.) At the time of this writing (summer 1978), the Witnesses are holding a massive convention at Riverfront Stadium in Cincinnati, and Garner "Ted" Armstrong, Herbert W.'s son and protégé, has again been expelled from the leadership of the Worldwide Church. For further reading on the Witnesses, see AHLSTROM, *Religious History,* pp. 807–808; ALAN ROGERSON, *Millions Now Living Will Never Die: A Study of the Jehovah's Witnesses* (London: Constable, 1969); LEE R. COOPER, "'Publish' or Perish: Negro Jehovah's Witnesses Adaptation in the Ghetto," in IRVING I. ZARETSKY and MARK P. LEONE, eds., *Religious Movements in Contemporary America* (Princeton, N.J.: Princeton University Press, 1974); JAMES A. BECKFORD, *The Trumpet of Prophecy: A Sociological Study of Jehovah's Witnesses* (Oxford, England: Blackwell, 1975); and BARBARA GRIZZUTI HARRISON, *Visions of Glory: A History and a Memory of Jehovah's Witnesses* (New York: Simon & Schuster, 1978). Two interesting but highly critical treatments of the Worldwide Church of God are JOSEPH MARTIN HOPKINS, *The Armstrong Empire: A Look at the Worldwide Church of God* (Grand Rapids: Eerdmans, 1974), and WILLIAM C. MARTIN, "The Plain Truth About the Armstrongs and the World Tomorrow," *Harper's,* (July 1973), pp. 74–82.

73. On Joseph Smith, see FAWN M. BRODIE, *No Man Knows My History: The Life of Joseph Smith* (New York: Knopf, 1945/71). On the Mormons, see AHLSTROM, *Religious History,* pp. 501–509; THOMAS F. O'DEA, *The Mormons* (Chicago: University of Chicago Press, 1957);* NELS ANDERSON, *Desert Saints: The Mormon Frontier in Utah* (Chicago: University of Chicago Press, 1942/66);* MARVIN S. HILL and JAMES B. ALLEN, eds., *Mormonism and American Culture* (New York: Harper & Row, 1972);* and NORMAN F. FURNISS, *The Mormon Conflict, 1850–1859* (New Haven, Conn.: Yale University Press, 1960).

74. On this sort of speculation, see ROBERT WAUCHOPE, *Lost Tribes and Sunken Continents: Myth and Method in the Study of the American Indian* (Chicago: University of Chicago Press, 1962).* See also MARTIN GARDNER, *Fads and Fallacies in the Name of Science* (New York: Dover, 1957).

75. See CROSS, *Burned-Over District,* Chap. 8 ("The Prophet").

76. The literature on urbanization and immigration is vast. Two older but still readable and useful introductions to these phenomena are ARTHUR MEIER SCHLESINGER, *The Rise of the City 1878–1898* (Chicago: Quadrangle, 1933/71)* and OSCAR HANDLIN, *The Uprooted* (New York: Grosset & Dunlap, 1951).*

77. Two contrasting interpretations of this fascinating woman are SYDNEY E. AHLSTROM, "Mary Baker Eddy," *Notable American Women,* Vol. I, 551-61, and the three-volume biography by ROBERT PEEL (New York: Holt, Rinehart & Winston, 1966) 71, 77. On Christian Science, see AHLSTROM, *Religious History,* Chap. 60 ("Harmonialism Since the Later Nineteenth Century"), and, for an "inside" perspective, STEPHEN GOTTSCHALK, *The Emergence of Christian Science in American Religious Life* (Berkeley and Los Angeles: University of California Press, 1973).
78. On Quimby and mind cure, see DONALD MEYER, *The Positive Thinkers* (Garden City, N.Y.: Doubleday, 1965),* and GAIL THAIN PARKER, *Mind Cure in New England: From the Civil War to World War I* (Hanover, N.H.: University Press of New England, 1973). See also PARKER's "Mary Baker Eddy and Sentimental Womanhood," *New England Quarterly,* 43 (March 1970), 3-18.
79. AHLSTROM, "Mary Baker Eddy," p. 554.
80. MARY DOUGLAS, *Natural Symbols: Explorations in Cosmology* (New York: Random/Pantheon, 1970), Chap. 4 ("A Rule of Method").
81. I believe that AHLSTROM has used this phrase in his class lectures. For a variant formulation, see his "Mary Baker Eddy," p. 559.
82. Ibid., p. 560.
83. On the sociology of Christian Science, see BRYAN WILSON, *Religious Sects* (New York and Toronto: McGraw-Hill, 1970), pp. 144-52, and his *Sects and Society* (Berkeley and Los Angeles: University of California Press, 1961), Part II.
84. A useful survey history of Methodism in America is FREDERICK A. NORWOOD, *The Story of American Methodism* (Nashville: Abingdon, 1974).* A provocative study of the English background of the movement is BERNARD SEMMEL, *The Methodist Revolution* (New York: Basic Books, 1973).
85. On this function, see T. SCOTT MIYAKAWA, *Protestants and Pioneers* (Chicago: University of Chicago Press, 1964), Chap. V ("The Methodists").
86. See *The Autobiography of Peter Cartwright* (Nashville: Abingdon, 1956), and consult the index of BYRNE, *No Foot of Land,* under "Cartwright, Peter."
87. On the emergence of Holiness within American Protestantism in general and in Methodism in particular, see TIMOTHY L. SMITH, *Revivalism and Social Reform: American Protestantism on the Eve of the Civil War* (New York: Harper Torchbooks, 1957/65),* and CHARLES EDWIN JONES, *Perfectionist Persuasion: The Holiness Movement in American Methodism, 1867-1936* (Metuchen, N.J.: Scarecrow Press, 1974). On particular Holiness denominations, see TIMOTHY L. SMITH, *Called Unto Holiness: The Story of the Nazarenes* (Kansas City, Mo.: Nazarene Publishing House, 1962), and JOHN W. V. SMITH, *A Brief History of the Church of God Reformation Movement* (Anderson, Ind.: Warner, 1956/76).*
88. On Bushnell, see BARBARA M. CROSS, *Horace Bushnell: Minister to a Changing America* (Chicago: University of Chicago Press, 1958), and AHLSTROM, *Religious History, passim* (see index). Recent editions of Bushnell's works include LUTHER A. WEIGLE, ed., *Christian Nurture* (New Haven: Yale University Press, 1888/1916/1967),* and H. SHELTON SMITH, ed., *Horace Bushnell* (New York: Oxford University Press [Library of Protestant Thought], 1965).
89. On Phoebe Palmer, see SMITH, *Revivalism and Social Reform, passim* (especially Chap. VIII), and JONES, *Perfectionist Persuasion,* Chap. 1.

90. On Holiness campgrounds, see JONES, ibid., Chap. 4.
91. Ibid., Chap. 6. See also JOHN THOMAS NICHOL, *Pentecostalism* (New York: Harper & Row, 1966), Chaps. 8 and 9.
92. On Moody, see JAMES F. FINDLAY, JR., *Dwight L. Moody: American Evangelist, 1837–1899* (Chicago: University of Chicago Press, 1969); McLOUGHLIN, *Modern Revivalism,* Chaps. 4 and 5; and WEISBERGER, *They Gathered at the River,* Chap. VII. See also AHLSTROM, *Religious History,* Chap. 44.
93. IRA D. SANKEY, *Sankey's Story of the Gospel Hymns* (also published as *My Life and the Story of the Gospel Hymns*) (Philadelphia: The Sunday School Times Company, 1906). For a provocative study of Moody/Sankey hymnody that complements my treatment, see SANDRA S. SIZER, *Gospel Hymns and Social Religion: The Rhetoric of Nineteenth Century Revivalism* (Philadelphia: Temple University Press, 1978). See also E. P. THOMPSON's more Freudian treatment of English Methodist hymnody in *The Making of the English Working Class* (New York: Pantheon, 1964).
94. On Crosby, see BERNARD RUFFIN, *Fanny Crosby* (New York: Pilgrim, 1976). The best general survey of American religious music is probably HENRY WILDER FOOTE, *Three Centuries of American Hymnody* (Cambridge, Mass.: Harvard University Press, 1940), but it is heavily weighted toward Unitarian and other "elite" traditions.
95. Most of the hymns referred to in what follows can be found in HOMER A. RODEHEAVER and CHARLES H. GABRIEL, compilers, *Awakening Songs* (Chicago and Philadelphia: Rodeheaver Co., 1917). Almost any such collection will serve the purpose, however.
96. See JONES, *Perfectionist Persuasion,* Chap. 5.
97. *Gemeinschaft* and *Gesellschaft* are technical sociological terms first used by FERDINAND TOENNIES in the book translated as *Community and Society* (New York: Harper Torchbooks, 1957/63).* *Gemeinschaft* refers to pre-industrial, traditional societies characterized by face-to-face relationships. *Gesellschaft,* on the other hand, is the ideal type of the modernized society, where relationships are impersonal and functional. *Gemeinschaft* is almost by definition rural, while *Gesellschaft* is urban.
98. *In His Steps,* ed. C. HUGH HOLMAN (New York: Odyssey, 1966);* ALICE PAYNE HACKETT, *Seventy Years of Best Sellers 1895–1965* (New York: R. R. Bowker, 1967), 12. See also pp. 83–86 for listings of best-selling fictional and nonfictional works on religion.
99. On the Social Gospel, see AHLSTROM, *Religious History, passim* (see index); ROBERT T. HANDY, ed., *The Social Gospel in America* (New York: Oxford University Press [Library of Protestant Thought], 1966); C. HOWARD HOPKINS, *The Rise of the Social Gospel in American Protestantism, 1865–1915* (New Haven, Conn.: Yale University Press, 1940/67);* HENRY F. MAY, *Protestant Churches and Industrial America* (New York: Harper Torchbooks, 1949/67);* AARON I. ABELL, *The Urban Impact on American Protestantism 1865–1900* (Cambridge, Mass.: Harvard University Press, 1943 [Archon reprint 1962]); and RONALD C. WHITE, JR., and C. HOWARD HOPKINS, *The Social Gospel* (Philadelphia: Temple University Press, 1976).*
100. WAYNE ELZEY, "'What Would Jesus Do?' *In His Steps* and the Moral Codes of the Middle Class," *Soundings,* 58 (Winter 1975), 463–89. See also PAUL S. BOYER, "*In His Steps:* A Reappraisal," *American Quarterly,* 13 (Spring 1971), 60–71.

101. Ann Douglas, *The Feminization of American Culture* (New York: Knopf 1977), pp. 3–4, 244–55, and *passim.*
102. Warner E. Sallman, born in Chicago in 1892 of Swedish and Finnish extraction, was inspired by the biblical illustrations of Gustave Doré, and was urged by his dean while a student at the Chicago Art Institute to create "a virile, manly Christ" as a counterpoint to the effete, sentimental portraits of Jesus that dominated the popular religious art of the time. Ironically, "Sallman's Head of Christ," originally drawn for the February 1924 issue of *The Covenant Companion* (of which he was art editor) in an attempt to show "the human side of Jesus," appears just as mawkish and effeminate to the contemporary viewer as did those against which Sallman himself was reacting. See Cynthia Pearl Maus, *The Church and the Fine Arts* (New York: Harper & Brothers, 1960), for a discussion of Sallman and his work, as well as for an abundant collection of poetry, paintings, and other materials expressive of popular middle-class Protestant taste and sensibility of the late nineteenth and early and middle twentieth centuries. (I am indebted to Cean Wilson for access to her religious artifacts and to Elizabeth Dean for her extremely helpful suggestions as to the place of these artifacts in the broader traditions of art history.)
103. On the history and character of Pentecostalism, see Ahlstrom, *Religious History,* pp. 819–22 and *passim;* John Thomas Nichol, *Pentecostalism* (New York: Harper & Row, 1966); Vinson Synan, *The Holiness-Pentecostal Movement in the United States* (Grand Rapids, Mich.: Eerdmans, 1971), and *The Old-Time Power* (Franklin Springs, Ga.: Advocate Press, 1973); W. J. Hollenweger, *The Pentecostals* (Minneapolis: Augsburg, 1969); and Nils Bloch-Hoell, *The Pentecostal Movement* (London: Allen & Unwin, 1964). Two recent social-scientific studies include Felicitas D. Goodman, *Speaking in Tongues: A Cross-Cultural Study of Glossalalia* (Chicago: University of Chicago Press, 1972) and John P. Kildahl, *The Psychology of Speaking in Tongues* (New York: Harper & Row, 1972). See also William G. McLoughlin, "Is There a Third Force in Christendom?", *Daedalus,* 96, 1 (Winter 1967), 43–68; articles by Bateson, Goodman, Garrison, Pattison, Gerlach, and others in Irving I. Zaretsky and Mark P. Leone, eds., *Religious Movements in Contemporary America* (Princeton: N.J.: Princeton University Press, 1974); and Robert Mapes Anderson, *Vision of the Disinherited: The Making of American Pentecostalism* (New York: Oxford University Press, 1979).
104. On shamanism, see Mircea Eliade, *Shamanism* (Princeton, N.J.: Princeton University Press, 1951/64).*
105. Turner, *The Ritual Process,* p. 132.
106. On postwar developments, see David Edwin Harrell, Jr., *All Things Are Possible: The Healing and Charismatic Revivals in Modern America* (Bloomington, Ind.: Indiana University Press, 1975).
107. Blair Boyd and Peter Adair, *Holy Ghost People,* Contemporary Films/McGraw-Hill, 1968.
108. A full-scale study of snake handling is Weston La Barre, *They Shall Take Up Serpents: Psychology of the Southern Snake-Handling Cult* (New York: Schocken, 1962/69).*
109. Wayne Elzey, "Liminality and Symbiosis in Popular American Protestantism," *Journal of the American Academy of Religion,* 43 (December 1975), 741–56.

110. On Neo-Pentecostalism, see JOSEPH H. FICHTER, *The Catholic Cult of the Paraclete* (New York: Sheed & Ward, 1975); VINCENT M. WALSH, *A Key to Charismatic Renewal in the Catholic Church* (St. Meinrad, Ind.: Abbey Press, 1974); FREDERICK DALE BRUNER, *A Theology of the Holy Spirit: The Pentecostal Experience and the New Testament Witness* (Grand Rapids, Mich.: Eerdmans, 1970); WILLIAM J. SAMARIN, *Tongues of Men and Angels* (New York: Macmillan, 1972); and JAMES W. JONES, *Filled With New Wine: The Charismatic Renewal of the Church* (New York: Harper & Row, 1974).* These are just a few of a large number of recent titles in this area.
111. Much of the following discussion of postwar faith-healing follows HARRELL, *All Things Are Possible.*
112. KEITH THOMAS, *Religion and the Decline of Magic,* Chap. 2 and *passim;* on the "King's Touch," Chap. 7 ("Magical Healing").
113. GENOVESE, *Roll, Jordan, Roll,* pp. 220–228.
114. THOMAS, *Religion and the Decline of Magic,* Chap. 22 ("The Decline of Magic.").
115. On "Sister Aimee," see WILLIAM G. MCLOUGHLIN's biographical sketch in *Notable American Women,* II, 477–80, and his "Aimee Semple McPherson: 'Your Sister in the King's Glad Service,'" *Journal of Popular Culture,* 1 (Winter 1967), 193–217.
116. For general treatments of this subject, see LOUIS ROSE, *Faith Healing* (Harmondsworth, Middlesex: Penguin, 1968/71),* and ARI KIEV, ed., *Magic, Faith, and Healing* (New York: Free Press, 1964/74).*
117. On Oral Roberts, see HARRELL, *All Things Are Possible,* pp. 41–52 and 150–58. See also JAMES MORRIS, *The Preachers* (New York: Saint Martin's, 1973), Chap. II.
118. HARRELL, pp. 198–99. On Allen, see HARRELL, pp. 66–74, 194–205, and *passim.* See also MORRIS, Chap. I.
119. HARRELL, p. 89. On Branham, see HARRELL, pp. 27–40 and 159–64. On demons, see plate preceding title page to sec. III.
120. See HARRELL, p. 202 (on Allen) and *passim.*
121. Ibid., p. 163.
122. Ibid., pp. 164–65.
123. Since the world of faith-healing tends to occupy the margins of the Evangelical-Fundamentalist world, it is perhaps not surprising that it has been the sphere in which women—McPherson, Stapleton, and Kathryn Kuhlman—should be able to achieve prominence. On STAPLETON, see her own works, *The Gift of Inner Healing* (Waco, Texas: Word Books, 1976),* and *Experiencing Inner Healing* (*ibid.,* 1979),* and the *Newsweek* feature article by KENNETH L. WOODWARD, *et al.,* "Sister Ruth." (17 July 1978, 58–66. MRS. STAPLETON has questioned this article's accuracy.) On KATHRYN KUHLMAN, see her own *I Believe in Miracles* (Englewood Cliffs, N.J.: Prentice-Hall, 1962),* and ALLEN SPRAGGETT, *Kathryn Kuhlman: The Woman Who Believes in Miracles* (New York: World, 1970).
124. THOMAS, *Religion and the Decline of Magic,* p. 641.
125. Recent witchcraft studies from both historical and anthropological perspectives in recent years have been numerous. Two good collections of such literature are MAX MARWICK, ed., *Witchcraft and Sorcery* (Harmondworth and Baltimore: Penguin, 1970),* and MARY DOUGLAS, ed.,

Witchcraft Confessions and Accusations (London: Tavistock, 1970). Some other useful studies include LUCY MAIR, *Witchcraft* (London: Weidenfeld & Nicolson, 1969), and "Witchcraft in the Study of Religion," *Cahiers d'Etudes Africaines,* 15, IV, no. 3 (1964), 335–48; and VICTOR TURNER, "Witchcraft and Sorcery: Taxonomy versus Dynamics," *Africa,* 34 (October 1964), 314-25.

126. The classic study of African witchcraft is E. E. EVANS-PRITCHARD, *Witchcraft, Oracles and Magic among the Azande* (Oxford, England; Clarendon Press, 1937).* See also MARY DOUGLAS, "Witch Beliefs in Central Africa," *Africa,* 37 (January 1967), 72-80.

127. A readable and useful interpretation of this phenomenon is H. R. TREVOR-ROPER, *The European Witch-Craze of the Sixteenth and Seventeenth Centuries* (New York: Harper Torchbooks, 1969),* pp. 90-192. Other recent studies of witchcraft and witch hunting in England and on the Continent include KEITH THOMAS, *Religion and the Decline of Magic,* Chaps. 14-18; ALAN D. MACFARLANE, *Witchcraft in Tudor and Stuart England* (London: Routledge & Kegan Paul, 1970);* E. WILLIAM MONTER, *Witchcraft in France and Switzerland: The Borderlands during the Reformation* (Ithaca, N.Y.: Cornell University Press, 1976); JEFFREY BURTON RUSSELL, *Witchcraft in the Middle Ages* (Ithaca, N.Y.: Cornell University Press, 1972); and H. C. ERIK MIDELFORT, *Witch Hunting in Southwestern German 1562-1684* (Stanford, Calif.: Stanford University Press, 1972). MIDELFORT is also the author of an exhaustive bibliographical study, "Recent Witch Hunting Research," *Papers of the Bibliographical Society of America,* 62 (1968), 373–420. Older but still useful studies include HENRY CHARLES LEA, *Materials Towards a History of Witchcraft* (Philadelphia: University of Pennsylvania Press, 1939); WALLACE NOTESTEIN, *A History of Witchcraft in England from 1558 to 1718* (New York: Russell & Russell, 1911/65); MONTAGUE SUMMERS, *The Geography of Witchcraft* (Evanston & New York: University Books, 1927/58); and GEORGE LYMAN KITTREDGE, *Witchcraft in Old and New England* (New York: Atheneum, 1929/72).*

128. THOMAS, *Religion and the Decline of Magic,* Chaps. 16 and 17.

129. New York: Braziller, 1969.*

130. This paragraph and the one preceding primarily follow Hansen. See also MARION L. STARKEY, *The Devil in Massachusetts* (Garden City, N.Y.: Doubleday Anchor, 1949/69), and, for background, FREDERICK C. DRAKE, "Witchcraft in the American Colonies, 1647-62," *American Quarterly,* 20 (Winter 1968), 694-725.

131. Published in Cambridge, Mass. by Harvard University Press.* The following account is based primarily on their study.

132. *Salem Possessed,* pp. 39–45.

133. Ibid., pp. 45-79.

134. Ibid., Chap. 4.

135. DOUGLAS, *Natural Symbols,* Chap. 4 (1st edition, 1970). On DOUGLAS, see also SHELDON R. ISENBERG and DENNIS E. OWEN, "Bodies, Natural and Contrived: The Work of Mary Douglas," *Religious Studies Review,* 3 (January 1977), 1-17.

136. DAVID BRION DAVIS, "Some Themes of Countersubversion: An Analysis of Anti-Masonic, Anti-Catholic, and Anti-Mormon Literature," *Mississippi Valley Historical Review,* 47 (September 1960), 205-24. (Reprinted in ab-

ridged form in Davis, ed., *The Fear of Conspiracy: Images of Un-American Subversion from the Revolution to the Present* [Ithaca, N.Y.: Cornell University Press, 1971],* pp. 9–22.) This is an excellent anthology which, in addition to further comment by Davis, contains a wide range of primary sources and extracts from Richard Hofstadter's essay "The Paranoid Style in American Politics" (pp. 2–9). See also Hofstadter's *The Paranoid Style in American Politics* (New York: Random/Vintage, 1967).*

137. Davis, "Countersubversion," in *Fear of Conspiracy,* pp. 23–34.

138. On Colonial anti-Catholicism, see Ray Allen Billington, *The Protestant Crusade 1800–1860* (Chicago: Quadrangle, 1938/64).*

139. For the Revolutionary period, see Davis, ed., *Fear of Conspiracy,* pp. 23 –34.

140. On the French Revolution, see Davis, ibid., pp. 35–65. On the Bavarian Illuminati, Vernon Stauffer, *New England and the Bavarian Illuminati* (New York: Russell & Russell, 1918/67). On Masonry, see Davis, section 4, and Lorman Ratner, ed., *Antimasonry: The Crusade and the Party* (Englewood Cliffs, N.J.: Prentice-Hall, 1969).* On Masonry, see also Bernard Fay, *Revolution and Freemasonry* (Boston: Little, Crown, 1935); Robert S. Ellwood, Jr., *Religious and Spiritual Groups in Modern America* (Englewood Cliffs, N.J.: Prentice-Hall, 1973),* pp. 62–64; Catherine L. Albanese, *Sons of the Fathers: The Civil Religion of the American Revolution* (Philadelphia: Temple University Press, 1976), pp. 129–36; and Dorothy Ann Lipson, *Freemasonry in Federalist Connecticut, 1789–1835* (Princeton, N.J.: Princeton University Press, 1977).

141. This and the following paragraphs follow Billington, *The Protestant Crusade.*

142. Ibid., pp. 361–62.

143. Davis, "Countersubversion," in *Fear of Conspiracy,* pp. 17–20.

144. Billington, *Protestant Crusade,* pp. 99–108.

145. Davis, pp. 17 and 100–101. See also Norman F. Furniss, *The Mormon Conflict, 1850–1959* (New Haven, Conn.: Yale University Press, 1960).

146. See Davis, sections 6 and 7. On nativism and the immigration restriction movement, see John Higham, *Strangers in the Land: Patterns of American Nativism 1860–1925* (New York: Atheneum, 1955/63);* Barbara Miller Solomon, *Ancestors and Immigrants: A Changing New England Tradition* (Chicago: University of Chicago Press, 1956/72);* and Ahlstrom, *Religious History,* Chap. 50.

147. On Prohibition, see James H. Timberlake, *Prohibition and the Progressive Movement, 1900–1920* (New York: Atheneum, 1963/70);* Andrew Sinclair, *Era of Excess: A Social History of Prohibition* (New York: Harper & Row, 1962/64);* and Joseph R. Gusfield, *Symbolic Crusade: Status Politics and the American Temperance Movement* (Urbana: University of Illinois Press, 1966).*

148. On the Klan, see Allen Trelease, *White Terror: The Ku Klux Klan Conspiracy and Southern Reconstruction* (New York: Harper Torchbooks, 1971);* Kenneth T. Jackson, *The Ku Klux Klan in the City 1915–1930* (New York: Oxford University Press, 1967);* and Richard Hofstadter, *Anti-Intellectualism in American Life,* pp. 124–25.

149. Judd Marmor, Viola W. Bernard, and Perry Ottenberg, "Psychodynamics of Group Opposition to Health Programs," *American Journal of Orthopsychiatry,* 30 (April 1960), 330–45.

150. On Kubrick and *Dr. Strangelove* (1963), see GENE D. PHILLIPS, *Stanley Kubrick: A Film Odyssey* (New York: Popular Library, 1975),* Chap. 6.
151. COLIN L. WESTERBECK, JR., "The Screen," *Commonweal,* 104 (August 5, 1977), 499.
152. On McCarthy, see RICHARD H. ROVERE, *Senator Joe McCarthy* (Cleveland and New York: World/Meridian, 1960). On McCarthy and American Catholics, see VINCENT P. DESANTIS, "American Catholics and McCarthyism," *Catholic Historical Review,* 51 (April 1965), 1-20; and DONALD E. CROSBY, "The Jesuits and Joe McCarthy," *Church History,* 46 (September 1977), 374-88, and, more extensively, *God, Church, and Flag: Senator Joseph R. McCarthy and the Catholic Church, 1950-1957* (Chapel Hill: University of North Carolina Press, 1978).
153. On McIntire, Hargis et al., see DAVIS, *Fear of Conspiracy,* Chap. 8; JAMES MORRIS, *The Preachers* (New York: St. Martin's, 1973, Chaps. V and VII); and BENJAMIN R. EPSTEIN and ARNOLD FOSTER, *The Radical Right: Report on the John Birch Society and Its Allies* (New York: Random Vintage, 1967).* See also SEYMOUR MARTIN LIPSET and EARL RAAB, *The Politics of Unreason: Right-Wing Extremism in America, 1790-1970* (New York: Harper Torchbooks, 1970/73).*
154. On Coughlin, see DAVIS, section 7, and SHELDON MARCUS, *Father Coughlin: The Tumultuous Life of the Priest of the Little Flower* (Boston: Little, Brown, 1973). See also DAVID J. O'BRIEN, *American Catholics and Social Reform: The New Deal Years* (New York: Oxford University Press, 1968).
155. See JOSHUA TRACHTENBERG, *The Devil and the Jews: The Medieval Conception of the Jew and its Relation to Modern Antisemitism* (New York: Harper Torchbooks, 1943/66).* See also RICHARD L. RUBENSTEIN, *After Auschwitz: Radical Theology and Contemporary Judaism* (Indianapolis, Ind.: Bobbs-Merrill, 1966),* Chap. 1 ("Religion and the Origins of the Death Camps, a Psychoanalytic Interpretation").
156. During the 1970s a new outburst of countersubversion has arisen on a rather small scale over the activities of the Reverend Sun Myung Moon and his Unification Church. Moon, a South Korean with thinly veiled messianic pretensions, presides over an international connection of religious communities which accept his leadership and his teaching that Jesus never was able to complete his mission, which involved marrying and having a family to rectify Eve's act of sexual infidelity with the serpent. The appeal of Moon's movement seems to stem less from this rather exotic exegesis of Genesis than from the movement's character as a "total institution," in which individual and family identity is subordinated in quasi-monastic fashion to total dedication to the life and work of the group. Several American families have engaged "deprogrammers" to abduct even adult children from the movement in an attempt to turn them against it. The fear aroused by an exotic, international, and closed community with unorthodox (though seemingly innocuous) sexual arrangements seems in many ways parallel to that of the countersubversive movements of earlier eras, though the ludicrous charges that emerged from earlier "crusades" do not seem to have appeared. On the "Moonies" and their opponents, see KENNETH L. WOODWARD et al., "Life with Father Moon," *Newsweek,* (June 14, 1976), pp. 60-66, and FREDERICK SONTAG, *Sun Myung Moon and the Unification Church* (Nashville: Abingdon, 1977). The revulsion that arose in the fall of 1978 from news of the mass suicides of the Reverend Jim Jones and his followers (the "Peoples' Temple") in Jonestown, Guyana, further

accentuated popular distrust of such "cultic" movements. See Jo THOMAS, "Practices of Cults Receiving New Scrutiny," *New York Times,* January 21, 1979, pp. 1 and 52.

157. Two standard works on the subject are NORMAN F. FURNISS, *The Fundamentalist Controversy, 1918-1931* (New Haven, Conn.: Yale University Press, 1954 [Archon reprint 1963]), and ERNEST R. SANDEEN, *The Roots of Fundamentalism, British and American* (Chicago: University of Chicago Press, 1970). See also SANDEEN's briefer treatment in his article "Toward a Historical Interpretation of the Origins of Fundamentalism," *Church History,* 36 (March 1967), 66-83, and AHLSTROM, *Religious History,* Chap. 48.

158. RICHARD QUEBEDEAUX, *The Young Evangelicals: Revolution in Orthodoxy* (New York: Harper & Row, 1974),* p. 10. QUEBEDEAUX is writing as a "Young Evangelical" hostile to Fundamentalism as he defines it.

159. See note 157 above.

160. AHLSTROM, *Religious History,* pp. 808-12, and C. NORMAN KRAUS, *Dispensationalism in America: Its Rise and Development* (Richmond, Va.: John Knox Press, 1958). See also SANDEEN, *Roots of Fundamentalism,* and TIMOTHY P. WEBER, *Living in the Shadow of the Second Coming: American Premillennialism 1875-1925* (New York: Oxford University Press, 1979).

161. AHLSTROM, *Religious History,* p. 814.

162. QUEBEDEAUX, *Young Evangelicals,* p. 22. This work is a good guide to the various strains of Evangelicalism and Fundamentalism.

163. See NICHOL, *Pentecostalism,* p. 80.

164. See MARTIN E. MARTY, *Righteous Empire: The Protestant Experience in America* (New York: Dial, 1970);* ROBERT T. HANDY, *A Christian America: Protestant Hopes and Historical Realities* (New York: Oxford University Press, 1971);* CLIFFORD S. GRIFFIN, *Their Brothers' Keepers: Moral Stewardship in the United States, 1800-1865* (New Brunswick, N.J.: Rutgers University Press, 1960); and AHLSTROM, *Religious History,* Chap. 51.

165. The best study of Sunday is WILLIAM G. MCLOUGHLIN, JR., *Billy Sunday Was His Real Name* (Chicago: University of Chicago Press, 1955). See also MCLOUGHLIN, *Modern Revivalism,* Chap. 8, and WEISBERGER, *They Gathered at the River,* Chap. VIII.

166. MCLOUGHLIN, *Billy Sunday,* Chap. 8.

167. WEISBERGER, *They Gathered at the River,* p. 258.

168. MCLOUGHLIN, *Billy Sunday,* Chap. 8.

169. RAY GINGER, *Six Days or Forever? Tennessee* v. *John Thomas Scopes* (Chicago: Quadrangle, 1958/69).* See also FREDERICK LEWIS ALLEN, *Only Yesterday* (New York: Harper & Row, 1931/64),* Chap. VIII, section 4.

170. Produced and directed by STANLEY KRAMER, 1960, starring Spencer Tracy and Frederick March.

171. On Graham, see MCLOUGHLIN, *Modern Revivalism,* Chap. 9, and the full-length biographical study, *Billy Graham: Revivalist in a Secular Age* (New York: Ronald, 1960). See also JOE E. BARNHART, *The Billy Graham Religion* (Philadelphia: Pilgrim, 1972), and DAVID FROST, *Billy Graham Talks with David Frost* (London: Hodder & Stoughton, 1966). On the dynamics of the "Crusades," see RONALD C. WIMBERLEY et al., "Conversion in a Billy Graham Crusade: Spontaneous Event or Ritual Performance?", *The*

Sociological Quarterly, 16 (Spring 1975), 162-70. Two recent works on Graham from very different perspectives are JOHN POLLOCK, *Billy Graham: Evangelist to the World* (San Francisco: Harper and Row, 1979), and MARSHALL FRADY, *Billy Graham: A Parable of American Righteousness* (Boston: Little, Brown, 1979). See also the review of the latter by GARRY WILLS, *New York Times Book Review,* 20 May 1979,1.

172. See WILLIAM M. CLEMENTS, "The Rhetoric of the Radio Ministry," *Journal of American Folklore,* 87 (October 1974), 318-27.

173. MCLUHAN, *Understanding Media: The Extensions of Man* (New York: New American Library/Signet, 1964),* Chap. 30.

174. For an autobiographical history of Campus Crusade, see BILL BRIGHT, *Come Help Change the World* (Old Tappan, N.J.: Revell, 1970). See also QUEBEDEAUX, *New Evangelicals,* pp. 30-31.

175. On this sort of symbiosis, see ELZEY, "Liminality and Symbiosis in Popular American Protestantism."

176. See QUEBEDEAUX, *New Evangelicals,* pp. 90-94. For historical background, see DOUGLAS JOHNSON, ed., *A Brief History of the International Fellowship of Evangelical Students* (Lausanne: I.F.E.S., 1964). I am indebted to my colleague Professor EDWIN M. YAMAUCHI of the Miami Department of History for bibliographical suggestions in this area.

177. See BRIGHT, *Come Help Change the World, passim.*

178. This series is distributed by Chick Publications, Chino, California. JACK T. CHICK is the author.

179. HAL LINDSEY, *The Late Great Planet Earth* (Grand Rapids, Mich.: Zondervan, 1970).*

180. BARNHART, *The Billy Graham Religion,* p. 52.

181. Although a considerable number of "Christian" bookstores have sprung up during the 1970s, it is significant that many Evangelical works are packaged identically with other mass-circulation paperbacks and sold in the same retail outlets with mysteries, cookbooks, and sex manuals. On the other hand, a *Christian Yellow Pages* urging selective buying aroused considerable controversy when it was publicized in newspapers and on network evening news programs, and an advertisement for an *Evangelical Marketing Report* recently arrived in my mail addressing me as "one of the key decision-makers in the Christian community." (I found this rather surprising.) These examples point to an ambivalence within Evangelicalism over whether to "infiltrate" or simply to imitate the broader popular culture, while utilizing its techniques of advertisement and distribution in all cases. The *Watchtower* of the Jehovah's Witnesses still comes on newsprint, but its graphics are of commercial quality.

182. See SIDNEY E. MEAD, *The Lively Experiment: The Shaping of Christianity in America* (New York: Harper & Row, 1963), Chaps. II and IV, for a seminal discussion of this question. See also the recent collection of MEAD's essays published under the title *The Nation with the Soul of a Church* (New York: Harper & Row, 1975).* The classic essay on Civil Religion is ROBERT N. BELLAH, "Civil Religion in America," in BELLAH and MCLOUGHLIN, eds., *Religion in America* (Boston: Beacon, 1968),* pp. 3-23. (See also BELLAH's more recent reflections in *The Broken Covenant: American Civil Religion in Time of Trial* [New York: Seabury, 1975].*) Recent writings on the subject are too

numerous to catalogue fully. A good sense of the state of the discussion can be obtained from Russell E. Richey and Donald G. Jones, eds., *American Civil Religion* (New York: Harper & Row, 1974),* and Martin E. Marty, *A Nation of Behavers* (Chicago: University of Chicago Press, 1976), Chap. 8.

183. See Carl Bridenbaugh, *Mitre and Sceptre: Transatlantic Faiths, Ideas, Personalities and Politics 1689–1775* (New York: Oxford University Press, 1962).*

184. See Ahlstrom, *Religious History,* Chap. 23.

185. A stimulating discussion of the symbolic system that was forged during the Revolutionary period is Catherine L. Albanese, *Sons of the Fathers: The Civil Religion of the American Revolution* (Philadelphia: Temple University Press, 1976), on which the following draws heavily. On the Revolutionary period, see also Ahlstrom, *Religious History,* Chap. 23; Peter N. Carroll, ed., *Religion and the Coming of the American Revolution* (Waltham, Mass.: Ginn-Blaisdell, 1970); Alice M. Baldwin, *The New England Clergy and the American Revolution* (New York: Ungar, 1928/58); Alan Heimert, *Religion and the American Mind: From the Great Awakening to the Revolution* (Cambridge, Mass.: Harvard University Press, 1966); and Edmund S. Morgan, "The Puritan Ethic and the American Revolution," *William and Mary Quarterly,* 3rd ser., 24 (January 1967), 3–43.

186. On the Enlightenment and American religion, see Ahlstrom, *Religious History,* Chap. 22; Henry F. May, *The Enlightenment in America* (New York: Oxford University Press, 1976); Daniel J. Boorstin, *The Lost World of Thomas Jefferson* (Boston: Beacon, 1948/60);* and the older, not always reliable G. Adolf Koch, *Religion of the American Enlightenment* (New York: Crowell, 1933/68).*

187. Albanese, *Sons of the Fathers,* Chap. 2.

188. Ibid., Chap. 5.

189. Mason L. Weems, *The Life of Washington,* ed. Marcus Cunliffe (Cambridge, Mass.: Harvard University Press, 1962).* See also Wesley Frank Craven, *The Legend of the Founding Fathers* (New York: New York University Press, 1956).

190. See Ruth Miller Elson, *Guardians of Tradition: American Schoolbooks of the Nineteenth Century* (Lincoln, Nebr.: University of Nebraska Press, 1964),* esp. Chap. 6.

191. These *Readers,* which have recently been enjoying a resurgence of popularity, have been reissued by Signet Classics and the American Book Company. Henry Steele Commager's introduction to the Signet Classic reissue of the *Fifth Eclectic Reader* (New York, 1962)* is especially helpful. See also Richard D. Mosier, *Making the American Mind: Social and Moral Ideas in the McGuffey Readers* (New York: King's Crown Press, 1947).

192. See glossary.

193. Henry Wilder Foote, *Three Centuries of American Hymnody* (Cambridge, Mass.: Harvard University Press, 1940), pp. 226–27; Albert Edward Bailey, *The Gospel in Hymns: Backgrounds and Interpretations* (New York: Scribner's, 1950), pp. 491–92.

194. Foote, pp. 252–54; Edward D. Snyder, "The Biblical Background of the 'Battle Hymn of the Republic,'" *New England Quarterly,* 24 (June 1951),

231–38; PAUL S. BOYER, "Julia Ward Howe," in *Notable American Women,* II, 225–29.

195. KATHERINE C. BALDERSTON, "Katherine Lee Bates," in *Notable American Women,* I, 114–15.
196. MARTY, *A Nation of Behavers,* p. 194.
197. On the War of 1812, see WILLIAM GRIBBIN, *The Churches Militant: The War of 1812 and American Religion* (New Haven, Conn.: Yale University Press, 1973). On the Spanish-American War, see AHLSTROM, *Religious History,* pp. 878–80, and ROBERT L. BEISNER, *Twelve Against Empire: The Anti-Imperialists, 1898–1900* (New York: McGraw-Hill, 1968/71).*
198. On the Civil War, see AHLSTROM, *Religious History,* Chap. 41; CHESTER F. DUNHAM, *The Attitude of the Northern Clergy toward the South, 1860–1865* (Toledo, Ohio: Gray, 1942); GEORGE FREDERICKSON, *The Inner Civil War: Northern Intellectuals and the Crisis of the Union* (New York: Harper Torchbooks, 1965/68);* WILLIAM J. WOLF, *Lincoln's Religion* (*The Almost Chosen People*) (Philadelphia and Boston: Pilgrim, 1959/63/70);* JAMES W. SILVER, *Confederate Morale and Church Propaganda* (New York: Norton, 1957/67);* WILLIAM A. CLEBSCH, "Christian Interpretations of the Civil War," *Church History,* 30 (June 1961), 212–22; CONRAD CHERRY, ed., *God's New Israel: Religious Interpretations of American Destiny* (Englewood Cliffs, N.J.: Prentice-Hall, 1971),* Part 4. (CHERRY is good on the general relationship between religion and war in the American experience.)
199. On World War I, see AHLSTROM, *Religious History,* Chap. 52, and RAY H. ABRAMS, *Preachers Present Arms* (Scottsdale, Pa.: Herald Press, 1933/69).
200. AHLSTROM, *Religious History,* Chap. 56. See also JOHN MORTON BLUM, *V Was for Victory: Politics and American Culture During World War II* (New York: Harcourt Brace Jovanovich, 1976).
201. W. LLOYD WARNER, *The Living and the Dead: A Study of the Symbolic Life of Americans* (New Haven, Conn.: Yale University Press, 1959). See also CATHERINE L. ALBANESE, "Requiem for Memorial Day," *American Quarterly,* 26 (October 1974), 386–98.
202. WESLEY FRANK CRAVEN, *Legend of the Founding Fathers,* Chap. 5.
203. In conversation.
204. A term coined by the folklorist RICHARD M. DORSON.
205. New York: Grosset & Dunlap/Universal, 1929/41/61.*
206. Ibid., pp. 194–95, 232–46.
207. Ibid., pp. 234, 239–41.
208. Ibid., pp. 259–60.
209. Ibid., pp. 43–44, 289–303.
210. Ibid., Chap. 10. On the *theios aner* motif, see ALBANESE, *Sons of the Fathers,* Chap. 6; MORTON SMITH, "Prolegomena to a Discussion of Aretalogies, Divine Men, The Gospels and Jesus," *Journal of Biblical Literature,* 90 (1971), 174–99; PETER BROWN, "The Rise and Function of the Holy Man in Late Antiquity," *Journal of Roman Studies,* 61 (1971), 80–101. See also DIXON WECTER, *The Hero in America* (Ann Arbor, Mich.: University of Michigan Press, 1941/63).*
211. LEWIS, *Myths After Lincoln,* Part Two ("The American Judas").

4

Post-Modern, Post-Puritan: Religion in Mass Society

RELIGION AND THE POST-MODERN ERA

Many of the scholarly interpretations of our present time—the twentieth century, and, more especially, the period that began after the end of the Second World War—converge around a common theme that we are living in a new era. Our own age is a period qualitatively different from that which began with the Renaissance and Reformation and which finally dissipated its energies and yielded to a new *Zeitgeist.* The previous epoch had been one of transition, of rapid and dizzying change, of confidence and optimism, of nation and empire building, of individualism and nationalism. For David Riesman, it was the age of the "inner-directed" personality; for Sydney Ahlstrom, it was the "Great Puritan Epoch"; for sociologists, it was the "age of modernity"; and for economists it was the time of the flowering of capitalism.[1]

Most scholars agree that something important did happen, that certain social forces did in fact converge during the twentieth century to result in a new incipiently universal culture. Much of this change was the result of the development of mass commications—telegraph, telephone, radio, television, motion pictures, computers—a process begun by Gutenberg that finally reached critical mass in our own century. As a result, the world has become, in Marshall McLuhan's phrase, a "global village" in which American audiences could watch the most recent episodes of the Vietnam War each night over the dinner table. Although it is a time of emerging national feeling, especially in the nations of the Third World, the process of modernization taking place in those nations is bringing their cultural "infrastructure" increasingly into conformity with that of the already developed countries.[2] A universal culture seems to be emerging, with the profoundest consequences for everyone even in the remotest corners of the planet. It is a culture based on technology, a force that does not respect traditionalistic or personal distinctions of any sort but demands only competence and efficiency for its maintenance. What the actual outcome of these developments will be is beyond prediction. What seems plausible, however, is that the tone of the emergent culture will be universalistic rather than particularistic; functional rather than personal; collective rather than individual; and socialist rather than capitalist. Whether its ultimate consequences will be humanizing or oppressive remains to be seen.

Just as the United States took the lead in the drive toward modernization during the nineteenth century, so does it seem to point the way toward the New Culture. As we have seen, America has from its beginnings been a pluralistic nation with a self-conscious and even artificial origin, although tendencies toward neo-tribalism have occasionally been extremely strong. The transformation of its capitalistic institutions with origins in "rugged individualism" into multinational conglomerates has pointed the way for an international economic order. Its relatively open social system, combined with at least theoretical opportunities for universal literacy and education, has resulted in a minimizing (though by no means an obliteration) of social distinctions. The mass media have in fact created a national (and incipiently international) culture that has increasingly been concentrated in television, and has thus provided a new common vocabulary of images and references for everyone. Finally, as David Riesman and his associates argued as long ago as 1950, a new personality type has been shaped by this new "mass culture," an "other-directed" person who responds neither to the dictates of tradition nor to an internalized set of values, but who rather takes cues from his peer group, and modifies his values and actions according to signals received from the world around him.[3]

Much of the groundwork for this new culture was established during the nineteeth century in the emergence of a middle class predominant not only economically and politically but also numerically. (It has been said that America is the first nation to have a middle-class majority.) The major correlation between religion and the emergence of this middle class has been Protestantism's role in helping to mold a disciplined personality type aimed toward mastery and achievement in this world.[4] With the proliferation of bureaucracy in the twentieth century and the concomitant erosion of the possibility of free action by the individual, together with the general achievement of a high level of economic well-being, the mainspring of this drive for achievement began to unwind a bit. Nevertheless, the culture—and the religion—of the later twentieth century still reflected many of the emphases and consequences of a bourgeois civilization that had lost much of its energy.

One of the primary consequences of the development of a middle-class culture might be called *privatization.* With the gradual separation of the family from the broader social and economic realm during the process of urbanization and industrialization, many people seemed to divide experience into two realms, the private and the public. (In a way, these form a parallel with the categories of sacred and profane.) The public realm of political, economic, and intellectual competition was reserved primarily for men; women and children were relegated to the domestic sphere, the hearth of which became almost as sacred as that of the ancient Romans. As the clergy became less and less effectual in the public realm, they also, together with the whole sphere of religion, came to be regarded by many as part of the private sphere.[5] As religious pluralism became increasingly real, a reticence about public discussion of religious matters became an increasingly important part of middle-class genteel reserve, and religion thus became ever more relegated to the private sector. For many of the "comfortable" middle class, the force of Protestantism as a communal bond and as an "inner gyroscope" gradually evaporated. What was left was an emphasis on the individual, alone with his family to contemplate eternal things.

The nearly universal literacy of the middle classes, together with an ever-advancing communications technology, helped to create a Protestant middle-class popular religion that was quite distinct from many of the other phenomena which we have been calling "popular." This new popular Protestantism reflected theological liberalism in that it was no longer supernaturalistic, no longer discontinuous with the natural and social orders. Charles Sheldon's *In His Steps,* which we discussed earlier, is a good example of the liberal picture of Jesus as exemplar and friend rather than savior, as is the Jesus-as-advertising-executive of Bruce Barton's *The Man Nobody Knows* (1925).

The ostensible message of Sheldon's novel is that all should take up the cross and follow Jesus, just as the novel's characters do, no matter what the worldly cost. Although this may in fact have been the consequence in some few cases, one seldom comes across accounts of people actually moved to do so by Sheldon's work. Yet millions of people did read Sheldon. One concludes that the actual religious function of *In His Steps* and similar works was not to stimulate people to action, but rather to induce them to comtemplate the (fictive) good works of others and to derive edification therefrom. In short, simply to read such a book as *In His Steps,* in the privacy of one's own living room or study, became a devotional act in itself. Where *Uncle Tom's Cabin* had moved people to act—where it had a demonstrably *public* effect—the enthusiastic yet socially ineffectual reception with which *In His Steps* met was a good indication of the emergence of a popular Protestant literature that was for the most part a substitute for rather than an ancillary to corporate worship or activity.

Where both Calvinistic Puritanism and liberal Unitarianism had been active faiths, the new religiosity that was beginning to emerge with an increasingly complex and intractable set of social institutions was characterized instead by an in-turning and a passivity. As cultural value was transferred from the act of production to that of consumption, so did religion also become a consumer product in many cases. Television, motion pictures, and novels, together with massive Billy Graham crusades, all required little of the spectators beyond their attention. Self-transformation often involved not so much the dramatic conversions induced by Charles Finney but rather a sort of internal psychological tinkering, à la Norman Vincent Peale, designed to bring about an adjustment to and acceptance of immediate circumstances rather than a determination to transform both the self and the environment. The introduction of courses entitled "Life Adjustment" into the high school curriculum during the 1950s epitomized this cultural tendency, which found religious as well as secular expression.

Another way in which this general cultural direction has expressed itself in American material culture has been in a confusion of categories. The historian Daniel Boorstin has cleverly pointed out that modern technology has in fact blurred all sorts of previously nearly absolute contrasts.[6] Air conditioning and plate-glass windows have diminished the force of the inside-outside dichotomy. Mobile homes are a *tertium quid* between stationary and transitional modes of being. Technology, in short, affects perception, and with perception the basic categories through which we interpret the world. In similar fashion, regional distinctions have been increasingly eroded not only by universalistic civil rights legislation but also by the development of an interstate system of divided highways with accompanying fast-food chains, motel franchises, and the like. Just as it is often difficult to know whether one is indoors or outdoors, it is similarly difficult to tell whether one is in Connecticut or Texas (or in a mobile home somewhere in between).

Not surprisingly, religion has not gone unaffected by these tendencies toward universalism and cultural homogeneity. Liberal and Neo-Orthodox churches, at the "elite" level, have generally taken a lead in endorsing various universalistic causes such as civil rights and women's liberation. The "mainline" denominations also for a brief period flirted with the "COCU" proposal (Consultation on Church Union) in which duplication of resources and facilities could be eliminated while individual traditions would still be preserved within a common bureaucratic structure.[7] The forces of particularism, however, proved to be too strong, and the ecumenical movement began to founder in the 1970s. The Roman Catholic Church has also recently lowered many of the barriers it had maintained against Protestantism before the Second Vatican Council, but the result seems to have been confusion about Catholic identity as much as anything else. From the vantage point of the later 1970s, it seems that interdenominational relationships have in fact improved, but that a considerable backlash in favor of traditionalism has also resulted. This conflict is as yet unresolved.

One of the phenomena of line-blurring against which the Neo-Orthodox movement arose as a protest was the general tendency in American (or perhaps any) culture for the lines between religion and society to erode. In the Puritan community, where Church and State and religion and culture largely coincided, the church attempted to balance its message of collective mission with the theme of collective judgment through the vehicle of periodic jeremiads. During the earlier nineteenth century, the Evangelicals who aimed at an informal religious hegemony over the mores and beliefs of the new nation viewed the new government as indifferent or even at times hostile to Evangelical causes (e.g., the abolition of Sunday mail delivery), and stood in a certain tension against the secular institutions of society. Many highly disparate religious subcultural groups—Catholics, Jews, Mormons, Fundamentalists—interpreted their mission in terms of keeping themselves pure from the contaminating influences of the culture at large and from other religious groups.

During the later nineteenth century, the theological movement known as "Liberalism" arose, with its principal strength in the seminaries and upper-middle-class churches. Liberalism deemphasized boundary symbolism of any sort, including that between the divine and human and between religion and culture.[8] Liberalism made some important contributions to the rapprochement between religion and science and to a Christian critique of social problems in the form of the Social Gospel. It was never a broadly popular movement, however, and its intellectual appeal was in large measure displaced by that of Neo-Orthodoxy, which seemed to speak more coherently to the dilemmas raised first by the Depression and then by the Second World War. Like Liberalism, Neo-Orthodoxy was not a popular creed, and was unable to compete on a broad scale with Evangelicalism during the post war period.[9]

Even Evangelicalism, however, was not able for long to maintain a distance between its teachings and the values and pressures of the culture at large. The aim of Evangelicals since the early nineteenth century had been the at least covert supervision and direction of national life, and the popularity of Billy Graham and his political well-wishers during the 1950s and 60s seemed to point to the achievement of this goal. Graham himself had been nurtured in a Fundamentalist atmosphere, and had begun his career as an evangelist with a strongly pre-millennial emphasis. The imminent threat of atomic war which overshadowed the 1950s seemed to lend plausibility to this message, and Graham rapidly achieved a considerable following across the social spectrum.[10]

With the passage of time, however, Graham's message began to change. As the mass media extended his recognition far beyond that which his urban "crusades" could have made possible, his friendship and at least tacit endorsement became increasingly valuable to political figures, especially those of a conservative bent. Graham's message was also spread through highly sophisticated feature films distributed through his organization, which employed the structures of the mass media to convey a message that (perhaps not surprisingly) did not stand in very great tension with that which the media ordinarily conveyed. "A Sure Defense" (Graham preaching at the Pentagon) emphasized military preparedness fortified by evangelical piety, while "Oiltown U.S.A." was an undisguised celebration of Texas-style capitalism. Graham's particular friendship with Richard Nixon and his frequent appearance at White House "prayer breakfasts" lent a note of legitimacy to Nixonian programs and rhetoric until that president's credibility foundered and finally sank in the wake of the Watergate debacle.

Graham's career was by no means fatally injured by his identification with the Nixon Administration, although his judgment did come into some rather serious question. His crusades were continuing into the later 1970s, with a message stressing the need for dedicating oneself to Christ and adhering to a style of life characterized by traditional evangelical moral emphases. The crusades, however, were now staged in locales that would have been unthinkable during his earlier career, and included the Notre Dame stadium and Communist Hungary. Just as Bishop Fulton J. Sheen had attracted an extremely wide audience with his "Life Is Worth Living" television programs during the 1950s, so did Graham now appeal to Catholics and Protestants alike who shared a nostalgia for "traditional American values."[11] The exclusivism of both Catholic and Evangelical was dissolved in mass-media appeals to a national constituency for which diffuse symbols such as "morality" and "anti-Communism" superseded those of theological particularities. (Oral Roberts has also become active in staging television spectaculars, the overt religious content of which is practically nonexistent.[12])

RELIGION AND MASS MEDIA

Both Graham and Sheen attained popularity and recognition on such a vast scale largely through their skillful use of the mass media. Syndicated newspaper columns have also contributed to the impact of religious "celebrities" on the public consciousness, and Graham's "My Answer" is often distinguishable from the advice given by Abby Van Buren and Ann Landers (twin sisters of Jewish descent) only through its overtly Christian vocabulary.[13] (The answers to personal problems given by all basically consist of middle-class common sense and what one might call "ecumenical moralism.") Andrew Greeley, a statistical-minded sociologist and Catholic priest, also achieved popularity during the seventies through columns syndicated both in Catholic diocesan newspapers and in the popular press.

Motion pictures, however, were the first major vehicle through which America's minority religious communities began to achieve equal respectability and acceptability in the minds of the general public. This process helped bring about the "triple melting pot" described by Will Herberg in his *Protestant Catholic Jew*.[14] Sports and entertainment, together with politics, were the principal channels through which members of minority communities—Catholics, Jews, and later blacks—first began to achieve success and recognition on a national scale.[15] We have already discussed briefly the role motion pictures played in an attempt to instill a pan-ethnic national consciousness among Americans of differing descent to help create a spirit of unity for the war effort during the 1940s. During that same period, a series of extremely popular films also helped to transform the image of American Catholicism from that of a rather suspect subculture to a gently traditional community presided over by winsome priests and amiable nuns. *Going My Way* (1944) achieved especial popularity as the story of two lovable Irish clerics portrayed by Bing Crosby and Barry Fitzgerald. (It had been anticipated in its success by Spencer Tracy as Father Flanagan in *Boys Town* [1938].) Such diverse personalities as Frank Sinatra, Ingrid Bergman, Rosalind Russell, and Debbie Reynolds joined this roster in later films, and the peculiar phenomenon of a flying nun even appeared briefly in a television series.

Protestant ministers, while appearing occasionally in feature films, have not been nearly as appealing to the Hollywood imagination as have Catholic priests and nuns. On the rare occasions when they have appeared, they have generally been portrayed as exponents and embodiments of the sort of muscular Christianity exemplified in Pat O'Brien as priest. (Frederic March as the firm but lovable Methodist preacher in *One Foot in Heaven* [1941] is a good example.) A film such as *Elmer Gantry,* which depicted a hypocritical, manipulative Billy Sunday-style evangelist, could not be made until 1960, although the Sinclair Lewis novel of the same name from which it was adapted had been first published in 1927. Rabbis have almost never been featured as leading characters in feature films, although one has become a popular detective on the model of Father Brown in Harry Kemelman's series of novels.[16]

The treatment of religious themes in humor is another indication of certain basic social and attitudinal shifts among the American public during the twentieth century. Until the time of the Second Vatican Council and the election of the first American Catholic president during the early 1960s, neither of those two bastions of mass-circulation humor, the *New Yorker* and the *Reader's Digest,* utilized religious themes very frequently. Such *New Yorker* cartoons that dealt with the subject usually depicted middle-aged, sexless, vaguely Protestant clerics involved in mildly incongruous situations. Though a certain expansion of scope and freedom of treatment came about roughly after 1960, religion as a major theme for humor never seemed to appeal to the "worldly" sensibilities of the *New Yorker* constituency.

The case of the *Reader's Digest* is considerably different. Where the *New Yorker* has traditionally adopted a pose of sophisticated skepticism toward "mainstream" American middle-class culture, the *Digest* has endorsed, even apotheosized, that culture consistently.[17] *New Yorker* humor in the post–Vatican II period has generally been *about* religion, and presented angels, devils, saints, Old Testament figures, and other characters from the American Sunday-School folk tradition in incongruous or anachronistic situations. *Digest* humor, on the other hand, may more properly be called *religious* humor in that it assumes that the reader is more likely to be involved in rather than simply amused by religion.[18] Its thrust, therefore, tends to be more didactic and corrective than that of the *New Yorker. Digest* jokes and anecdotes, when not simply bad puns, are often used to chastize moderately deviant behavior on the part of both clergy and laity, and to recall these offenders to their appropriate norms.[19] Clergy, for example, may have fun poked at them for preaching dull sermons, for falling a bit short of the standards they are expected to live up to, or for taking a sanctimonious, "holier-than-thou" attitude toward others. Cardinal Cushing and Pope John XXIII were great *Digest* favorites because, although exemplary in their personal lives, they often deflated the pretensions of others who pretended that they held a monopoly on holiness or purity. The *Digest,* in short, consistently advocates a "middle road" similar in form if not exactly in content to *In His Steps:* one should not yield to temptation, but one should also not pretend that one is never tempted.

Specifically religious themes are only one entree into what might be called the religious dimensions of mass-circulation periodicals if we regard "religion" broadly. Many periodicals whose concerns are not narrowly technical or specialized in fact convey to their readers a broad interpretation of experience which may plausibly be regarded as a worldview. The *Reader's Digest* is in many ways the most successful example of this effort, since its circulation is so massive. In what follows, we will take a closer look at the *Digest* from this point of view, together with two newspapers of considerable but very different constituencies: the *National Enquirer* and the *New York Times.*

A look at any tabloid available at supermarket checkout counters everywhere should be sufficient to demonstrate that magic, in the broad sense of the word, is by no means dead. Almost every issue of the *National Enquirer* and its relatives features on the front page several recurrent themes.[20] First, "miracle" cures for cancer abound. Cancer has taken on a demonic quality in popular thought, since it remains in large measure uncurable by medical science. As such, it is not surprising that it can continue to provoke great anxiety, and take on symbolic significance as the representative of all that is maleficent and uncontrollable in the cosmos. That science should promise "miraculous" cures illustrates the "mystical" aura which continues to surround that realm of investigation, and it is paradoxical that the quintessence of disciplined, rational inquiry should be a contemporary locus of the miraculous.

Secondly, these tabloids abound in predictions of future events. (Astrological predictions and advice are by no means restricted to tabloids, but can be found in almost every daily newspaper.[21]) The "seeress" Jeanne Dixon prophesies about national events and the futures of public figures with great regularity, but few of these predictions ever seem to materialize.[22] Her continued popularity is evidence that accuracy is by no means the issue: the phenomenon of prophecy is itself the object of fascination. (As Dr. Johnson once remarked in a slightly different context, one wonders not that she does it well, but that she does it at all.) An occasional successful prediction is enough to outweigh the considerably larger number that come to naught. The popularity of the psychic diagnostician Edgar Cayce is a similar example of this continuing interest in magical (as opposed to ethical) prophecy.[23]

A third recurring feature in the tabloids is the cult of celebrities. Jacqueline Kennedy Onassis has been by far the most prominent of these in recent years, and will doubtless remain so for some time. Such celebrities seem to live in a world of their own, in which the rules that govern and restrict ordinary mortals are suspended. Their activities seem at least remotely analogous to those of the Olympian gods, who were scarcely models of moral probity by Christian standards, but who lived instead as exaggerated mortals in a timeless realm. The Biblical epics produced by Hollywood (e.g., DeMille's 1956 remake of *The Ten Commandments,* and the 1961 *King of Kings,* with Tab Hunter as Jesus) are also versions of this mode of representation of divinity.[24] In these films, religious heros are appropriately played by celebrities, and the continuity between player and played is fitting. Also, this *theios aner* motif— the superhuman hero with divine attributes— is very much in harmony with one important mode of popular piety of the early Christian centuries.[25]

Gambling is another form of symbolic behavior with magical affinities or overtones, and the tabloids often feature stories about lottery winners.[26] Casting lots has a venerable lineage in many religious traditions, and the hope that one may suddenly acquire fabulous wealth through no effort is an important underground countercurrent in American popular culture. That it goes against the grain of evangelical morality, which teaches that unearned wealth is illegitimate and tainted, has led to a considerable amount of cultural conflict over such issues as legalized gambling and public lotteries. The entire state of Nevada is a refuge for "big-time" gambling, and stands out against its moralistic neighbor Utah as an island where the ordinary mores of American middle-class life are permanently suspended. (Nevada's traditionally liberal divorce laws have also enhanced this reputation.[27]) Gambling is also associated with subcultures that reject standard Protestant mores, such as aristocrats, the underworld, and the Catholic Church. The latter's sponsorship of bingo tournaments is a reflection of that church's traditional tolerance for peasant folkways, and has been a longstanding point of contention in Catholic-Protestant relations in many communities.[28]

One magazine has stood out for decades as *the* representation of middle-class life and values: the *Reader's Digest.*[29] The *Digest* was established in 1922 by DeWitt and Lila Acheson Wallace, and rapidly achieved pre-eminence among all nonspecialized American journals in circulation and general prestige. In many ways, the *Digest* stands in continuity with the McGuffey *Readers* of the previous century. Both are compilations rather than original compositions, and consist of items selected from the general literary materials available in the culture at large. These materials are then edited and assembled in such a way as to represent the themes and values of that culture in readily available form. In both cases, the editors were thoroughly imbued with the ethos of midwestern Presbyterianism, and this evangelical bias is clearly reflected in their editorial policies. In neither case, however, is the bias expressed in explicitly theological terms. Rather, a system of values derived from implicit religious assumptions is disseminated as an unspoken frame of reference which underlies all of the other aspects of culture and society that are dealt with explicitly. Each, in short, is a vehicle for promoting *diffuse* religiosity, and each in its time has been phenomenally successful.

The basic preoccupation of the *Digest* is *order.* Where the world of the tabloids is fundamentally disorderly, a world in which miracles happen frequently and the rules of nature may be reversed at any time, the *Digest* instead celebrates the ordinary and shudders at deviations from the norm. The seemingly extraordinary personalities celebrated in "The Most Unforgettable Character I've Met" features turn out in fact to be quite ordinary after all. Celebrities turn out to be not demigods, but down-to-earth people possessed of the homely virtues shared (or at least admired) by all of us. Although the *Digest* is often associated with a right-wing political stance by liberal critics, it is better characterized as conservative with regard to the proper performance of duly assigned roles as defined by the culture at large. Although Harry Truman's policies were hardly in accord with the general tone of the *Digest,* he has been proclaimed "unforgettable" because he carried out his presidential duties with reasonable faithfulness. The more congenial Spiro Agnew, who had once been praised as "Vice-President Extraordinary" (i.e., he had performed his assigned functions with a certain exuberance), lived to see his fall from grace chronicled in the *Digest* in a condensation of an article from the "left-wing" *New York Times.* Agnew had, in short, strayed from his proper place, and thus rapidly became "forgettable" (i.e., no longer usable as a moral paradigm).

For the *Digest,* the various categories of life—mechanical, physical, moral, social, political, religious—are all linked together in their common governance by principles of order, and each realm is potentially usuable as a metaphor for another. A popular recurrent feature which illustrates this principle is the "I Am Joe's Pituitary Gland" or "I Am Jane's Ovary" series, in which the functions of the various parts of the body are lucidly and engagingly described in anthropomorphic language. The "structural" principle that emerges from these articles is the necessity of correct functioning in prescribed fashion. If bodily parts do not function in this fashion, the result is disorder—i.e., disease and ultimate death. The same principles, of course, hold true for the social order.

Order can be maintained or re-established at a number of different levels. Much attention is given to medicine and technology, the pragmatic disciplines that concern themselves with material problem solving. Governmental agencies such as the police and FBI are generally portrayed favorably as instruments of social order, but bureaucracies such as the Internal Revenue Service are suspect since they can easily compromise the realm of individual freedom and initiative. Religion of all sorts is naturally a good thing, and is presented primarily as a problem-solving tool. For example, religion provides a remedy for cognitive disorders in explaining the positive moral significance of apparently meaningless misfortunes. More generally, it is a vehicle for "inspiration," for instilling a state of mind that leads to a healthy, positive approach to life. The *Digest's* approach to religion, in short, is instrumental and diffuse: all religions are good insofar as they produce good results.

The *Digest* stands in continuity with that vast popular religious literature of the twentieth century which is generally classified as "inspirational." This sort of religiosity has affinities with Christian Science and the "mind-cure" movements of the earlier part of the century, the aim of which was primarily pragmatic. The best-known representative of this school is Norman Vincent Peale, whose *The Power of Positive Thinking* (1952) had sold over two and a half million copies by 1965, and thus became the third most popular nonfictional religious work in twentieth-century America.[30] Peale's message was nonsectarian and basically nontheological. He presented a series of practical techniques of auto-suggestion which would result in relaxation and confidence for middle-class people plagued by self-doubt and nervous tension. This practical, individualistic approach aimed at fitting people into the social and economic order as it was given, and had no implications for social change or criticism. Like the *Digest,* Peale is basically conservative in his acceptance of the world order and his focus on adjusting individuals so that they may fit smoothly and uncritically into the functioning of that order.

A third level of publications, whose appeal is primarily to the upper middle class, really takes us beyond our working definition of popular religion and culture, but should be mentioned briefly for comparative purposes. Such periodicals as the *New York Times,* the *New Republic,* and, in the explicitly religious sphere, *Commonweal* and the *Christian Century,* all share the liberal (or Neo-Orthodox) outlook that is primarily concerned with ethical reflection on social events.[31] The underlying assumption is that social problems are the result of ignorance and bad faith, and that individual human decisions are a major factor in setting right what has gone wrong. Broad social forces are real causal agents, but they can be mastered through informed analysis and through an ethical conscience based on principles commonly shared by Christianity and Judaism. Religious events are commonly treated in terms of their social and political ramifications, and the goal of the churches is tacitly assumed to be the promotion of positive social change. Political and religious institutions in which power and wealth tend to aggregate are viewed with suspicion as potentially corrupt, and the role of journalism is to keep the trustees of this power honest. The "investigative journalism" that was instrumental in the exposure of Watergate was perhaps the culmination of this attitude in actual political results. Although this worldview is influential among many who in fact make major decisions, it is by no means a "popular" outlook despite its propagation through the vehicles of the mass media.

Although it is impossible to make any precise statements about the impact of the diffuse religiosity we have been discussing, such as that represented by the *Reader's Digest,* it seems likely that the functional worldview of many middle-class Americans has been shaped at least as much by such forces as by the institutions of formal, organized religion. Religion itself has been influenced by the advent of mass culture and mass media, as a Sunday morning spent randomly watching television will indicate. Traditional religious symbols often become subsumed into nostalgic subcultural practices, such as "eating Jewish," or are absorbed into such broader cultural forms as the "American Christmas."[32] The public messages conveyed by spokespersons for particular organized groups are often couched in terms of broad, if not universal, appeal, and public issues such as abortion and school prayers generally polarize conservatives of all persuasions, Catholic, Protestant and, to a lesser extent, Jewish, against liberals from the same communions. Diversity of worldview still exists, but it now cuts across confessional boundaries rather than coinciding with them.

It seems likely that most Americans share the basic premises of one of the varieties of popular religion and culture which we have outlined above, with various admixtures of confessional particularity. All three of the modes discussed above share a basic acceptance of the social order as given, and all regard themselves in at least sentimental continuity with one of the major traditions of Western religion. Fundamentalists, Mormons, and members of other sectarian groups are by no means negligible exceptions to this pattern. Their own practical beliefs and actions, however, are in large measure coincident with these paradigms, although they may adhere more strenuously to their explicit and particularistic symbolic systems than do others.

Where three class-linked worldviews are indicative of continuing differences among Americans, another thrust of the mass media has been to overcome rather than accentuate such distinctions. *Sentimentalism* is a cultural mode which has been characterized as typical of the middle class, and which has permeated all manner of behavior and expression across the various gradations of the American social spectrum.[33] Sentimentalism may be defined as a falsification of emotion, an attribution of powerful sentiment to that which cannot carry or does not deserve such a burden, or the pretension that all is right with the world when other evidence would indicate that such, indeed, is not the case. Although the nineteenth century, in which a vast audience of women with the leisure to read readily-available popular fiction began to emerge, is often pointed to as the great age of sentimentality, the current age has its own version as well.

We have already mentioned in other contexts a number of examples of sentimental religious expression, such as *Uncle Tom's Cabin* and Victorian chromolithographs. Much of religious liberalism partook of the sentimental fashion in its emphasis on the basic goodness of the world and of human nature, and helped to fashion that American social and cultural milieu to which George Santayana forever fixed the label "The Genteel Tradition."[34] But where Victorian and early twentieth-century popular literature, such as *In His Steps,* often had a more or less explicit religious message or was built upon such a set of assumptions, that of the middle and late twentieth century abandoned many of those religious references which earlier generations would have expected and taken for granted. In some ways, the age of the mass-market paperback can be read as another manifestation of secularization.

It is possible to come to a somewhat different conclusion, though, if one examines exactly what does sell well in the mass market. It is certainly true that best-sellers with an overtly religious content are confined primarily to the large Evangelical sub-culture. However, many extremely popular writers serve a purpose or convey a message which in many ways resemble those of religion. One of the best examples of this phenomenon is the continuing popularity of the writings of the Lebanese "mystic," Kahlil Gibran.[35] Gibran's best-known work, *The Prophet* (1923), consists of the observations of one Almustafa on practically every aspect of life, and his wisdom about marriage has frequently been incorporated into contemporary wedding services. Both Gibran's prose and his accompanying sketches share a certain fuzziness of contour, a blurring of sharp distinctions in the interest of uttering "beautiful thoughts" the precise import of which is somewhat elusive. Both, moreover, are derivative: his drawings are sexless, effete imitations of William Blake's, while his writing listlessly echoes the cadences of the King James Bible. The general effect is that of a sentimental mysticism, designed to evoke vaguely religious thoughts and emotions but having roots in no coherent tradition. One writer has remarked about Gibran's popularity, "As organized religion loses its authority, disorganized religion fills its place."[36]

Other examples of the success of artifacts of popular culture as a sort of surrogate religion are the works of Erich Segal and Rod McKuen.[37] Segal's *Love Story* (1970), enormously popular in both book and film versions, is essentially a Victorian "tear-jerker" with a liberal admixture of four-letter words to convey a "tough" image. The immortal message of the book—"love is never having to say you're sorry"—is exactly the sort of unfocussed, ill-conceived "beautiful thought" which is characteristic of the sentimental tradition. Another extremely successful practitioner of the art is Rod McKuen, who writes and sings "poems" completely lacking in form, structure, and disciplined emotion. Though Segal is the son of a rabbi, neither he nor McKuen deal directly with religious themes. On the other hand, their traffic in "beautiful thoughts" places them in continuity with the sentimental liberal religious tradition, and they convey a message of universal but unfocussed "love" which overcomes such problems as evil with a misty sadness about suffering and death. (McKuen informs us that "It doesn't matter who you love or how you love but that you love.")[38]

Two final features of later twentieth-century sentimentalism which are worth notice are its increasingly personalistic focus and its greater "democratization" in comparison with its Victorian forerunners. Such an example of the latter as Henry Van Dyke's *The Story of the Other Wise Man* (1896) is typical of genteel American Victorianism not simply in its sentiment but its ethical thrust, its limited but nevertheless genuine sense of social responsibility.[39] Works such as *Love Story* and Richard Bach's *Jonathan Livingston Seagull* (1970), on the other hand, focus almost entirely on the individual—or the loving couple—as the locus of significance. Feelings seem to be all that matter, with little sense of any external, objective set of moral or ethical obligation other than being true to one's self (or "each other"). ("Situation Ethics" is more explicitly theological version of the same attitude.)

Secondly, where much Victorian literature was at least implicitly aimed at a reasonably comfortable middle class audience, or to those who aspired to such a status and already shared its values, the vast expansion of the American reading public during the twentieth century—as well as the even broader audience reachable through film, radio, television, and records—has muted the note of aspiration and effort which characterized Victorian culture. Social class distinctions are triumphantly, albeit transiently, overcome in *Love Story,* and Rod McKuen's wistful melancholy and memories of a lonely fatherless childhood reach out to a vast audience, mostly young, white, and of the middle class, but no longer particularly troubled by status anxiety or the need for social self-definiton. This is not to say that class distinctions have disappeared in contemporary America; rather, it is to point out that the middle class has expanded to such vast proportions that its taste and values dominate American popular culture almost completely. (Such aberrations as the "counter-culture" of the 1960s have been rapidly co-opted.)

Sentimentalism, then, is another good example of the erosion of symbolic boundaries which writers such as Boorstin have perceived as characteristic of twentieth-century culture. The works of Gibran, McKuen, Segal, Bach and others are all characterized by an absence of expressive, emotional, and conceptual rigor, a seeming withdrawal from the sharpnesses of the external world into a soft, misty interior realm where lovers never need to beg one another's pardon. Similarly, the natural/supernatural distinction of earlier American culture, whether folk or sophisticated, disappears in a benevolent metaphysical haze, and even sexual distinctions seem to disappear in the androgynous figures of Gibran's illustrations. Where androgyny may have a liminal quality in some cultures, here it only seems to point to an inability or unwillingness to make distinctions.

THE TRANSFORMATION OF SACRED TIME: THE HOLIDAY CYCLE IN THE POST-MODERN ERA

One of the major shifts in symbolic behavior which marked the transition from the medieval to the Protestant era was a reinterpretation of the idea of sacred time, which took the concrete form of the Puritan abolition of most of the holidays that were celebrated in the course of the liturgical year. During the past century or so, the emergence of new cycles of holidays, some new, others metamorphoses of traditional celebrations, began to refill the symbolic vacuum that had resulted from the impact of Puritan iconoclasm on American public life.

One example drawn from film provides a useful tie-in with the subject matter of the previous section, and illustrates nicely this change in conception in "sacred" or festal time. *White Christmas,* a movie first released in 1954 and still seen every December, featured the Irish Catholic Bing Crosby and the Jewish Danny Kaye (born David Daniel Kaminsky). The sentimental plot involves the machinations of two ex-GIs (Crosby and Kaye) to rally their old unit to the support of the postwar enterprise (a ski lodge) of their old commander. Their effort, after many comic and romantic complications, is naturally successful, and the film ends with a rendition of the title song. (Crosby's version of this song remains to this day the best-selling recording by a solo vocalist.)

Although *White Christmas* had no overt religious message, its theme and its popularity are a good example of the topics we have been discussing. For a nation torn by internal confusion and suspicion, the reminiscence of wartime cooperation and courage was extremely appealing, and the film's characters sang of army life with a mixture of humor and nostalgia. The role-reversal motif, in which former enlisted men get together to help out a general fallen on hard times, was equally appealing (in part, perhaps, simply because it demonstrated that rank and power are transient in a democratic and socially mobile society).

The curious thing about the film was the fact that it was *not* in fact overtly religious, despite the inclusion of one of the principal feasts of the Christian liturgical year in its title (and title song). This omission points to the development of a holiday cycle in America parallel to and partially coincident with that of the "Civil Religion"—namely, the family-centered festival. Independence Day, Memorial Day, Armistice (later Veterans') Day, and the birthdays of Washington and Lincoln (with the later formal addition of Martin Luther King Day and the informal remembrance of the assasination of John F. Kennedy on 22 November 1963) constitute the bulk of the one cycle, and all commemorate events of national significance. Sydney Ahlstrom has commented that the rescheduling of many of these occasions to convenient Mondays is an indication of their secularization into "long or lost weekends."[40]

Thanksgiving Day provides a link with the second, or family, cycle. The idea of a day of thanksgiving (together with its converse, the communal fast day, which has long since fallen into disuse) dates back in this country to the earliest of Puritan times. In recent years, however, Thanksgiving has come to be associated with overflowing supplies of food (especially turkey, the first preparation of which has emerged as a rite of passage for young women[41]), family reunions, and televised football games.

Halloween, Mother's and Father's Day, and even Easter have also arisen or been modified from their traditional meanings to emphasize one or more members of the family as their central focus. (Easter often seems to have more to do with rabbits and egg-rolling than the resurrection of Jesus, as the annual event on the White House lawn demonstrates.[42]) The primary family festival, however, is certainly Christmas.[43] The original dating of Christmas was itself artificial, and was chosen to correspond with, build on, and supersede the Roman feast of Sol Invictus ("the Unconquered Sun").[44] The Puritans, admittedly with some logic, suppressed its celebration because of these pagan associations, and declared that only the Sabbath was to be observed as sacred.[45] By the third and fourth decades of the nineteenth century such considerations began to lose their force, and the nostalgic descriptions of Christmas by Dickens and Irving provided the groundwork for a distinctively American celebration.[46] Dutch and German folklore helped shape the modern "Santa Claus," who received definitive form in Clement Moore's "A Visit from Saint Nicholas" (1822) and cartoonist Thomas Nast's subsequent illustrations thereof.[47] Theological liberalism, the Sunday-School movement, and the general sentimental mood of the middle and later years of the nineteenth century gradually resulted in the canonization of these images into popular religious (and general) culture.[48]

Over the centuries, Christmas also acquired a highly diverse canon of music. Latin hymns, English folksongs, Wesleyan compositions, Phillips Brooks' "O Little Town of Bethlehem," and numerous others all were explicitly religious, although the latter reflects some of the sentimentality and nostalgia that was characterisic of Victorian culture and that persists to this day.[49] During the twentieth century, Christmas songs (to call them "carols" would be stretching a point) dealt increasingly with "fakelore" themes such as Frosty the Snowman, Rudolph the Red-Nosed

Reindeer, and Angie the Christmas-Tree Angel (who enjoyed a brief popularity during the fifties). These and other artificial creatures occupied an indeterminate place in the chain of being with folklore figures and Disneyesque theriomorphs. That the motivation for many of these creations was primarily commercial needs little substantiation.

The iconography and imagery of Christmas, like that of the Civil Religion, is clearly eclectic, and was a long time in developing. "White Christmas" ends with an image that perhaps best captures its import: young girls dressed in fairy-princess costumes performing a ballet. They are surrounded by a large surrogate family (the reassembled World War II regiment and their nuclear families), and dance in front of a large Christmas tree. The divine child motif is evoked, but any explicit religious reference is deliberately omitted. The group is presumably drawn from all faiths (Kaye and Crosby being good examples); even Jews can participate in this celebration, since it clearly has little to do with Christian doctrine or practice. It is instead a nostalgic representation of Americans assembled into a voluntaristic rather than a biological family, bound together by common sacrifice in war. They are now united in a common festival, drawn from a wide variety of sources, the meaning of which is purely human. Whiteness, as Joel Kovel has pointed out, is an apt symbol for the obliteration of all distinctions in a mass culture (although its meaning here is perhaps less sinister than some of those which Kovel develops[50]—nevertheless, there are no blacks in the scene, since they fought in segregated regiments during the war). The title song is filled with images of winter scenes (perhaps linking it indirectly with New England as the archetypal setting of the American past); of children; of past celebrations ("just like the ones I used to know"); and of generalized good wishes toward its auditors. The quest for a return to mythic origins, to the "strong time" of the childhood of Christianity and its founder, has become attenuated into a nostalgic desire simply to return to individual and national childhood.

DEATH IN THE POST-MODERN AGE

Other examples of the blurring of symbolic boundaries in American culture can be found in attitudes toward death. During the Middle Ages, and the Puritan period, death was regarded both as an inescapable natural process and as a time at which the last of the major life crises was passed.[51] The Catholic Church had provided symbolic mediation for these crises in the form of the sacraments (in the case of death, Extreme

Unction), which simultaneously called attention to the seriousness of the event and provided symbolic and social mediation in order to ease the accompanying tensions.[52] Puritanism eliminated much of the mediation, but nevertheless continued to stress the gravity of death in the preaching of funeral sermons and in the iconography with which tombstones were decorated.[53]

By the end of the eighteenth century, however, the skulls and Latin exhortations of American funerary art began to yield to floral and arboreal motifs, as well as cherubs and personal portraits. Corpses were no longer deposited in neglected churchyards, but rather in picturesque rural gardens.[54] By the time of the Civil War, the spectre of hellfire was becoming obscured by the new, smiling visage of heaven conjured by Elizabeth Stuart Phelps in *The Gates Ajar* (which Mark Twain described as depicting a "mean little ten-cent heaven about the size of Rhode Island"[55]). In a Victorian culture where death was uncomfortably associated with such unpleasant bodily realities as corpses, euphemisms such as "passing on" began to supplant the more direct "dying." Death, in short, was becoming a private rather than a public matter. Like all Victorian private matters, it was discreetly concealed behind a screen of avoidance and evasion.

During the twentieth century, the fine art of avoidance reached new levels in the emergence of the profession of funeral directing.[56] In one sense, this new art of cosmetics and embalming resulted in a much more direct confrontation with the physical reality of death, since the body was displayed rather than discreetly cremated. On the other hand, however, the image which the contents of the open coffin were intended to convey was that of artificially sustained or re-created life. The highest praise that could be applied to such corpses was that they appeared "lifelike" and "natural"—anything, in short, except dead. The elaborate pretense that death was something other than the end of life reached its culmination in Los Angeles's Forest Lawn "Memorial Park," which carried the rural cemetery movement of the nineteenth century to what was perhaps its logical conclusion.[57]

Charles H. Lippy has also recently called attention to the role sympathy cards play in the contemporary American encounter with death.[58] On the one hand, they fill the cultural expectation that *something* ought to be done when a friend or acquaintance "passes on." On the other, their general strategy is to avoid serious or controversial theological issues through rather bland sentiments which seldom mention the phenomenon of death directly. In general, they function to fill the symbolic vacuum left by the disappearance of the Catholic sacraments, while at the same time blurring the boundaries and distinctions (in this case, between life and death) those sacraments affirmed.

CALIFORNIA: THE LAST RELIGIOUS FRONTIER?

One other paradigm of contemporary popular religion remains to be considered before we come to an end. California has for some time been a symbolic alternative for Americans, a final cultural frontier where the rules of ordinary life might be suspended or transcended.[59] Hollywood, Forest Lawn, Disneyland, Orange County, and Haight-Ashbury have all constituted alternative worlds, very different from one another, but all sources of an at least temporary escape from the laws of time, space, and causality that govern our mundane existence.

In general terms, California has functioned as a literal and symbolic frontier, a zone where the past is nonexistent and irrelevant, where the old ways may be rejected with impunity and new beginnings undertaken at will.[60] In many ways it is the fulfillment of the Adamic motif of much nineteenth-century American literature, a world where innocence may be recovered after the moral, conceptual, and social baggage of the past has been cast off. The dangers of this vision as realized in California have been pointed out in such fictional works as Evelyn Waugh's *The Loved One,* Nathanael West's *The Day of the Locust,* and Aldous Huxley's *After Many a Summer Dies the Swan.* Such cautionary tales have not managed to impede very seriously the "California dreaming" of many, however, and new experiments and visions continue to proliferate.

Los Angeles especially provides a physical and social correlative for this religious and cultural impulse.[61] In these terms, it is the polar counterpoint of the New England towns to which we referred earlier. Where the latter were self-consciously layed out in geometrical order with the church demarcating the geographical and moral center, Los Angeles has no such center. It is in many ways the archetypally *anomic* city, a collection of individuals and groups linked together loosely by a common system of freeways. Although many Angelenos undoubtedly live lives in substantial conformity with the broader American norm, the possibility of experimentation, of a "protean" lifestyle, is certainly abetted by the lack of physical structures that conduce toward a settled, traditionally ordered way of life.

The openly or covertly religious expressions California has fostered are too numerous to discuss here in any detail. What we shall do instead is suggest a few common features which many of the groups, movements, and more general climates of opinion that have emerged recently in this context seem to share. No generalization will hold true for *every* group, but the correlation between symbolic expression and social experience—the probability that a given cultural matrix will produce a symbolic expression congruent with its social infrastructure—

makes it likely that even hostile and opposed groups will share some common features.

One of the common features of these groups and movements is their nearly unanimous rejection of history and tradition. In the case of Asian religions adapted to the American context, this takes the form of a coherent metaphysical system which denies significance to the historical process and the realm of earthly time.[62] Truth lies outside and beyond the realm of history, and earthly events are simply delusory appearances, *maya,* or illusion that veils ultimate reality. For groups with a revolutionary political orientation, history is the record of broken promises, a chronicle of exploitation and class privileges, whose precedent is invoked by the capitalistic enemy as an excuse for the established order.[63] For other, therapeutically oriented groups, history is simply irrelevant.[64] The "existential now" is all that matters, and techniques must be learned which make possible its full experience.

Similarly, the social order as it is currently constituted is irrelevant or offensive to these groups. For the politically oriented, it represents the triumph of privilege and power over justice and equity. For the metaphysically inclined, it is also part of the realm of illusion. Both groups have experimented with "alternate lifestyles" and social arrangements, especially of the commune variety. Communes have also been popular with the more radical segments of the "Jesus people," and the followers of the Korean messiah Sun Myung Moon have chosen to withdraw from the mainstream of society (although they, like the devotees of Krishna Consciousness, help to support themselves through the manufacture and sale of goods to the outside world.)[65] Therapeutic groups such as Scientology generally require substantial financial contributions from their members and clients, but make neither positive nor negative evaluations of the economy that generates these resources.[66]

Another (very American) emphasis that unites many of these groups is a concern with specific techniques for attaining religious experience or a transformation of consciousness. In this sense, they are in a rather unlikely continuity with Charles Grandison Finney, who devised his own techniques for bringing about immediate conversions to Evangelical Christianity. Unlike such older movements as Vedanta, Theosophy, and Rosicrucianism, which arose out of the same social context and shared many of the metaphysical assumptions of Christian Science, these groups have little patience with abstraction or metaphysics for their own sake. Rather, they are interested in attaining a new consciousness, a new state of being that is immediate and "tangible." The nature of the consciousness may be interpreted or described in a variety of ways, and the way thereto may consist of yoga exercises, drug "trips,"[67] chanting devotions to Krishna, massages, primal screams, or the "E-Meters" of Scientology. Once attained, this new consciousness may be simply an end in itself. For groups with an explicitly religious orientation, such as those of Asian origin, it often implies an ethical transformation as well. For others, which lack a formal theological tradition or ecclesiastical structure, the experience may be self-sufficient, although it may enable the experiencer to function more effectively and painlessly in the outside world.

Paradoxically, this phenomenon of transformation of consciousness as an end in itself may apply in groups that have defined their goals in terms of practical political action. In some cases, political groups have fallen victims to Freud's "narcissism of minor differences," and have dissipated their energies in a fruitless quest for ideological purity. Others, such as the ill-fated Symbionese Liberation Army, seem to have chosen as their tacit goal the achievement of a "revolutionary consciousness" in themselves and a few more-or-less willing converts such as the unfortunate Patricia Hearst, and finally elected death as a grand rhetorical gesture. Other more pragmatic and less "religious" movements such as Women's Liberation have utilized a less than ontological program of "consciousness raising" as a means to a reasonably well-defined set of social and political ends, and have already made a much more lasting impact on the American scene.

Some groups, such as the Scientologists, exhibit a direct continuity with many dominant themes in American society, such as a fascination with technology, and give their particular emphases a thin coating of metaphysical legitimation. Others—for example, some groups of Asian origin—have tacitly transformed their exotic religious sources into an indigenous product by stressing immediacy and practicality over an authentically Asian metaphysical perspective on the cosmos. Some of the politically oriented groups have simply expressed an adolescent exasperation with the gap between American ideals and realities, although they may have experienced genuine discomfort over America's rather unfortunate overseas involvements and racial policies during the 1960s. In short, it can be argued that all these groups, however exotic or radical their rhetoric and symbolism, have authentic roots in the American experience. Almost all of their emphases, in fact, have antecedents in the Transcendentalist "counterculture" of the antebellum period. (Drugs are a probable exception, although opium use was common among English literary figures such as Coleridge and De Quincey.)

That these movements have been possible at all is a reflection of the increasingly anomic character of significant segments of American life and culture. Although some of the new West Coast religious movements have taken the form of introversionist communities, others are really loose aggregates of individuals with a common interest, much like the Vedantists and Christian Scientists of an earlier generation.[68] Much of the "religious" literature available in paperback at supermarkets and shopping centers—on occultism, parapsychology, self-improvement, and "inspiration"—is oriented toward individual consumption. Like the clientele of religious television programs and "drive-in churches," its designated audience is composed of isolated people who may never communicate even indirectly with their like-minded fellows. The ancient linkage between symbolic expression and communities united by those symbols has begun to dissolve in America during the twentieth century. This may in fact be something genuinely new under the sun.

NOTES

1. DAVID RIESMAN, with NATHAN GLAZER and REUEL DENNEY, *The Lonely Crowd* (New Haven: Conn.: Yale University Press, 1950/61);* AHLSTROM, *Religious History* (New Haven: Yale University Press, 1972), Chap. 1. Important recent studies in the sociological and economic realms are DANIEL BELL, *The Coming of Post-Industrial Society: A Venture in Social Forecasting* (New York: Basic Books, 1973/76)* and JOHN KENNETH GALBRAITH, *The New Industrial State* (New York: New American Library/Signet 1967/68).* An extremely provocative appraisal of the age from a somewhat different sociological angle is PETER BERGER, BRIGITTE BERGER, and HANSFRIED KELLNER, *The Homeless Mind: Modernization and Consciousness* (New York: Random/Vintage, 1974).*
2. See BERGER et al., *The Homeless Mind.*
3. RIESMAN et al., *The Lonely Crowd,* pp. 19–24 and *passim.*
4. This, of course, is the "Weber thesis" developed by MAX WEBER in *The Protestant Ethic and the Spirit of Capitalism.*
5. On these developments, see CHRISTOPHER LASCH, *Haven in a Heartless World: The Family Besieged* (New York: Basic, 1977); RICHARD SENNETT, *The Fall of Public Man* (New York: Knopf, 1976); and ANN DOUGLAS, *The Feminization of American Culture* (New York: Knopf, 1977).
6. DANIEL J. BOORSTIN, *The Americans: The Democratic Experience* (New York: Random, 1973), Part V ("Leveling Times and Places"). See also RIESMAN, *Lonely Crowd,* pp. 157–58.
7. See WINTHROP S. HUDSON, *Religion in America,* 2nd ed. (New York: Scribner's, 1965/73),* p. 389 f.
8. On theological Liberalism, see AHLSTROM, *Religious History,* Chap. 46. See also KENNETH CAUTHEN, *The Impact of American Religious Liberalism* (New York: Harper & Row, 1962); LLOYD J. AVERILL, *American Theology in the Liberal Tradition* (Philadelphia: Westminster, 1967); and WILLIAM R. HUTCHISON, ed., *American Protestant Thought: The Liberal Era* (New York: Harper Torchbooks, 1968),* and *The Modern Impulse in American Protestantism* (Cambridge, Mass.: Harvard University Press, 1976).
9. On Neo-Orthodoxy, see AHLSTROM, *Religious History,* Chap. 55.
10. See note 171 in Chapter 3 for a general bibliography on GRAHAM. For a "transitional" statement of GRAHAM's position, see his *World Aflame* (Garden City, N.Y.: Doubleday, 1965).*

11. On Sheen, see E. C. PARKER, DAVID W. BARRY, and DALLAS W. SMYTHE, *The Television-Radio Audience and Religion* (New York: Harper & Brothers, 1955), pp. 125–30 and *passim.* Transcripts of Sheen's television programs have been published under the title *Life is Worth Living,* 2 vols. (New York: McGraw-Hill, 1953/54).*
12. On the later career of Oral Roberts, see DAVID EDWIN HARRELL, JR., *All Things Are Possible* (Bloomington, Ind.: Indiana University Press, 1975), pp. 150–59.
13. BILLY GRAHAM, *My Answer* (Garden City, N.Y.: Doubleday, 1960).*
14. Garden City, N.Y.: Doubleday Anchor, 1955/60.*
15. Jewish religion and culture did not become popular motion-picture subjects until the late fifties, though Jewish actors and actresses were successful long before this. The success of Otto Preminger's production of LEON URIS's *Exodus* in 1961 is worth noting in this regard. See also NORMAN L. FRIEDMAN, "Hollywood, the Jewish Experience, and Popular Culture," *Judaism* (Fall 1970), pp. 482–87.
16. *Friday the Rabbi Slept Late* (1964) and, to date (1979), six others.
17. See the fuller discussion of the *Digest* that comes later in this section.
18. Another way of describing *New Yorker* religious humor is to characterize it as more playful than satiric. In a broad sense, it stands in the tradition of Saints Francis of Assisi and Philip Neri, "fools for Christ" who implicitly recognized the common anti-structural elements of religion, play, and humor. The newspaper cartoon "Brother Juniper," whose creator is himself a Franciscan, is an example of religouis humor directly in this tradition.
19. One favorite theme of such humor is the disparity between the "counsels of perfection" of the Gospels and the inability of ordinary mortals to live up to them. A good example can be found in a collection of stories entitled "Quakers Feel Their Oats" in *Fun Fare: A Treasury of Reader's Digest Wit and Humor* (New York: Simon & Schuster, 1949), p. 100:

    > A gentle Quaker, hearing a strange noise in his house one night, got up and discovered a burglar busily at work. So he went and got his gun, then came back and stood quietly in the doorway. "Friend," he said, "I would do thee no harm for the world, but thee standest where I am about to shoot." (*The Kellogg Messenger*)

    (The story does not explain what a Quaker was doing with a gun in the first place.)
20. One reader of this manuscript commented that the *National Enquirer* was "the Bible" of one of her relatives, and did not recognize the appropriateness of the remark until I called it to her attention. I am reminded of one of my students who observed of a friend that "he goes to church religiously."
21. On astrology in America, see WILLIAM D. STAHLMAN, "Astrology in Colonial America: An Extended Query," *William and Mary Quarterly,* 13 (October 1956), 551–63, and ROBERT S. ELLWOOD, JR., *Religious and Spiritual Groups in Modern America* (Englewood Cliffs, N.J.: Prentice-Hall, 1973),* pp. 57 and 183–85. For background, see KEITH THOMAS, *Religion and the Decline of Magic* (New York: Scribner's, 1971), Chaps. 10–12.
22. See RUTH MONTGOMERY, *A Gift of Prophecy: The Phenomenal Jeanne Dixon* (New York: Bantam, 1965/66).*

23. See THOMAS SUGRUE, *There is a River: The Story of Edgar Cayce* (New York: Dell, 1942/67).*
24. See WILLIAM LEE MILLER, "Hollywood and Religion," *Religion in Life,* 22 (1953), 273–79, for a rather hostile appraisal of this phenomenon.
25. I am indebted to my colleague Roy Bowen Ward for this observation. See also bibliographical references in note 210, Chapter 3.
26. For studies of gambling in two very different American social contexts, see T. H. BREEN, "Horses and Gentlemen: The Cutural Significance of Gambling Among the Gentry of Virginia," *William and Mary Quarterly,* 3rd ser., 34 (April 1977), 239–57, and JAMES M. HENSLIN, "Craps and Magic," *American Journal of Sociology,* 73 (November 1967), 316–30. On lotteries in America, see JOHN S. EZELL, *Fortune's Merry Wheel: The Lottery in America* (Cambridge, Mass.: Harvard University Press, 1960).
27. On Nevada, gambling, and divorce, see BOORSTIN, *The Americans: The Democratic Exerience,* Part I, Chap. 7.
28. Another recurring topic in the tabloids is UFOs (unidentified flying objects or "flying saucers"). On this phenomenon, see ELLWOOD, *Religious and Spiritual Groups,* Chap. 4, and CARL G. JUNG, *Flying Saucers: A Modern Myth of Things Seen in the Sky* (New York: Harcourt Brace Jovanovich, 1969).* I am indebted to Kathi Fields for this observation.
29. The following discussion is based in large part on an article by my colleague Wayne Elzey which resulted from our collaboration on a study of the *Digest.* See WAYNE ELZEY, "The Most Unforgettable Magazine I've Ever Read: Religion and Social Hygiene in *The Reader's Digest,*" *Journal of Popular Culture,* 10 (Summer 1976), 181–90. For background on the *Digest,* see JAMES PLAYSTED WOOD, *Of Lasting Interest: The Story of the Reader's Digest* (Garden City, N.Y.: Doubleday, 1958), and JOHN BAINBRIDGE, *Little Wonder: Or, The Reader's Digest and How It Grew* (New York: Reynal & Hitchcock, 1946).
30. On "mind cure" and "new thought," see DONALD MEYER, *The Positive Thinkers* (Garden City, N.Y.: Doubleday, 1965);* LOUIS SCHNEIDER and SANFORD M. DORNBUSH, *Popular Religion: Inspirational Books in America* (Chicago: University of Chicago Press, 1958/73);* and AHLSTROM, *Religious History,* Chap. 60. On Peale in particular, see MEYER, Chap. XXIII; SCHNEIDER and DORNBUSCH, *passim;* and AHLSTROM, pp. 1033–34.
31. On religious periodicals, see MARTIN E. MARTY et al., *The Religious Press in America* (New York: Holt, Rinehart & Winston, 1963).
32. NORMAN L. FRIEDMAN, "Jewish Popular Culture in Contemporary America," *Judaism,* 24 (Summer 1975), 263–77 (on "eating Jewish," see pp. 266–68).
33. On sentimentalism, see E. DOUGLAS BRANCH, *The Sentimental Years 1836–1860* (New York and London: Appleton-Century, 1934),* and DOUGLAS, *The Feminization of American Culture.*
34. SANTAYANA, "The Genteel Tradition in American Philosophy" (1911) and other essays collected in DOUGLAS L. WILSON, ed., *The Genteel Tradition: Nine Essays by George Santayana* (Cambridge, Mass.: Harvard University Press, 1967). On American gentility, see also STOW PERSONS, *The Decline of American Gentility* (New York and London: Columbia University Press, 1973);* GORDON MILNE, *George William Curtis and the Genteel Tradition* (Bloomington, Ind.: Indiana University Press, 1956); and JOHN TOMSICH,

A Genteel Endeavor: American Culture and Politics in the Gilded Age (Stanford, Calif.: Stanford University Press, 1971.

An interesting footnote to the story of the American genteel tradition is contained in the 1977 General Theological Union doctoral thesis of WILLIAM MICHAEL HALSEY, entitled "The Survival of American Innocence: Catholicism in an Age of Disillusionment, 1920–1940," which at this writing is scheduled for publication by the University of Notre Dame Press in book form. HALSEY argues that, as "mainstream" American writers were beginning to abandon "gentility" and to bring about what HENRY F. MAY has called "the end of American Innocence," Catholic writers were adopting the same cultural values on a wide scale. (See MAY, *The End of American Innocence* [New York: Knopf, 1960].*)

35. For a sympathetic biography of Gibran, see JEAN GIBRAN and KAHLIL GIBRAN, *Kahlil Gibran: His Life and World* (Boston: New York Graphic Society, 1974). For a considerably less appreciative interpretation, see STEFAN KANFER, "But Is it Not Strange That Even Elephants Will Yield, and that The Prophet Is Still Popular?" *New York Times Magazine,* 25 June 1972, 8-9+, and replies, *ibid.,* 16 July 1972, 4.
36. KANFER, "But Is It Not Strange," 28.
37. A good account of MCKUEN and his work is WILLIAM MURRAY, "Says Rod McKuen: It Doesn't Matter Who You Love or How You Love, But That You Love," *New York Times Magazine* 4 April 1971, 32–34+. Two rather hostile treatments of the genre are JOSH GREENFELD, "The Marshmallow Literature and the Gang that Whipped It Up: Rod McKuen, Walter Benton, and Kahlil Gibran," *Mademoiselle* 68, 5 (March 1969), 206–207+, and NORA EPHRON, "Mush," *Esquire,* June 1971, 89–92+.
38. See MURRAY, "Says Rod McKuen," *supra.*
39. Henry Van Dyke (1852–1933), Presbyterian minister and later Professor of English at Princeton, is a good example of the genteel alliance of liberal religion and literature which ANN DOUGLAS writes about in *The Feminization of American Culture.* On Van Dyke, see TERTIUS VAN DYKE, *Henry Van Dyke: A Biography* (New York and London: Harper & Brothers, 1935), and EDWIN MIMS, ed., *The Van Dyke Book* (New York etc.: Scribner's, 1906).
40. AHLSTROM, *Religious History,* p. 1085.
41. I am indebted to MARIA FLEMING TYMOCZKO for this observation.
42. On Easter, see FRANCIS X. WEISER, *Handbook of Christian Feasts and Customs* (New York: Harcourt, Brace & World, 1952/58), Part II, chaps. 16 and 17, and JAMES H. BARNETT, "The Easter Festival: A Study in Cultural Change," *American Sociological Review,* 14 (February 1949), 62–70.
43. A good study of this phenomenon is JAMES H. BARNETT, *The American Christmas: A Study in National Culture* (New York: Macmillan, 1954). See also MARK BENNEY, ROBERT WEISS, ROLF MEYERSOHN, and DAVID RIESMAN, "Christmas in an Apartment Hotel," *American Journal of Sociology,* 65 (December 1959), 233–40, and notes 44 and 45 *infra.*
44. WEISER, *Handbook,* pp. 60–62, as well as his extended discussion of Christmas in Part II, Chaps. 6–10.
45. BARNETT, *American Christmas,* pp. 2–6; J. A. R. PIMLOTT, "Christmas under the Puritans," *History Today,* 10 (December 1960), 832–39; and IVOR DE-

BENHAM SPENCER, "Christmas, the Upstart," *New England Quarterly,* 8 (December 1935), 498–517.

46. BARNETT, *American Christmas,* pp. 14–18 and 26 f.
47. Ibid., pp. 24–31.
48. Ibid., pp. 6–9.
49. On Christmas Carols, see WEISER, *Handbook,* Chap. 7; BARNETT, *American Christmas, passim;* HENRY WILDER FOOTE, *Three Centuries of American Hymnoldy* (Cambridge, Mass.: Harvard University, 1940) and ALBERT EDWARD BAILEY, *The Gospel in Hymns* (New York: Scribner's, 1950), *passim.* On "O Little Town of Bethlehem," pp. 545–48.
50. JOEL KOVEL, *White Racism: A Psychohistory* (New York: Random/Vintage, 1970).*
51. A good general treatment of this subject is PHILIPPE ARIES, *Western Attitudes Towards Death* (Baltimore: Johns Hopkins Press, 1974).* On the Middle Ages, see T. S. R. BOASE, *Death in the Middle Ages* (New York: McGraw-Hill, 1972). On Puritanism, DAVID E. STANNARD, *The Puritan Way of Death: A Study in Religion, Culture, and Social Change* (New York: Oxford University Press, 1977),* and citations in note 53 *infra.*
52. See KEITH THOMAS, *Religion and the Decline of Magic,* pp. 36–40. See also ARNOLD VAN GENNEP, *The Rites of Passage* (Chicago: University of Chicago Press, 1960).*
53. See DICKRAN and ANN TASHJIAN, *Memorials for Children of Change* (Middletown, Conn.: Wesleyan University Press, 1974), and ALLEN I. LUDWIG, *Graven Images: New England Stonecarving and Its Symbols 1650–1815* (Middletown, Conn.: Wesleyan University Press, 1966).
54. On the rural cemetery movement, see STANLEY FRENCH, "The Cemetery as Cultural Institution: The Establishment of Mount Auburn and the 'Rural Cemetery Movement,'" *American Quarterly,* 26 (March 1974), 37–59, and THOMAS BENDER, "The 'Rural' Cemetery Movement: Urban Travail and the Appeal of Nature," *New England Quarterly,* 47 (June 1974), 196–211.
55. ELIZABETH STUART PHELPS, *The Gates Ajar,* ed. HELEN SOOTIN SMITH (Cambridge, Mass.: Harvard University Press, 1964), p. xxii and n. 21.
56. On the development of the funeral profession and allied practices, see JESSICA MITFORD, *The American Way of Death* (Greenwich, Conn.: Fawcett/Crest, c. 1963).*
57. On Forest Lawn, see MITFORD, Chap. 10; RALPH HANCOCK, *The Forest Lawn Story* (Los Angeles: Angelus Press, 1964);* and, for a fictionalized account, EVELYN WAUGH, *The Loved One* (Boston: Little, Brown, 1948).*
58. "Sympathy Cards and Death," *Theology Today,* 34 (July 1977), 167–77.
59. See PETER W. WILLIAMS, "Reflections in/on/of a Golden State," *American Quarterly,* 28 (Fall 1976), 496–503. One reader of this manuscript has suggested that the culture of most of California is really no different from the mass culture in which the rest of the country participates, and that those specifically California attitudes and phenomena described here are largely restricted to the Los Angeles and San Francisco Bay area.
60. See KEVIN STARR, *Americans and the California Dream 1850–1915* (New York: Oxford University Press, 1973).

61. On Los Angeles, see REYNER BANHAM, *Los Angeles: The Architecture of Four Ecologies* (Baltimore: Penguin, 1973).* See also ELLWOOD, *Religious and Spiritual Groups,* "Foreword."
62. On American religious groups of Asian origin, see ELLWOOD, *Religious and Spiritual Groups,* Chaps. 7 and 8; JACOB NEEDLEMAN, *The New Religions* (Garden City, N.Y.: Doubleday, 1970);* MARTIN E. MARTY, *A Nation of Behavers,* Chap. 6; AHLSTROM, *Religious History,* pp. 1047–54; EMMA McCLOY LAYMAN, *Buddhism in America* (Chicago: Nelson-Hall, 1977);* CHARLES Y. GLOCK and ROBERT N. BELLAH, eds., *The New Religious Consciousness* (Berkeley and Los Angeles: University of California Press, 1976), Part I; and articles in Section 5 of IRVING I. ZARETSKY and MARK P. LEONE, eds., *Religious Movements in Contemporary America* (Princeton, N.J.: Princeton University Press, 1974).*
63. See ROBERT N. BELLAH, "The New Consciousness and the Berkeley New Left," in GLOCK and BELLAH, eds., *New Religious Consciousness,* pp. 77–92.
64. On therapeutic groups, see DONALD STONE, "The Human Potential Movement," in GLOCK and BELLAH, *New Religious Consciousness,* pp. 92–115; THOMAS C. ODEN, *The Intensive Group Experience: The New Pietism* (Philadelphia: Westminster, 1972); NATHAN ADLER, *The Underground Stream: New Life-Styles and the Antinomian Personality* (New York: Harper Torchbooks, 1972);* KURT BACH, *Beyond Words: The Story of Sensitivity Training and the Encounter Movement* (Baltimore: Penguin, 1973);* SEVERIN PETERSON, *A Catalogue of the Way People Grow* (New York: Ballantine, 1971)* and MORTON LIBERMAN, *Encounter Groups: First Facts* (New York: Basic Books, 1973). For a brief, journalistic survey, see KENNETH L. WOODWARD et al., "Getting Your Head Together," *Newsweek,* 88 (September 6, 1976), 56–62.
65. On the "Jesus People," see DAVID F. GORDON, "The Jesus People: An Identity Synthesis," *Urban Life and Culture,* 3 (July 1974), 159–78; ROBERT S. ELLWOOD, JR., *One Way: The Jesus Movement and Its Meaning* (Englewood Cliffs, N.J.: Prentice-Hall, 1973); and DONALD HEINZ, "The Christian Liberation Front," in GLOCK and BELLAH, eds., *New Religious Consciousness;* on the "Moonies," see note 156, Chapter 3.
66. On Scientology, see ELLWOOD, *Religious and Spiritual Groups,* pp. 168–75, and HARRIET WHITEHEAD, "Reasonably Fantastic: Some Perspectives on Scientology, Science Fiction and Occultism," in ZARETSKY and LEONE, eds., *Religious and Spiritual Groups,* pp. 547–90, and ROY WALLIS, *The Road to Total Freedom: A Sociological Analysis of Scientology* (New York: Columbia University Press, 1977). For more popular treatments, see DR. [sic] CHRISTOPHER EVANS, *Cults of Unreason* (New York: Delta, 1973),* Chap. I, and GEORGE MALKO, *Scientology: The Now Religion* (New York: Delacorte, 1970). The sociologist BRYAN WILSON classifies such movements as "manipulationist,"—that is, using religious or metaphysical themes and techniques as a way of better adjusting to the social environment as given and thus becoming happier and more successful in "secular" life. (See WILSON, *Religious Sects,* Chap. 8.)
67. On the religious implications of consciousness-transforming drugs, see WILLIAM BRADEN, *The Private Sea: LSD and the Search for God* (New York: Bantam, 1967/68).*
68. ELLWOOD defines his subject matter in *Religious and Spiritual Groups* as "cults"—i.e., groups that have doctrines and teachers but little experience

of community (p. 5). Christian Science, at least in its early phases, closely approximated this definition, since its solution to the problem of social dislocation and urban *anomie* lay in denying the importance (and even the existence) of society rather than adopting the sectarian strategy of creating *communitas* in the midst of an increasingly impersonal social environment. This sort of metaphysical escapism probably finds its closest contemporary parallel in astrology and occultism, but generally lacks even the minimal institutional base which it possessed during the last century. The currently popular Transcendental Meditation movement (see ELLWOOD, pp. 231–34) is equally individualist, but its affinities are closer to the manipulationism of PEALE's "Positive Thinking" than to the older Vedanta or Rosicrucianism. See J. STILLSON JUDAH, *The History and Philosophy of the Metaphysical Movements in America* (Philadelphia: Westminster, 1967). On cult theory, see also ALLAN W. EISTER, "Culture Crises and New Religious Movements: A Paradigmatic Statement of a Theory of Cults," in ZARETSKY and LEONE, eds., *Religious and Spiritual Groups,* pp. 612–27 (with bibliographical note, pp. 626–27).

5

Some Concluding Observations

In the course of the preceding sections we have surveyed a wide variety of data, and tried to arrange them into an order which helps to make them comprehensible. It might be profitable now to take a retrospective look at some of the assumptions we have been making, the interpretive tools we have been using, and the tentative conclusions to which we have come.

In the first place, this study has not been carried through with any intentional normative purpose. One principle of selection we have been using, however, has been the divergence of various groups and movements from the mainstreams of middle-class American culture. In one sense, Judaism would be more deviant from this culture than Pentecostalism in that the latter shares the basic symbol system of mainstream Christianity. However, the basic assumptions about religion which most Jews—except for a few extreme groups, such as the Hasidim—make about the nature of religion, about the sources of religious knowledge, and about the implications of religion for everyday life are far closer to that of their middle-class Christian brethren than are those of many "fringe" Christian sects. I must add, however, that if one shares in the assumptions of middle-class culture, especially the academic subculture, it is difficult to suppress completely one's own judgment and inclinations. The best one can hope, perhaps, is that the assumptions can be kept as explicit as possible, and therefore separable from the analytical process. Nevertheless, one's judgment as to what is "marginal" or "popular" must to some extent be tied to one's own cultural presuppositions.

Secondly, the enterprise of the study of what Victor Turner calls "symbolic activity" and Bryan Wilson calls "comparative symbolics" constitutes what one might perhaps call a "discipline once removed." Students of religion or, more broadly, of symbolic activity, are by the nature of their activity dependent upon other disciplines for their data, since religion (or "religious studies" or "religiology") has no unique method of data collection it can call its own. Therefore, we must go to the historian, the philologist, the sociologist, the ethnologist, and the psychologist for our raw materials, since all these disciplines have concerned themselves with religious phenomena. The study of religion, in short, has not arisen around a unique or peculiar system of data collection. It clearly does have its own particular data, but it relies on skills developed in other fields for its accumulation.

Thirdly, since we have been primarily concerned with the social dimensions of the symbolic process, we have utilized theories developed in the contexts of sociology and social anthropology, specifically those of the Weber and Durkheim traditions. From Weber, we have taken up the notion that there are several basic broad paradigms of social organization which have emerged historically, and that each of these forms of organization has its own corresponding set of religious and cultural implications. From Durkheim and his followers we have adopted the idea that different types of social organization, disorganization, or transformation have similar consequences for symbolic behavior, although these modalities of symbolism may occur in any of Weber's paradigmatic societies. What both systems share is the hypothesis that ways of knowing, of believing, and of acting symbolically correlate with and reflect collective social experience.

Fourthly, we have deliberately chosen a loose working definition of popular religion—namely, that of extra-ecclesiastical symbolic activity. Popular religion, in short, is that carried on outside the formal structures provided by most societies for such activity. Such religion is usually an expression of the inadequacy of formal structures for the satisfactory ordering of the cosmos for all. For the "elite" who have experienced alienation or dissatisfaction, there have been the alternatives of philosophy, such as Stoicism, Neo-Platonism, or Ethical Culture, or the founding of new religious groups based on theological reformulations more often than on fresh revelation.

For the less sophisticated or less formally educated, however, something more tangible has usually been in order. This may take the form of mass movements with chiliastic expectations; of new revelation, often accompanied by personal devotion to the bearer of that insight; of direct experience of the numinous or divine, as in tongue-speaking or conversion; of manipulative techniques for self-transformation, such as the achievement of inner peace or greater energy; or in other forms of immediate perception or experience of the activity or manifestation of the divine in the arena of this world. When this experience takes place in the context of acute social dislocation, popular movements may adopt a symbolic expression directly translatable into action—e.g., witchcraft accusations, revolutionary movements, or other forms of attack on the extant structures of religion and society.

Aside from these characteristics, which are of the broadest sort, it is nearly as difficult to make any comprehensive statements about popular religion as about religion itself. Each is a term to which usage has given a meaning, but that meaning is best regarded as ranging over a spectrum or continuum of possibilities rather than as reducible to a pithy kernel of essence. No matter how neat a definition of either phenomenon we may formulate, we always find some borderline cases which we recognize intuitively, through "common sense," as pertinent even though they do not conform exactly to our carefully crafted formulation. It is perhaps fitting that we should conclude with the observation that, just as organized religion tends to break down at its margins and boundaries, so does our definition of popular religion.

Glossary

Although I dislike jargon as much as anyone, this attempt to deal with American religious phenomena by utilizing comparative typologies and analytical tools derived from the behavioral sciences has necessitated my using a considerable number of terms that may not be familiar. Although their overuse may grate on the humanistically trained ear, in moderation they are of great value in conveying specific and rather complex concepts with considerable economy. What follows is a glossary of terms occurring in the text of this work—derived from such disciplines as sociology, anthropology, philosophy, and theology—which may not be part of the reader's everyday working vocabulary, or which take on a somewhat different sense in technical usage than they may have in ordinary speech. I have avoided listing names of specific historical groups and movements, and refer the reader instead to such reference works as E. A. Livingstone, ed., *The Concise Oxford Dictionary of the Christian Church* (Oxford, London, New York: Oxford University Press, 1977), or Jerald C. Brauer, ed., *The Westminster Dictionary of Church History* (Philadelphia: Westminster, 1971).

abstinence Refraining from the use of something attractive—e.g., meat during Lent. (As opposed to *fasting,* which refers to a general refraining from eating.)

accommodationist (adj.; also n.) Designed or inclined (such as a movement) to come to terms with a neighboring and often more powerful culture without necessarily adopting all the features of the new culture; one who makes such an accommodation.

acculturation The process of cultural accommodation; adjustment to the presence of a new culture, sometimes to the point of absorption into it. (Cf. **assimilation.**)

alienation Psychological estrangement; more specifically, disaffection of a worker from the work process through loss of control over the finished product. (Marx)

anarchism A political philosophy advocating decentralization and individual autonomy; more popularly, the advocacy of social chaos.

anchorite A monk living in isolation; a religious hermit; as opposed to **c(o)enobite,** a monk living in community.

androgyne A person with characteristics of both sexes. (Cf. **hermaphrodite.**)

anomie The disorienting psychological experience of the lack of norms and guidelines for belief and conduct. (Durkheim)

anthropomorphism The attribution of human qualities to nonhumans—e.g., gods or animals. (Cf. **theriomorph.**)

anticlericalism Hostility to the clergy as an established caste.

antinomianism The belief that the experience or conviction of election to salvation exempts the believer from all norms of conduct. Specifically (caps.), the version of this belief held by Anne Hutchinson and her followers in the Massachusetts Bay Colony during the 1630s. **antinomian** (n. and adj.)

anti-structure Forces in a society or social movement that contradict or negate the **structure** (q.v.) of that society. (Victor Turner)

apocalyptic (n. and adj.) (Writing) pertaining to a cataclysm, often divinely initiated, that marks the end of an age or the world.

apotheosis The elevation of a person or idea to divine status. **apotheosize** (v.)

archetype A model or paradigm for a given action or artifact which exists eternally outside time. (Eliade, Jung)

architectonic Possessing a large, complex, inclusive structure.

asceticism Self-discipline achieved through self-denial of various sources of gratification. Weber distinguished two principal types: **world-rejecting** (or **other-worldly**)—i.e., aimed at salvation in the world to come; and **this-worldly** (**inner-worldly**), i.e., aimed at the transformation of the present world and taking place within this world's life and activities.

assimilationism The doctrine or practice of losing one's individual or collective cultural identity through absorption into another culture. **assimilationist** (n. or adj.)

astrology The systematic attempt to discern the influence of heavenly bodies on the course of earthly life.

axis mundi (Latin) The symbolic point around which all that exists revolves and in which it finds its center, meaning, or source of existence. (Eliade)

boundary maintenance The sociological phenomenon of a group's careful, even obsessive regulation of its definition and membership.

bourgeoisie (French) The entrepreneurial class in a capitalist society; the middle class. (Marx) **bourgeois** (adj. and n.)

calling See **vocation.**

cargo cult A group possessed of a millenarian hope in the coming of agents of modern civilization (ships, planes) to usher in a new era in which native peoples will suddenly become heirs to the material culture of the new civilization in abundance. (Primarily in Melanesia.)

caste A social group whose membership is defined by heredity or other special, fixed status such as that provided by ordination. (Opposed to **class** [q.v.].)

casuistry Deduction of specific applications from general principles, usually in the realm of morals and ethics.

celibacy Systematic abstinence from marriage and sexual activity, often reinforced by a special vow.

c(o)enobite See **anchorite.**

charisma A special power that gives legitimacy and potency to an office or its holder. Charisma may reside in the personality of a leader or be a function of the office that leader holds. (Weber)

chiliasm Millenarianism (q.v.); **chiliastic** (adj.)

church

1. An assembly for religious worship.
2. The building in which such an assembly takes place.
3. Any organization for such worship. (Durkheim)
4. An inclusive religious organization, usually coextensive with a given sociopolitical unit, membership in which usually comes by virtue of birth into both groups. As opposed to **sect** (q.v.). (Troeltsch)

Civil Religion The loose collection of rites, ceremonies, and beliefs derived from and pertaining to the collective experience and destiny of a particular nation. (Robert Bellah)

class A status group in which membership is dependent primarily on acquirable characteristics and qualifications; according to Weber, a group with similar "life chances." (Cf. **caste.**)

clerico-popular A term used in this work to designate a type of religious culture characterized by a mixture of popular and folk styles of religiosity shaped strongly by clerical influence.

communitarian (adj., also n.) Characterized by life in common, often including common residence and collective ownership of goods; **communitarianism** is the advocacy of such practices.

communitas (Latin) The condition or experience of total participation by individuals in a group so that individual identity is absorbed in the group. This experience may be momentary and evanescent (**spontaneous communitas**); routinized into an ongoing enterprise (**institutional communitas**); or made into a normative program for social organization (**ideological communitas**). (Victor Turner)

condensed symbol A concrete image, often material and visual, which "condenses" into itself a wide range of reference and connotation, and which usually reflects a strong sense of social solidarity. (Cf. **diffuse symbol.**) (Mary Douglas)

confessional

1. (n.) a booth in which the sacrament of penance is administered.
2. (adj.) pertaining to a specific religious group or tradition.

conversion The transformation of an individual from one religious state or group to another. Conversion may be highly emotional and be interpreted as a change from a state of sin to one of grace, or may simply involve a decision to change one's religious allegiance or affiliation.

cosmology A metaphysical framework for interpreting all that exists in its totality; a **Weltanschauung** or comprehensive world picture. **cosmological** (adj.)

cosmos An organized, comprehensible universe (opposed to **chaos**).

countersubversion Activity or ideology directed against suspected subversive forces at work within a society—e.g., anti-Communism. (David Brion Davis)

covenant A personal alliance entered into between two parties, often of unequal strength, in which mutual loyalty and assistance is pledged. Opposed to **contract,** an agreement of strictly limited scope involving no personal allegiance.

cult

1. Worship or ritual around which a religious group is organized (also **cultus**).
2. Devotion to a particular deity or other object of worship or veneration—e.g., the Blessed Virgin or Krishna.
3. A loose religious organization with little sense of community,—one in which individual salvation through the acquisition of esoteric knowledge or techniques is central.
4. A **sect** (q.v.) centered on a charismatic leader and that person's teachings, which are usually radical departures from the orthodoxy of the broader community.

culture The matrix of beliefs, orientations, values, rules, practices, and patterns which a coherent social group holds in common and through which it expresses and maintains its identity.

demigod (literally, "half-god") A figure partly divine and partly human.

demotic Of the people; pertaining to the mass of working people in a differentiated society, in contrast to the elite.

denomination A religious group, usually Protestant, coexisting within a pluralistic society with other such groups often only marginally distinguishable in belief, practice, and organization from one another.

deprivation, relative A state in which a group (or individual) regards itself as lacking in comparison with others in some vital way, but not necessarily inferior to others in material terms. Psychological rather than material deprivation.

desacralization The process through which individual objects or a whole world picture loses its status as sacred or divine.

determinism The philosophical doctrine that all worldly events are predetermined and therefore unalterable. (Cf. **predestination.**)

devotionalism A kind of religious behavior characterized by devotion to a divine or sacred figure. (Cf. **cult,** 2.)

dialectic A process in which two or more elements are involved in mutual interaction. (An important concept in the philosophical systems of Marx and Hegel.)

diaspora A process of scattering, or condition of being scattered. Specifically (caps.), the dispersal of the Jewish people into exile after the Babylonian captivity.

diffuse symbol A general symbol or formula, usually verbal, which evokes a response more universalistic and ethical than that called forth by a **condensed symbol** (q.v.). (Mary Douglas)

diffusion

1. The process of spreading over a broad area.
2. The dilution of the force of that which is diffused in sense (1) above.

ecclesiastical Having to do with a church or other organized religious body.

ecclesiastic (n.), a cleric.

ecstatic Characterized by extreme emotional frenzy, such as that produced by possession by a spirit.

ecumenical Favorably inclined toward the cooperation or union of different, often previously hostile or competitive religious bodies. Synonym of **irenic.**

effervescence A state of great collective excitement, often of a religious sort. (Durkheim)

empirical Derived from observation through the senses.

empiricism

1. The philosophical doctrine that all that is real is knowable through the senses. (Locke, Hume)
2. A method of investigation, or an inclination, relying on empirical observation. (Opposed to **rationalism.**)

enthusiasm Behavior, especially religious behavior, characterized by a state of high emotional excitability and demonstration. **enthusiastic** (adj.)

eschatology The branch of theology dealing with last things—e.g., death, judgment, Heaven and Hell. **eschatological,** oriented toward such concerns.

esoteric Secret, reserved only for initiates, as in "esoteric knowledge (or teaching)."

ethics The branch of philosophy or theology concerned with norms of human conduct.

ethnology The branch of anthropology concerned with the study of the cultures of primitive and peasant communities. Loosely synonomous with "cultural" or "social anthropology." Most simply, "descriptive anthropology."

evangelical (n. and adj.) [One who is] committed to the aggressive communication of religious beliefs to others, and concerned with bringing about the conversion of others. When capitalized usually referring to the branch of British and American Protestantism stressing proselytization, Biblical centrality, and the person of Jesus.

evil eye (malocchio) (Italian) Power, possessed by certain classes of people, which can bring misfortune to those with whom it comes in contact. This power is not usually voluntarily controllable. (Cf. **witchcraft.**)

existential
1. Experiential.
2. (caps.) Pertaining to the philosophical school of **Existentialism,** which teaches that existence precedes essence. Existential philosophy may be theistic (Buber, Marcel) or atheistic (Camus, Sartre).

exorcism The process through which the hold of a demon or other malevolent spirit is removed from a person or object. **exorcise** (v.)

exoteric Public, open to all. Opposite of **esoteric.**

fissiparous Subject to repeated division.

folk culture Culture transmitted orally, as in primitive and peasant societies. (Redfield)

formulaic Composed of verbal units that may be repeated frequently wherever appropriate, as in an epic.

functionalism A sociological approach that explains all aspects of social behavior in terms of that behavior's role in helping society to carry out functions necessary for its maintenance and preservation, regardless of the ostensible meaning of that behavior.

Gemeinschaft (German) An **ideal type** (q.v.) of society characterized by strong kinship ties, multibonded relationships, and small-scale agriculture—e.g., a **peasant** or **folk** society. Opposed to **Gesellschaft** (q.v.). **gemeinschaftlich** (adj.) (Toennies)

Gesellschaft (German) An **ideal type** (q.v.) of society characterized by urbanization, literacy, industrial-commercial economy, and impersonal, functional relationships. Opposed to **Gemeinschaft** (q.v.). **gesellschaftlich** (adj.) (Toennies)

ghetto (Italian) An urban district in which members of a particular ethnic group, such as Jews or blacks, elect or are compelled to live. More broadly, the area occupied by a subcultural group, such as Catholics, differentiated from the dominant culture by its particular beliefs and practices, and usually reinforced at least partially by separate institutions and **vicinal segregation** (q.v.).

glossolalia The practice of speaking in a flow of sounds unintelligible to all except those with a "gift of discernment" or interpretation as an expression of religious ecstacy. Characteristic of **Pentecostalism.** (**Xenoglossia** involves speaking in a real language that is unknown to the speaker.)

gnostic (adj.) Characterized by the possession of esoteric saving knowledge.

Specifically (n., caps.), a member of any of a number of religious groups in the Hellenistic world characterized by such teaching, collectively known as **Gnosticism.**

Great Tradition The sophisticated interpretation of a religious or cultural system developed by that system's intellectual elite. Opposed to **Little Tradition** (q.v.). (Robert Redfield)

grid A measure of the degree of social stratification possessed by a particular group. (Mary Douglas)

group Generally, a collection of people with a shared identity or common culture; as used here, a measure of the degree of a sense of belonging to and identification with a clearly defined social unit. (Mary Douglas)

hagiography The life of a saint or holy person, usually following a set pattern or formula. **hagiographic** (adj.)

henotheism Allegiance to a specific god, usually associated with a particular territory, while acknowledging the existence of other gods.

heresy Religious or ideological teaching which deviates from that established by a group as normative. **heretic,** one who holds such teaching. **heretical** (adj.) (Cf. **schism.**)

hermaphrodite A person or animal possessing the generative organs of both sexes. **hermaphroditic** (adj.) (Cf. **androgyne.**)

heterodoxy Heresy (q.v.).

heuristic Stimulative of further interest in and investigation of a subject.

hierarchy A form of stratified social organization in which power increases in quantity as the number of those holding it diminishes. **hierarchical** (adj.)

hierophany An earthly manifestation or appearance of divinity or divine power.

high religion A complex religious system characterized by a high or creator god, a distinct caste of religious functionaries, and a rationalized system of theology. Usually used to describe the religions of complex societies characterized by "Great" and "Little Traditions."

homily A brief sermon or piece of moral instruction. **homiletics,** the study of preaching.

iconoclasm

1. Literally, the breaking of images or idols; opposition to the use of visual or physical representations of the deity or divine beings in worship and devotion.
2. Figuratively, a posture of skepticism or cynicism toward all established and received beliefs and practices in a culture.

iconography A standardized system of conventions for depicting sacred persons, objects, or topics in art.

ideal type A model or paradigm, usually of a social phenomenon, in which that phenomenon is characterized by its essential qualities apart from any particular examples. (Weber)

illud tempus (Latin) Literally, "that time." The primordial period at the creation of the world when the gods performed those actions which provided the **paradigms** for all subsequent human activity. **In illo tempore,** "at that time"—i.e., at the beginning of the world; also the **strong time.** (Eliade)

infrastructure The elements or forces that hold a system together at its foundations.

in-migrant A person migrating from one part of a country to another without leaving the country's boundaries. (also adj.)

introversionism Turning inward; closing in on one's self; avoiding all unnecessary interaction with outsiders; maintaining high social boundaries. Used especially of **introversionist sects.** (Bryan Wilson)

irenic Inclined toward the promotion of cooperation and harmony. (Cf. **ecumenical.**)

itinerant Mobile, on the move, not restricted to one locale.

jeremiad (from Hebrew prophet Jeremiah) A form of sermon, usually delivered at Colonial New England elections, in which the sins of the community are ritually denounced, disasters and misfortunes are attributed to such unfaithful behavior, and repentance is called for. (Perry Miller)

justification The process whereby a sinner is freed from the consequences of sin and reconciled with God.

laity Members of a religious community who have not received ordination to clerical status. **lay** (adj.)

legend A traditional story, usually transmitted orally, about heroic figures of an earlier or primordial period in a people's history or prehistory.

legitimation, legitimization The process of making legitimate, as political authority. **legitimate, legitimatize** (v.)

liminal That which stands outside the usual categories of thought or social organization; marginal; possessed of a "betwixt-and-between" quality, often with an uncanny or sacred dimension. (Victor Turner)

Little Tradition The adaptation of a civilization's general, sophisticated culture, by peasant communities within that civilization. (Robert Redfield)

liturgy The collective components of a religious ritual, including prayers, music, preaching, and sacramental activity.

macrocosm A complex of things represented or manifested on a large scale. (Opposed to **microcosm.**) **macrocosmic** (adj.)

magic The manipulation of supernatural powers for individual ends.

manipulationist sect A religious or quasi-religious group whose teaching is oriented toward the achievement of specific this-worldly ends such as health and wealth. (Bryan Wilson)

mass culture A form of culture in which standardized products, artifacts, ideas, and, especially, entertainment are made available on a wide scale through sophisticated technical means of production and distribution; culture disseminated through the **mass media.** Often used pejoratively, with connotations of slickness and commercial exploitativeness.

matriarchy A system of governance in which women, especially elderly ones, predominate. Opposed to **patriarchy** (q.v.)

matrilineal Characteristic of a kinship system in which descent is traced through the female (maternal) line.

matrilocal Characteristic of a social system in which a married couple resides with or near the family of the wife.

messiah An anointed one, usually called by the deity to perform some divine function.

metaphysics The branch of philosophy that deals with the ultimate nature and underlying principles of reality as a whole.

microcosm A system that contains all the elements of a larger system in miniature. (Opposite of **macrocosm.**)

millennium A long or indefinite period or time (in Christian thought, 1000 years) of peace and harmony on earth, ushered in by or culminating in the coming of a messiah (e.g., Jesus Christ). **Millennialism** or **millenarianism:** belief in the coming of such a period. (Cf. **post-millennialism** and **pre-millennialism.)**

miracle An event or occurrence in violation of the order of nature, often attributed to supernatural causes.

modernization The process through which a society becomes literate, technologically sophisticated, politically centralized, urbanized, and industrialized.

monasticism A type of religious life characterized by withdrawal from the world and the practice of an ascetic regimen. (Cf. **asceticism; anchorite; c(o)enobite.**)

monism The philosophical doctrine that all reality is fundamentally one. Opposed to **dualism** and **pluralism.**

monotheism Belief in a single divinity. (Opposed to **polytheism** and **henotheism.**)

moralism A religious or ethical attitude stressing personal or collective conduct, with an emphasis on the maintenance of purity; more loosely, conduct as opposed to **piety** (q.v.).

mundane This-worldly; **profane** (q.v.).

mysticism Religious practice aiming at unity with the divine through prayer and ascetic exercises. A **mystic** is one who seeks such union.

myth A narrative recounting in symbolic terms the origins of the universe, of particular aspects of human life and experience, or any other problematical aspect of existence. (also **mythos.**)

nativism

1. Hostility toward those of alien origin.
2. Revival of tribal or patriotic feeling among a people encountering a more modernized people. (Cf. **revitalization movement.**)

numerology The study of the magical attributes of numbers and their manipulation. **numerological** (adj.)

occult Hidden; secret; specifically, referring to practices and beliefs dealing with supernatural forces outside the scope of science or religion. **occult** (n.); **occultism** (n.)

oneiric Having to do with dreams, particularly in terms of their revelatory or predictive value.

ontology The branch of philosophy dealing with the nature of being. **ontological** (adj.), pertaining to fundamental properties of being.

orthodoxy Teaching or belief accepted as correct by a religious or ideological group.

pan-ethnic Encompassing all or many ethnic groups in its scope—e.g., the Roman Catholic Church.

pantheon The collectivity of divinities of a polytheistic religion.

paradigm An examplary instance; a model or **archetype.**

parochial

1. Limited in scope or vision.
2. Pertaining or confined to a parish, or basic organizational unit, particularly of a church.
3. Pertaining to a religious structure based on territorial subdivision.

particularism Investing of value or significance in the specific—e.g., one's tribe or family—rather than in all members of a class. Opposed to **universalism** (q.v.). (Weber)

patriarchy A society characterized by governance by elder male authority figures. (Opposed to **matriarchy.**)

peasant (n.) A member of a society that is preliterate, engaged predominantly in agriculture, but living in **symbiotic** tension with a modernized society. (adj.) pertaining to or characteristic of such a person, society, or culture.

perfectionism The belief or doctrine that total freedom from sin is possible in this life. (Cf. **sanctification.**)

pietism Religious practice characterized by cultivation of the religious affects or emotions, often through introspection and **devotionalism.** (Cf. **moralism, devotionalism.**)

piety Pietistic religious practice; more generally, a devout attitude and demeanor. **pious** (adj.)

pluralism

1. A social or political situation in which a wide variety of opinions or practices are permitted or tolerated.
2. A philosophical position which maintains that reality is not unified, but consists of an indefinite number of different elements

polygamy A system of marriage that permits a person of either sex to have more than one spouse.

polytheism A religious system in which many gods are acknowledged.

post-millennialism The belief that the **millennium** (q.v.) will be ushered in gradually, with the second coming of Christ taking place at its end. This belief is usually associated with an optimistic attitude toward human progress.

post-modern A type of social structure in which the modernization process has been generally completed; characterized by security, egalitarianism, and a preoccupation with the dissemination of information. (Daniel Bell)

pragmatism

1. An attitude toward experience based on the premise that all difficulties can be resolved through resourcefulness and common sense.
2. Specifically (caps.), the philosophical position that ideas can be evaluated only in terms of their useful practical consequences or **cash value.** (William James)

predestination A deterministic theological position which maintains that God has ordained all people to salvation or damnation from the beginning of time. (Characteristic of Calvinism.)

pre-millennialism The belief that the **millennium** (q.v.) will take place only after the second coming of Christ. (Usually associated with a pessimistic attitude toward human possibilities.)

primitivism Admiration for or an advocacy of a return to the conditions characteristic of an earlier, purer phase of human existence.

privatization A process of making private—i.e., taking some aspect of human activity such as religion out of the public arena.

profane

1. Impure, defiling, offensive, blasphemous. (popular)
2. Secular, mundane; having no religious significance. (Eliade)

prophet

1. The bearer of a revelation.
2. One who preaches divine judgment and punishment if offenses are not repented of.

proselytization Evangelization; aggressive seeking of converts. (Cf. **Evangelical.**)

providence Divine guidance or intervention in worldly affairs. **Special providence** refers to divine intervention in specific situations; **general providence** refers to divine guidance of the totality of human affairs and their ultimate outcome.

puritan

1. An advocate of a strict moralistic behavior.
2. (caps.) A follower of a variety of Calvinism practiced in Old and New England during the seventeenth century which was characterized by a close coordination of Church and State, an emphasis on sound knowledge and upright conduct, and a revulsion from all traces of Roman Catholic usage.

rationalization A process through which all means are systematically oriented toward achievement of a specific goal. (Opposed to **traditionalism,** in which actions are patterned and justified on the basis of precedent, and in which the instrumental use of certain things is prohibited by beliefs in their sacrality.) (Weber)

relative deprivation See **deprivation, relative.**

Religionswissenschaft (German, "science of religion") The empirical, comparative study of religious phenomena with no normative intent.

resocialization A change, usually rapid, in the sense of values and identity of a person, often brought about under extreme and deliberate stress such as "brainwashing." (Cf. **socialization.**)

revelation Disclosure of the divine will through human agency; also, the means, such as Scripture, through which such disclosure is conveyed.

revitalization movement A religious movement, usually among primitive peoples, which calls for a return to traditional practices, customs, and beliefs, after partial erosion of such practices through contact with more modernized cultures—e.g., the Ghost Dance movement.

rites of passage Rituals or ceremonies designed to mediate symbolically the transition from one state of life to another.

ritual A ceremony with a fixed form performed at regular intervals.

routinization Making regular, routine, unspontaneous, of fixed form. **Routinization of charisma** is the process through which the special attractive gifts of personality of the founder of a (religious) movement are transformed into a pattern of leadership based not on personality but on the authority and legitimacy inherent in an office. (Weber)

sacrality The state or quality of being sacred—i.e., endowed with divinity or religious power. **sacralization,** the process through which a person or object is endowed with sacrality.

sacrament A process or object through which divine power or grace is mediated to an earthly recipient.

sanctification

1. The process through which grace or blessings are acquired; the state of being blessed.
2. More particularly, the Wesleyan (Methodist) doctrine of the "second blessing" (or "entire sanctification"), through which a **justified** person goes on to attain complete freedom from sin.

schism A split in an ecclesiastical body based on differences with regard to organization or governance rather than doctrine or belief. (Cf. **heresy.**) **schismatic,** a promoter or supporter of a schism. (also adj.)

scholasticism A method of theological or philosophical investigation based on the careful drawing of distinctions and development of arguments from first premises based on deductive logic. Specifically (caps.), the body of thought developed by St. Thomas Aquinas and others during the thirteenth and fourteenth centuries. (Cf. **syllogism.**)

sect A religious group, usually small in number, characterized by exclusiveness, adult initiation, strict regulation of belief and conduct, and rejection of the institutions and customs of the broader culture. (Opposed to **church.**) (Troeltsch) **sectarian** (n. and adj.)

secular Pertaining to the mundane or profane world; devoid of religious or symbolic significance. **secularism,** advocacy of the secular as normative; hostility to religion as a source of meaning and value. **secularization,** the process through which everyday life is deprived of religious or symbolic significance.

seeker A person unsure of religious truth and actively seeking it through experimentation with various forms of religious belief and practice.

shaman Among primitive peoples, a religious specialist capable of entering into trances, performing miraculous acts, and curing sickness. (Eliade)

shtetl A small community, usually composed mainly of Jews, existing in the agricultural areas of traditional Eastern Europe. (Cf. **ghetto.**)

sin

1. An act in violation of the norms of a religion.
2. A state of being alienated from or out of harmony with the divine.

socialization The process through which a person (usually a child) comes to learn and internalize the customs and norms of a particular culture. (Cf. **resocialization.**)

soteriology The branch of theology dealing with the question of salvation. **soteriological** (adj.)

spiritualism Beliefs and practices related to communication with the spirits of the dead.

status One's subjective sense of rank or standing in society, often described in terms of social class; a measure or sense of prestige. **ascribed status** is usually inherited; **achieved status** is attained through individual effort. (Cf. **caste, class.**)

strong time See **illud tempus.**

structuralism A method of analysis—e.g., of literary texts or of religious myths or rituals, in which the interrelationships among the internal components of the phenomenon being analyzed are taken as the key to that phenomenon's nature or meaning.

structure The roles, norms, and institutions that constitute a given society. (Cf. **anti-structure.**) (Victor Turner)

subculture A group—or its beliefs and practices—existing within a broader society and culture, but deviating from the norms of that culture in a significant fashion.

supernatural A realm of being apart from the visible which can be communicated with only through religious or magical means.

superstition Vestiges of magical beliefs and practices manifesting themselves in modern society. Usually used pejoratively, to designate disapproved-of religious beliefs and practices.

syllogism A form of reasoning based on the conjunction of "major" and "minor" premises and the conclusions drawn from their juxtapostion. Characteristic of **scholasticism** (q.v.).

symbiosis A relationship of mutual dependence between two entities.

symbol A person, place, thing, event, or relationship carrying a meaning or significance that cannot be verified or disproved empirically, or that points to something beyond itself.

syncretism The combination of components from two or more religious or symbolic systems to form a new unity. **syncretistic** (adj.)

thaumaturgy Healing through religious means. **thaumaturge,** one who heals in this fashion.

theios aner (Greek) A divine man.

theism Any religious or philosophical system involving belief in a deity. **theist** (n.); **theistic** (adj.)

theocracy A political system in which power is vested in a deity or (more practically) its representatives—e.g., a priestly caste. (Often used pejoratively.)

theodicy The branch of theology that deals with the explanation of the existence of evil.

theology The systematic study of the nature of divine things, usually through the transformation of revelation into propositional form.

theriomorph A being represented in animal form. **theriomorphic** (adj.); **theriomorphism** (n.)

tongue-speaking See **glossolalia.**

total institution An institution (e.g., a monastery, prison, concentration camp, mental hospital) in which all aspects of the lives of the inmates are regulated by the institution. (Erving Goffman)

totem A symbol representing a tribe or other social group, usually in the form of an animal or plant.

traditionalism Adherence to custom as the source of norms for all activity. **traditionalistic** (adj.)

transcendence The realm of being standing beyond and against the mundane or profane realm; the quality of partaking in such a realm. **transcendent, transcendental** (adjs.)

tribalism Behavior based on and reinforcing a sense of belonging to a specific nation, group, or clan.

trickster A figure in African and Amerind folklore, often in animal form, which mediates between the divine and human and engages in humorous, often scatological exploits.

typology A model or paradigm used as a means of classification.

universalistic Pertaining to that which is equally available or applicable to all people. Opposed to **particularism** (q.v.). **universalism** (n.), the belief that all will ultimately be saved.

utopian Idealistic; believing in or pertaining to belief in the achievement of a perfect society.

vicinal Pertaining to place of residence. **vicinal segregation,** a drawing apart from others into a physically separate community, as a **sect.**

virtuoso (Italian) A person extraordinarily skilled in or dedicated to a particular talent, practice, or way of life. (Weber)

vocation (or **calling, Beruf** [German]) Divine legitimation of one's occupation, whether religious or secular, or the sense thereof. (Weber)

voluntarism A mode of social organization, especially with reference to religious affiliation, in which one's institutional allegiances are based on free choice rather than tradition or compulsion. (also **voluntaryism**) **voluntaristic** (adj.), based on free choice.

witchcraft A sort of magical practice in which good or bad effects are called down on a person through the manipulation of supernatural forces.

xenophobia Fear of the strange or foreign. **xenophobic** (adj.)

Index